SMARTPHONE LINK

PRO TREK Connected

After installing the PRO TREK Connected app on your phone, you can link with the watch and automatically adjust its time setting.

Phone linking simplifies a number of operations, including FISH MEMO record management, quick access to the current time in 300 cities around the globe, and time setting configuration.

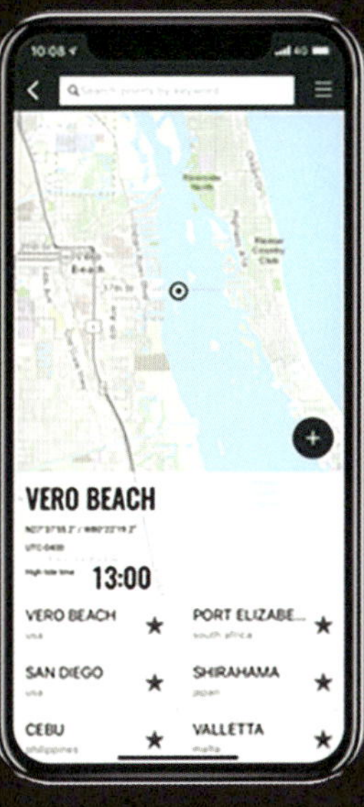

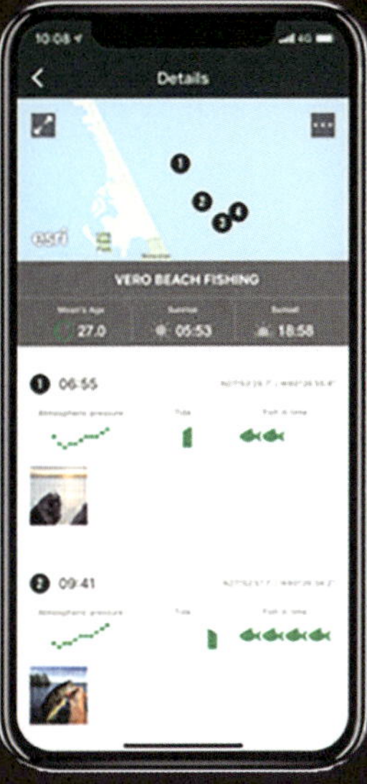

FISHING POINT SETTING

After you have downloaded the App you can specify any one of approximately 3,300 points at ports around the world. Simply select a port on a map to access Best Fishing Times, Tide Graph information, Moon data, and sunrise and sunset times for that location.

SMART WATCH

PRT-B70-1D

PRT-B70-2D

PRT-B70-5D

FISHING GUIDE TO
SOUTH AUSTRALIA

SHANE MENSFORTH & JAMIE CRAWFORD

ACKNOWLEDGEMENTS

Many thanks to Len Vanderwaal and Bill Classon for photographs and their input on the Far West Coast of South Australia. Thanks also to Brad Smith for input and images for the Spencer Gulf section.

Also special thanks to Bob Hutchinson of Port Lincoln for his help with the fishing information on the maps for this area.

First published 2010
Revised 2017, Reprinted 2022

Published and distributed by
AFN Fishing and Outdoors
PO Box 544 Croydon, Victoria 3136
Telephone: (03) 9729 8788
Email: sales@afn.com.au
Website: www.afn.com.au

ISBN: 9781 8651 3307 2

Printed in China

CONTENTS

Beach at Point Drummond

NAVIGATION AIDS FOR MAPS

Port When lighted exhibits

Starboard When lighted exhibits

Beacons, Bouys

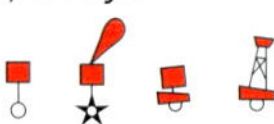

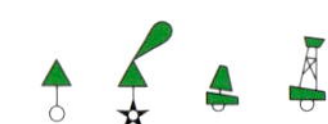

CARDINAL MARKS Indicate navigable water for the area beyond the mark in the direction depicted.

North

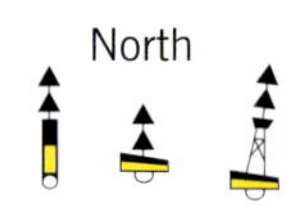

West

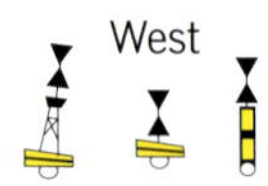

East

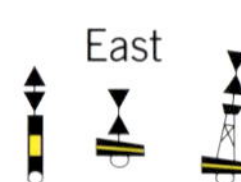

South

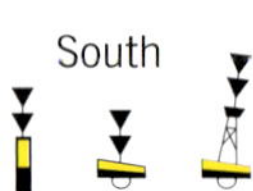

Lighted marks all exhibit a WHITE light.

SPECIAL MARKS Indicate several features (eg: pipe outfall) where navigable water is usually evident from the map.

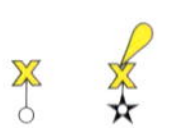

When lighted exhibits

ISOLATED DANGER MARKS Are stationed over a submerged hazard. KEEP CLEAR.

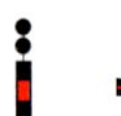

When lighted exhibits

SAFE WATER MARKS

When lighted exhibits

MARINE PARK BUOYS

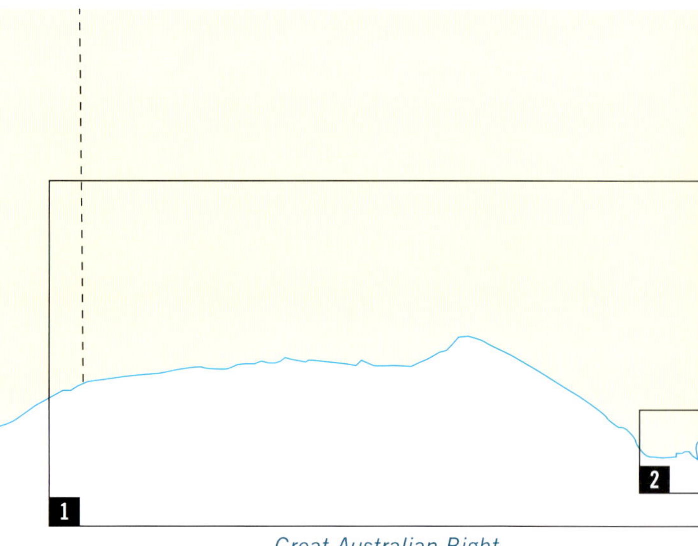

Key for map positioning

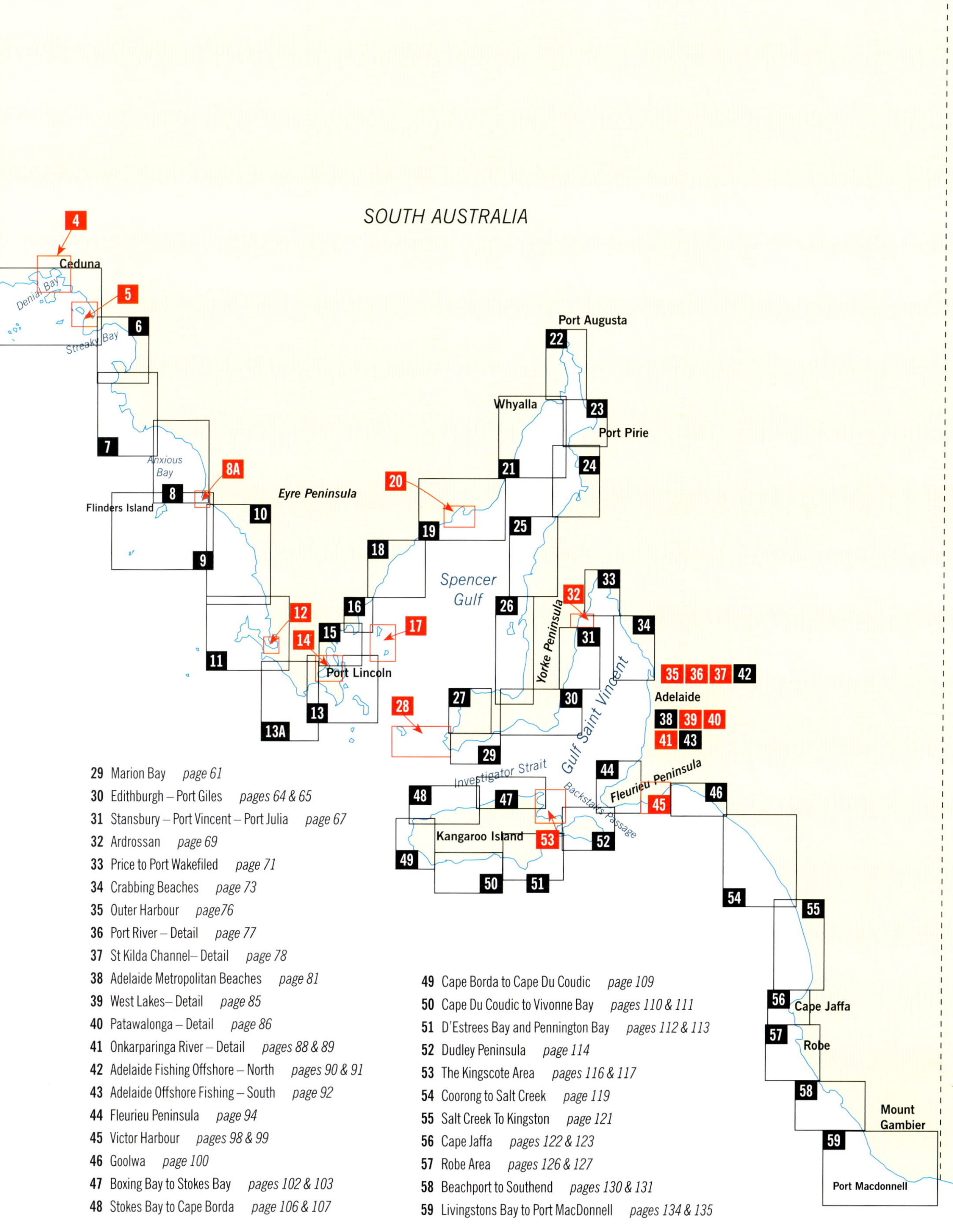
SOUTH AUSTRALIA
Ceduna
Denial Bay
Streaky Bay
Anxious Bay
Flinders Island
Eyre Peninsula
Port Augusta
Whyalla
Port Pirie
Spencer Gulf
Yorke Peninsula
Port Lincoln
Gulf Saint Vincent
Adelaide
Investigator Strait
Backstairs Passage
Fleurieu Peninsula
Kangaroo Island
Cape Jaffa
Robe
Mount Gambier
Port Macdonnell
4
5
6
7
8A
8
9
10
11
12
13
13A
14
15
16
17
18
19
20
21
22
23
24
25
26
27
28
29
30
31
32
33
34
35 36 37 42
38 39 40
41 43
44
45
46
47
48
49
50
51
52
53
54
55
56
57
58
59

INTRODUCTION

SA's western waters has some wild islands.

It's a fact that more than 90 per cent of South Australians live on or near the coast. This is the driest state in the nation, with very few inland waterways and an annual rainfall that's less than a third of Queensland's. Despite a relative lack of fresh water, however, SA's marine fishery is among the most vibrant in the country and now draws thousands of interstate angling visitors annually.

While it was once just the mighty snapper on which South Australia's fishing reputation was built, horizons are now far broader. Nowhere else in the country will you find King George whiting, mulloway and yellowtail kingfish in such abundance or consistently large sizes. Southern bluefin tuna are regular visitors offshore, huge samson fish can be caught on many deep water reefs and then there are the 'bread and butter' varieties like garfish, yellowfin whiting, bream, tommy ruffs and copious amounts of southern calamari.

While SA was once regarded as the poor relation in national fishing circles, it is now emerging as one of the very best.

We have a coastline length that's double that of Victoria, but less than one third of the population, so pressure on angling resources of all types is extremely low. Combine this with highly efficient Fisheries management and you come up with a fishery that remains healthy and shows very few signs of over exploitation.

Unlike the eastern states, which have many substantial coastal towns and small cities, South Australia has relatively few and these are well spread. Most of our coastal settlements are small and quite sparsely populated, but they do offer a terrific range of services and accommodation options for visiting anglers and their families. Charter operations are available in most coastal centres and there are well stocked tackle stores to provide the right bait and gear, as well as up to date local information.

Thanks to many of the regional councils and significant Government input, SA's boat launching and mooring facilities are now top class; in fact, many visitors comment that ours are the best in the country. There aren't too many coastal resorts – even the smaller ones – that don't have a multi-lane, all-tide ramp, so you can tow a boat here and feel confident about launching and retrieving.

Most forms of fishing are available, although fresh water is limited. There are trout in a number of streams to the north and south of Adelaide, but there is no Government-funded stocking program and our trout fishery remains in the hands of a private body, the SA Fly Fishers' Association. Access to the trout streams is limited, but each year some really nice browns and rainbows are landed.

Cod are present in the SA section of the Murray, along with callop (golden perch), silver perch and, of course, European carp. The cod are subject to an annual closed season, but most caught year-round are unhooked and released. The Murray's water flow is far less reliable these days than ever before in the history of white settlement and there is grave concern that our mightiest river may be facing a grim future. Being at the seaward end of the Murray's south-westward journey, our section is influenced significantly by user groups upstream, particularly cotton farmers and similar irrigation-heavy agriculturists. The steady decline of both water quality and water volume is one of our Government's greatest headaches and finding a workable solution to the problem is indeed a daunting challenge.

South Australia's weather patterns are really quite unique and play an important role in determining how, when and where most of us go fishing. Generally speaking, autumn and early winter offer the most stable and predictable weather, while summer and spring can be windy and more difficult to forecast. Fresh to strong afternoon sea breezes dominate between November and March, making boating on both St Vincent and Spencer Gulfs quite uncomfortable after lunch. By far the calmest months are April, May and June, when the mornings are generally calm and the influence of coastal sea breezes has diminished.

This is the period when our long range charter skippers plan extended voyages out of locations such as Kangaroo Island, Port Lincoln and Coffin Bay. The deep reefs and offshore islands accessible in large boats from these areas can provide mind-blowing action on all manner of pelagic species, and particularly on southern bluefin tuna. Bluefin to over 100 kilograms have been caught well offshore in recent years and there are plenty to be had in the 15-20kg range for those with smaller boats. As a lot of the tuna fishing is done 20 miles or more from the coast, calm weather and a high degree of offshore knowledge are mandatory for the trailer boat brigade.

Winter time sees sustained periods of good weather punctuated by regular north-westerly storms, but it's a great time to target one of our iconic local species, the King George whiting. Both gulfs carry good numbers year-round, but the fish tend to be easier to find during the cooler months and particularly along the inshore weed beds and areas of broken bottom. Winter also sees Adelaide's Port River at its best, with giant mulloway available to both lure casters and live baiters. Jewies to 30 kilos are quite common between late April and August and these are extremely popular targets with our estuary specialists.

Fisheries regulations are strict, but sensible in South Australia. We have an expanding network of Marine Parks, which influence where we can and can't go, but generally speaking, access to most of the coastline and offshore areas remains good. There's no fishing licence required here and only a few seasonal closures apply to various species and specific areas.

In short, South Australia is an excellent place to fish. We may not have traditionally enjoyed as much of the angling limelight as our neighbours to the north, east and west, but you can rest assured, SA has plenty to offer any visiting angler with a sense of adventure and a liking for top quality seafood!

Sunset session

CHAPTER 1
THE FAR WEST COAST

A chunky bronze whaler caught from the surf on the Far West Coast

As far as remote fishing areas go, SA's Far West Coast rates right up there with the best in the country, particularly for the beach, rock and jetty angler. This stretch begins in the township of Ceduna and concludes some 900 kilometres westward at the WA border. Most of the fishing is done between Ceduna and the head of the Great Australian Bight, where pristine surf beaches are punctuated by spectacular headlands that eventually give way to rugged, inaccessible cliffs.

This is big mulloway territory; in fact, the surf beaches between Yalata and the head of the Bight are generally regarded as the best mulloway producers in the country. The beaches are often difficult to access due to rough, ill-maintained tracks with unpredictably soft sand and a stint on any of the beaches definitely isn't for the unprepared or ill equipped. However, the rewards can be high for those who invest the time, planning and effort and this area seems to lure more and more angling adventurers each season.

Big Australian salmon also are readily available on many of the Far West Coast beaches, especially in the cooler months when they school in their thousands and invade the prolific surf gutters. There are literally dozens of beaches between Ceduna and the head of the Bight that attract salmon specialists in the winter and springtime, as the fish are generally big and full of fight. Eight and ten pounders are common and it's not unusual to hook 30 or 40 in a single session.

This is also a land-based shark fisher's paradise. Large bronze whalers constantly patrol the surf beaches in search of an easy feed and hooking one is often as simple as beaching a fresh salmon, baiting it up alive on heavy tackle and sending it back out into the surf. Sharks to ten feet long and 250 kilograms in weight are hooked from the beaches regularly and although most escape due to unprepared anglers and sub-standard equipment, they provide the ultimate land-based challenge.

Gummy and school sharks are also caught in good numbers from these western beaches, and are a more manageable target than the bigger whalers. These smaller sharks become more active at night, and by laying a good berley trail and fishing baits after dark, it's possible to beach some nice 'table' sharks from the surf. Most of these sharks are in the 5 to 10kg size, but you will get some bigger gummies and schoolies on occasions.

Although the Far West Coast beaches are a year-round proposition, there are distinct seasons for some species. Mulloway, for example, are at their best from late October to February, while the salmon fishing is best from Easter through until early spring. Big snapper are available in some locations as well, particularly those beaches with substantial inshore reef systems, and rocky headlands fronting deep water. These can be caught for most of the year, but seem best in the summer months.

Tailor are occasional visitors to these beaches, but they are the exception rather than the rule. Most caught are quite large, often topping pre-metrics double figures, but their needle-sharp teeth regularly make short work of the monofilament traces used for salmon and mulloway. A light wire trace is mandatory equipment if tailor are known to be in a specific area.

Jetty anglers are well catered for along this stretch of coastline, with several long piers providing access to great light tackle action. Fowlers Bay, in particular, is a renowned producer of good sized squid, big tommy ruffs, snook, salmon and the occasional kingfish. Point Sinclair jetty is also a good one to try, as there have been both sharks and mulloway taken there by those using heavy tackle.

There is naturally some great offshore fishing to be had along the state's Far West Coast, but boat launching facilities are few and far between. There is beach launching in some of the more protected coves and bays, but no concrete ramps for larger vessels. Big yellowtail kingfish, samson fish, blue groper, sharks and southern bluefin tuna are available to keep sport and game fishers happy and there are plenty of snapper and big King George whiting for those with lighter tackle. When the weather is kind, a five metre boat will take you to most of the better inshore reefs, but a larger vessel is preferable for travelling out wide.

The bottom line with most of our Far West Coast areas is remoteness. Anyone planning an extended stay west of Ceduna should be well prepared. Accommodation options are limited, available supplies are basic at best and it's a long way back for help should something go wrong. However, the fishing is fantastic, which is why countless keen anglers return, year after year.

A mulloway caught from the surf at night from a Far West Coast beach.

THE HEAD OF THE BIGHT TO FOWLERS BAY

Each winter thousands of tourists flock to the cliffs fronting the Nullarbor Plain at the head of the Great Australian Bight. Migrating southern right whales are the major attraction, as literally hundreds of pregnant females travel there from cooler waters to give birth. It's a spectacular sight and facilities for viewing have been upgraded to make this area a *must* for trans-Nullarbor travellers between June and September. However, there are far more than just whales along this windswept and often foreboding stretch of coastline.

It's a surf fisher's paradise and has been for as long as four wheel drive vehicles have been available. Although there are few officially named beaches between Twin Rocks and the Dog Fence, there are many locations that bear titles bestowed upon them by locals. Most of these now have their own camping grounds, which must be used by visiting anglers or general tourists wishing to stay overnight. To the west of Twin Rocks it's largely inaccessible cliffs and limited fishing opportunities.

Legendary fishing locations such as 'Geues', 'The Hilton' and 'The Granites' are typical of what you'll find as you venture further from civilisation and each sees plenty of visiting surf fishermen annually. The tracks into these locations aren't marked, and the condition of each varies a lot – usually from bad to worse. If you're planning an extended stay, as most serious mulloway chasers do, you'll need a four wheel drive vehicle with enough 'grunt' to tow a decent trailer through soft sand. You will also need a tent, refrigeration, enough supplies to last you for the entire stay and, if possible, a quad bike for traversing beaches and sand dunes. Due to the remoteness of this region, a satellite phone will provide the ultimate in security, as standard cell phones have no service.

The nearest towns to most of the more popular Far West Coast surf beaches are Penong and Nundroo, neither of which offer much except petrol and take away food. The Yalata roadhouse used to offer fuel and food as well, but has been closed for a number of years now. You'll need to take in fuel for both quad bikes and generators and there is absolutely no fresh water available, so be prepared to carry plenty.

This is all aboriginal land, so permits are mandatory for those intending to enter and fish the beaches. These can be obtained in Ceduna and being caught without one can result in a hefty fine. All aboriginal lands here are alcohol free and it's an offence to possess any alcohol outside the designated hotels. Rangers patrol the beaches and camp grounds to enforce the no alcohol restriction and also to check that all campers are carrying the appropriate permits. Yalata Beach has restricted access, but most of the others can be fished, so long as you have the appropriate paperwork. Permits can be purchased on the internet at *www.yalata.org/permits.htm*

Whereas camping was once available on an ad-hoc basis throughout this region, it is now restricted to designated areas only and the number of campers at any one time is limited. Most who intend to fish and camp throughout the popular November-January period secure their camping permits and allocated sites early. Trying to get a permit a few weeks before you plan to visit usually results in disappointment, so booking well in advance is always prudent.

Wild camels, dingoes, wombats, emus and other Australian outback fauna are prolific in this region and most who travel there to fish will interact with all or any of them. The camels, in particular, are quite spectacular. They are the descendants of stock brought in by Afghan herders back in the nineteenth century and now roam the sand dunes and saltbush flats in vast mobs. Due to their isolation for over a century, these camels are considered to be the purest strain in the world and are sought after by overseas breeders. They are wild and unpredictable and should always be given a wide berth if you happen across them.

MAP 1 THE HEAD OF THE BIGHT TO FOWLERS BAY

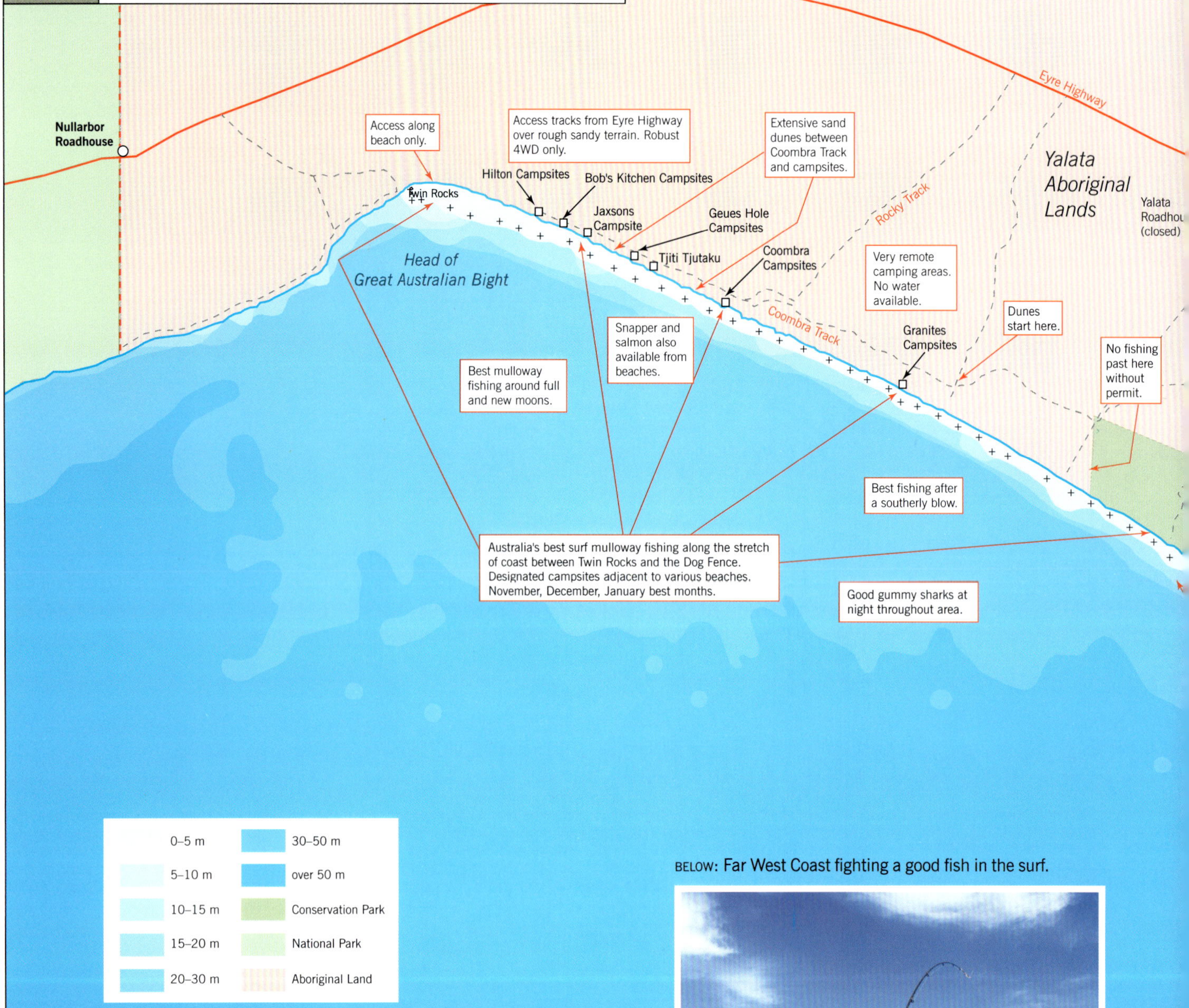

Nullarbor Roadhouse
Access along beach only.
Access tracks from Eyre Highway over rough sandy terrain. Robust 4WD only.
Extensive sand dunes between Coombra Track and campsites.
Eyre Highway
Yalata Aboriginal Lands
Yalata Roadhou
(closed)
Twin Rocks
Hilton Campsites
Bob's Kitchen Campsites
Jaxsons Campsite
Geues Hole Campsites
Tjiti Tjutaku
Coombra Campsites
Rocky Track
Very remote camping areas. No water available.
Dunes start here.
Head of Great Australian Bight
Coombra Track
Granites Campsites
No fishing past here without permit.
Snapper and salmon also available from beaches.
Best mulloway fishing around full and new moons.
Best fishing after a southerly blow.
Australia's best surf mulloway fishing along the stretch of coast between Twin Rocks and the Dog Fence. Designated campsites adjacent to various beaches. November, December, January best months.
Good gummy sharks at night throughout area.
0–5 m
5–10 m
10–15 m
15–20 m
20–30 m
30–50 m
over 50 m
Conservation Park
National Park
Aboriginal Land

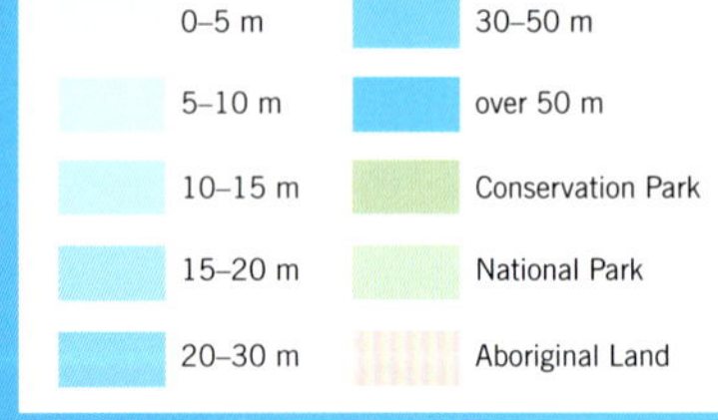

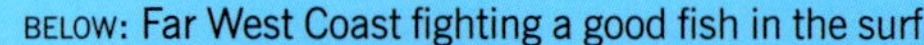

BELOW: Far West Coast fighting a good fish in the surf.

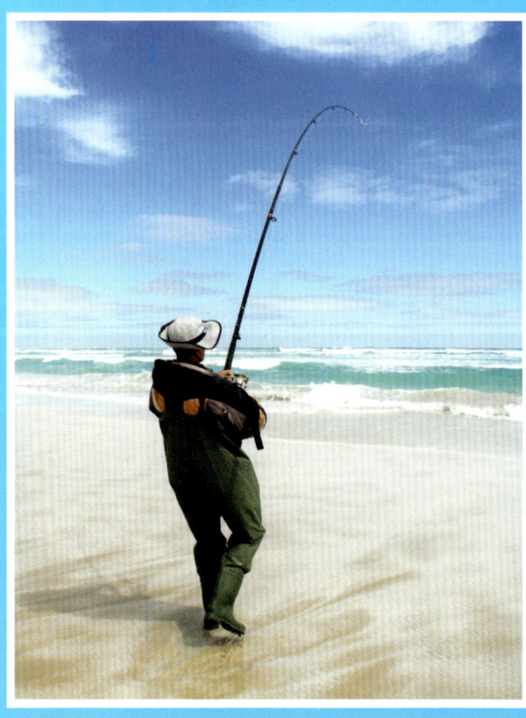

BELOW: A typical camp set up along one of the beaches along the Far West Coast.

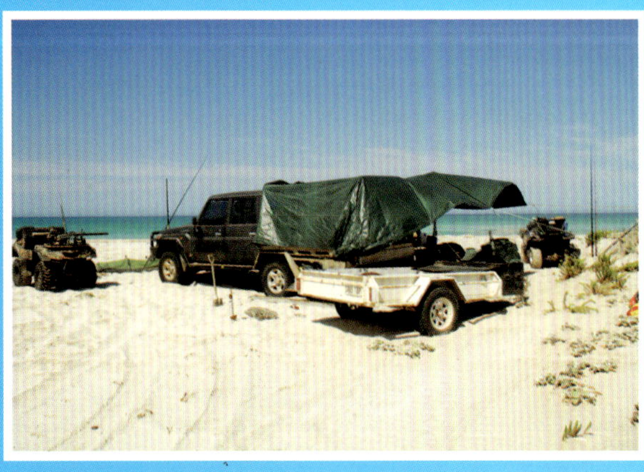

Yalata
DINGO FENCE
DINGO FENCE
DINGO FENCE
Good mulloway beaches. Public access is allowed through this whole area. Extreme sand dunes between tracks and beaches.
Nundroo
Fuel and caravan park.
Bookabie
(breaks with heavy swell)
Very good surf fishing. Excellent mulloway, salmon, snapper and sharks.
Coorabie
(Awash at HW)
D'Entrecasteaux Reef
(breaks)
(breaks)
(breaks)
Cape Adieu
(breaks)
Big kingfish, tuna, groper around reef system. Big boat territory only.
(seldom breaks)
(seldom breaks)
Cape Nuyts
(seldom breaks)
Scott Point
Scott Bay
Fowlers Bay
Port Eyre
Fowlers Bay
Point Fowler
Clare Bay
Nuyts Reef
(Awash at HW)
(breaks)
N
NW
NE
W
E
SW
SE
S
0
10
20
Kilometres

The camping areas along the Far West Coast beaches are generally tucked in behind the sand dunes and well protected from harsh onshore summer winds. Most have room for three or four groups of anglers, so sharing with others you may not know is always a possibility.

Setting up a comfortable, secure camp is usually first priority after trekking into the beach from the Eyre Highway. You'll need shelter from both sun and rain, somewhere to cook, somewhere to install your refrigeration (be it electric or simply a large capacity ice box) and an area where you can unwind and relax after a long day on the beach. Camping areas can get very hot on summer afternoons, with temperatures out of the wind often exceeding 50 degrees, so it's wise to spend much of the day out in the breeze if possible and return to camp as the sun goes down.

An off-road bike, preferably a four wheeler, will definitely open up the fishing possibilities along the Far West Coast beaches. Heavier four wheel drives simply can't go where quad bikes can and the mobility quads provide can often mean the difference between fish and no fish. The mulloway action in this region is generally confined to the deeper gutters on most beaches and these can often be many kilometres apart. Walking to find the best fishing water isn't really an option, so it pays to buy, borrow or hire a quad bike to facilitate exploration.

Although big mulloway can be caught during the hours of darkness on most of the Far West Coast beaches, this is also the period when stingrays and sharks are most active. Those anglers who are targeting mulloway only and don't wish to break their backs (and tackle) on sharks and rays generally fish through the day, then pack up and head for camp as the sun goes down. Prime time for mulloway seems to be around the change of high tide, when the inshore gutters are full and the baitfish are most accessible. Fresh baits of Australian salmon fillets, trevally fillets, mullet, whiting, squid and squid heads are the most popular offerings and, of course, small live fish can be deadly.

The usual beach mulloway fishing day consists of an early breakfast in camp, followed by a three or four hour fishing session around the morning high tide. It's then back to camp for lunch and a rest and back out again for a shorter session in the afternoon. With any luck, you will have a big, golden mulloway or two to celebrate that evening and a camp roast to round out a productive and enjoyable day. That's the ideal situation, of course, but as with most things in fishing, it doesn't always turn out that way!

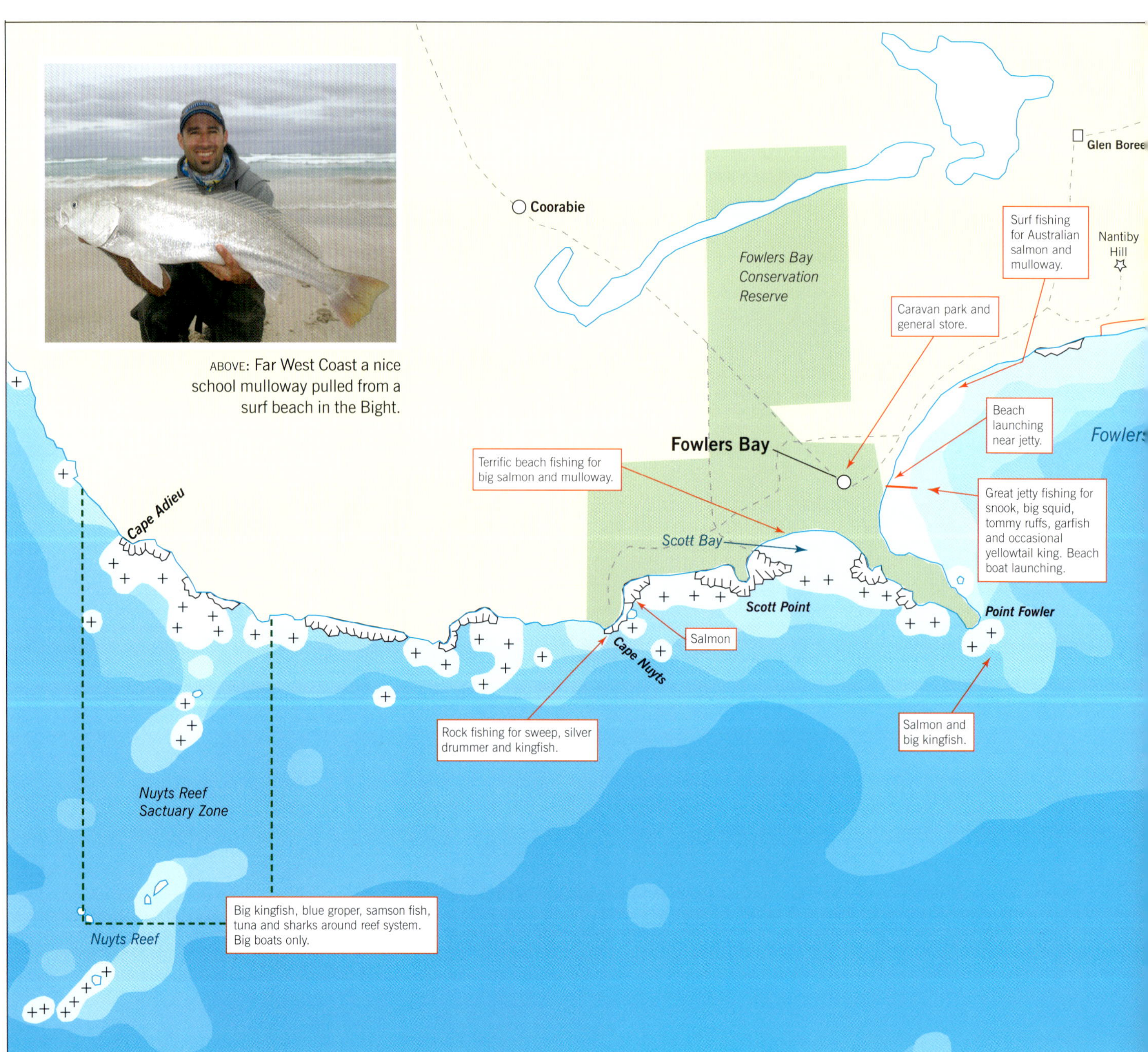

ABOVE: Far West Coast a nice school mulloway pulled from a surf beach in the Bight.

FOWLERS BAY TO CEDUNA

The coastal terrain begins to change a little as you leave the spectacular Nullarbor surf beaches and head eastward. There are more sheltered bays and rocky headlands that provide excellent fishing, as well as a couple of jetties for those with lighter tackle. This is still a remote part of South Australia, but it's all within a comfortable day trip of Ceduna, so you don't have to be quite as prepared and well equipped as those travelling further west.

MAP 2 SCOTT'S BAY

This is a beach that produces some huge mulloway during the warmer months, but not with the same regularity as the beaches at the head of the Bight. Situated just a few kilometres from Fowlers Bay, it is readily accessible to four wheel drivers. Most of the better mulloway come from the deeper gutters at night, but they can also be caught around tide changes during the day. Big slabs of Australian salmon and fresh squid heads are the preferred baits and, of course, the jewies will eagerly grab a live salmon or mullet if you can get your hands on one.

Scotts is also a first rate salmon beach during the cooler months. Big schools generally show up in winter time and are still around in early spring. Most of the salmon are big ones, with 3.5 kilograms about average and 4–5 kg specimens reasonably common. They will take both lures and pilchard baits and definitely bite best around dusk and dawn.

Big sharks patrol Scotts Bay regularly, especially when the salmon schools are in residence. Most are bronze whalers, but this is also white shark territory, which local surfers are constantly aware of. Big whaler sharks are hooked from the beach and occasionally landed by those well equipped to tackle them, but most break free or bite through nylon traces in short order.

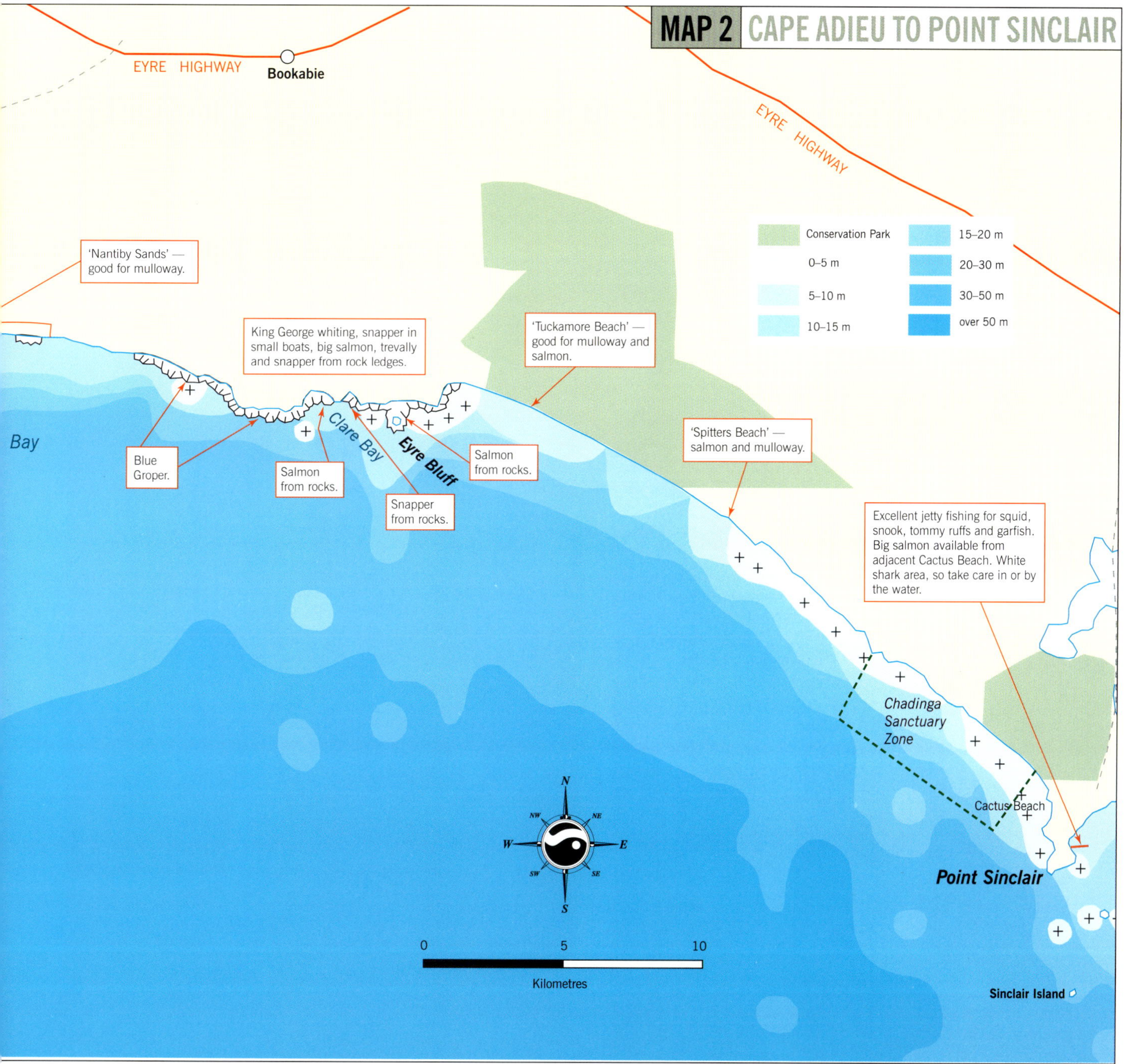

ABOVE: Launching a boat from the beach at Fowlers Bay.

MAP 2 FOWLERS BAY

Established as a base camp by explorer, Edward John Eyre, in 1840, Fowlers today is a thriving little holiday settlement with a lengthy jetty. It has around 22 permanent residents, but attracts many visitors to its holiday accommodation annually. It has a general store/cafe that provides basic grocery needs.

Fowlers has beach launching adjacent to the jetty and though it frequently weeds up creating difficulties, it's still possible to launch sizeable trailer boats with four wheel drive tow vehicles. There's a very popular charter operation that attracts plenty of visiting offshore anglers, most of whom target samson fish, yellowtail kings, bluefin tuna, big salmon, snapper and sharks. The reef systems wide of Fowlers Bay offer some fabulous fishing, but only when the weather is favourable.

There are some big King George whiting in the bay for those with smaller boats and it's not unusual to pull kilogram-plus fish from the inshore sand patches. Trolling around the headlands will often produce big salmon, snook and the occasional kingfish and there are plenty of crayfish for divers.

ABOVE: The reef systems wide of Fowlers Bay house some solid groper.

LEFT: Most of the salmon caught along the west coast are big.

Fowlers Bay jetty is a major holiday attraction and many who go there are satisfied to fish the pier exclusively. It is one of the best locations for big southern calamari in the state, with specimens of two kilograms and more taken regularly. Most squidders use a teaser line in conjunction with an imitation prawn jig and often take home the daily bag limit of 15 per person. Best squidding time is late afternoon through into the evening, but calamari can be expected throughout the day in reasonable numbers.

Big tommy ruffs often turn up after dark, along with snook and garfish. It's possible to catch a good feed of all three varieties, provided you have plenty of berley and the right bait. Gents (blowfly maggots) are undoubtedly the best for gar and tommies, while strips of squid, fish fillets, blue bait or small minnow lures will nearly always catch snook. A few 'oddballs' turn up from the jetty at times, including giant herring and Atlantic salmon. Exactly why a warm water fish like a giant herring and a cold water fish like a salmon would venture to Fowlers Bay is anyone's guess, but it has happened more than once.

Fowlers is the ideal jumping off point for those who enjoy fishing further west, but don't wish to camp overnight. There are several holiday rental properties and a caravan park that offers 25 powered sites and four on-site caravans. It's a neat place to stay and is the ideal location in which to break the lengthy trip across the Nullarbor.

You will need to have confidence in your 4WD and driving abilities to tackle the beaches of the Far West Coast.

MAP 2 Clare Bay

This is a picturesque location that's popular with both anglers and general holiday makers. It's an easy drive from Ceduna and a popular weekend get-away. There is a handful of shacks situated along the cliff tops and a protected bay that's ideal for both land-based and small boat fishing. There are several easily accessed rock ledges that produce hectic action on big salmon at times, as well as lots of blue groper, silver trevally, snook, the occasional yellowtail king and snapper.

Most of the better salmon catches are made by anglers using pilchard baits set beneath styrene floats and it's not unusual to pull 4-5 kilogram fish, so light tackle isn't a viable option. Berleying with crushed pilchards or fish scraps will generally attract the salmon in numbers and there is always the chance of hooking a decent snapper. A long handled gaff can be a definite asset while fishing the Clare Bay rock ledges.

Big King George whiting and small to medium snapper are the main catch offshore, with good fishing available from small trailer boats when conditions are right. Summer winds can be a problem at Clare Bay, particularly in the afternoons, so it's wise to be on the water early and back in cleaning the catch by lunchtime. There are plenty of big snook for lure trollers as well and enough squid to make a few drifts over the inshore weed beds a good option.

MAP 2 Tuckamore Beach

Along with Scotts Bay, Locks Well and Sheringa, Tuckamore enjoys legendary status among SA's keen surf fishers. It's a magnificent beach with pure white sand and a reputation for producing big Australian salmon year-round. The fishing is generally most reliable during the cooler months, when salmon schools move in and take up temporary residence. The fish vary in size from what South Aussies call 'salmon trout' all the way up to five kilos and beyond, with 3.5kg a reasonable average.

A decent four wheel drive vehicle is mandatory for fishing Tuckamore, as the deep, fish-holding gutters can often be spread over several kilometres. It's wise to survey most of the beach prior to fishing and select a gutter that will fill quickly on the rising tide. If high water coincides with dusk, conditions are ideal, but you can expect salmon at any stage of the making tide.

Many who fish Tuckamore regularly do so with metal lures and in most cases there is little need to vary this approach. However, it's always wise to have a block of pilchards on hand in case the fish are in a fickle mood. Berleying from the beach will definitely increase the chance of a consistent salmon bite, but it can also attract sharks and rays, both of which are a nuisance and may put the salmon off the bite.

Big mulloway are also taken from Tuckamore at times, with some of the better catches occurring earlier in the year around September/October onwards than the beaches further west. 60 and 70 pounders are hooked by those prepared to put in the time, with the most consistent catches coming from late afternoon through into the evening. The usual baits of fresh salmon fillets and squid seem to work well and it's not often that long casts are required here, as the better surf gutters are often quite close.

Light tackle, smaller hooks and plenty of berley will often produce nice yellow eye mullet, big tommy ruffs, salmon trout and the occasional King George whiting. Both the tommies and salmon trout will respond well to small soft plastic lures and can provide plenty of light line fun. The southern end of Tuckamore Beach, just before a rocky headland, is called 'Spitters Beach' where salmon and mulloway can be found.

MAP2 Point Sinclair

Situated off the Eyre Highway about 20 kilometres south of Penong, Sinclair is one of the most beautiful coves along SA's Far West Coast. It's close to Cactus Beach, one of the most famous surfing locations in the country, and within an easy drive of Ceduna for day trippers. There is a camping ground (unpowered) that is quite popular with visiting anglers and surfers and one of the most productive jetties in the state.

Huge snook can be taken from the jetty on hard-body minnow lures, soft plastics and natural baits like pilchards, squid and blue bait. The best time is late afternoon and you'll need reasonably heavy line, as some of these fish are over a metre long and can weigh better than three kilograms. Sinclair jetty has no lights, so you'll need a torch or lantern to fish there after dark.

Big tommy ruffs, garfish and squid make up the remainder of the jetty catch for those with lighter gear and there are some big sharks available for the more adventurous. A young boy was tragically taken by a great white while swimming from the Point Sinclair jetty back in 1975, so care should always be taken while landing large fish in this area. Mulloway have also been hooked here and it's a good idea to have a live bait set on the bottom while you're fishing for other species.

Cactus Beach itself, while generally better known for the world-class waves it produces, can also be a terrific location for big Australian salmon during winter and spring. Quite often visiting surfers find themselves sharing the waves with salmon schools, which must be a little un-nerving considering the number of sharks in this area!

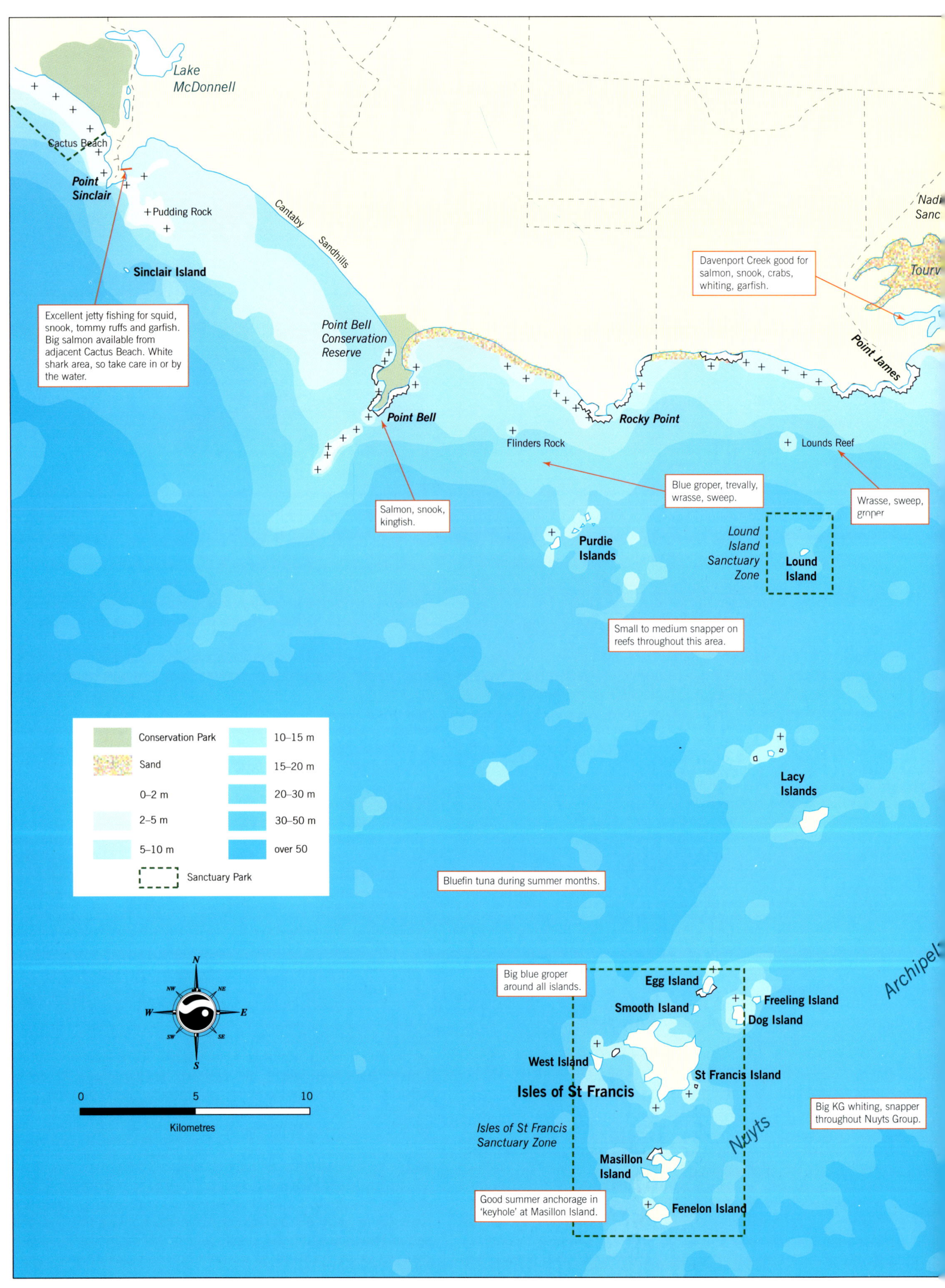

Lake McDonnell
Cactus Beach
Point Sinclair
Pudding Rock
Sinclair Island
Cantaby Sandhills
Point Bell Conservation Reserve
Point Bell
Rocky Point
Flinders Rock
Lounds Reef
Point James
Davenport Creek good for salmon, snook, crabs, whiting, garfish.
Excellent jetty fishing for squid, snook, tommy ruffs and garfish. Big salmon available from adjacent Cactus Beach. White shark area, so take care in or by the water.
Salmon, snook, kingfish.
Blue groper, trevally, wrasse, sweep.
Wrasse, sweep, groper
Purdie Islands
Lound Island Sanctuary Zone
Lound Island
Small to medium snapper on reefs throughout this area.
Lacy Islands
Conservation Park
Sand
0–2 m
2–5 m
5–10 m
10–15 m
15–20 m
20–30 m
30–50 m
over 50
Sanctuary Park
Bluefin tuna during summer months.
N
NE
E
SE
S
SW
W
NW
0
5
10
Kilometres
Big blue groper around all islands.
Egg Island
Smooth Island
Freeling Island
Dog Island
West Island
St Francis Island
Isles of St Francis
Isles of St Francis Sanctuary Zone
Masillon Island
Fenelon Island
Good summer anchorage in 'keyhole' at Masillon Island.
Nuyts
Big KG whiting, snapper throughout Nuyts Group.

MAP 3 POINT BELL TO GASCOIGNE BAY
EYRE HIGHWAY
FLINDERS HIGHWAY
Jetty fishing for tommies, snook, crabs, squid.
Deep water jetty good for tommies, snook, squid, garfish, occasional snapper.
Wandana
Maltee
Denial Bay
KG whiting, blue swimmers.
Murat Bay
Ceduna
Boat ramp
Matts Point
Creek Flat Sanctuary Zone
Thevenard
Bosanquet Bay
Cape Beaufort
Point Peter Sanctuary Zone
Point Peter
Snook trolling.
Cape Vivonne
Wittelbee Point
Yatala Channel
Denial Bay
Decres Island Bay
Laura Bay
Big snapper on channel edges.
Snook, KG whiting.
Cape D'Estrees
Snook trolling.
St Peter Island
Waterwitch Channel
Smoky Bay
KG whiting, gar, snook, squid.
Goat Island
Eyre Island
Smoky Bay
Evans Islands
Flinders Reef
snapper, KG whiting.
Groper, sweep, wrasse, trevally.
Goalen Rocks
Cape Missiessy
Good jetty fishing for tommies, gar, snook, squid.
Franklin Islands
KG whiting, big snook.
Barlows Beach Sanctuary Zone
Point Dillon
Point De Mole
Gascoigne Bay
Mary Bay
Point Brown
Edward Bay
Point Collinson
Salmon, snook trolling.

MAP 3 POINT BELL

This is a delightful location that provides some excellent rock and small boat fishing opportunities. Big Australian salmon frequent this stretch of coast year-round and can turn up at virtually any time. They are caught from the rock ledges on both lures and pilchard baits set beneath bobby corks and vary in size from 1-5 kilograms. There is also some excellent sweep fishing around the Point Bell rocks and these are generally targeted using medium weight tackle, floating rigs and either squid, cockle or cray tail baits. Sweep to over a kilogram are reasonably common and make great sport when hooked in turbulent water.

Also targeted from the rocks here are snook, silver drummer, tommy ruffs and the occasional kingfish, although most kings hooked are lost due to inadequate tackle. The rock platforms and ledges are generally safe, but it's a good idea to fish in the company of others and never venture on to rocks that are wet from spray or ocean swell.

It's possible to launch a small boat in the corner of the beach, just inside the point, and when sea conditions are good, you can catch some amazing fish off Point Bell. Big King George whiting are a prime target and it's not unusual to catch them over 50 centimetres and a kilogram in weight. Snook, squid, salmon and snapper are also available not far from the beach and most are of good size. Yellowtail kingfish patrol the reefs and ledges, especially during the warmer months, and some beauties to over 30 kilograms have been taken by those with the right tackle and technique.

Further offshore lies some of the best deep reef fishing in South Australia. The Purdie Islands are home to some thumping blue groper, while southern bluefin tuna are regular visitors between Christmas time and February. There are plenty of sharks of various sizes and species and samson fish are often hooked by those targeting snapper over reefy bottom. Mulloway are also caught from September through the summer. It's a real 'mixed bag' situation as you venture further offshore, but low swell and light winds are mandatory.

MAP 3 DAVENPORT CREEK

Situated about 40 kilometres west of Ceduna and at the entrance to Tourville Bay, Davenport Creek is a favourite recreation area for thousands of visiting anglers, holiday makers, campers and picnickers. It's essentially the southerly arm of the multi-channel connection between Tourville and Denial Bays and is generally a reliable light tackle fishing venue. It's busy most fine weekends, but continues to fish well, despite the pressure.

Davenport is flanked by magnificent sand dunes nearer the mouth, which give way to an extensive (and very important) mangrove system. It's a significant fish nursery area for species like King George and schoolwhiting, gar, mullet, juvenile salmon, squid and blue swimmer crabs. The creek meanders inland and eventually becomes an extensive salt marsh, which again is environmentally important.

You'll need a four wheel drive vehicle to access Davenport Creek proper, but conventional vehicles can get through to both Ocean and Cockleshell Beaches. Ocean Beach produces some good surf fishing at times, with salmon, school mulloway, mullet and flathead among the regular catch. It can produce mulloway up to 30 kg, but there are only

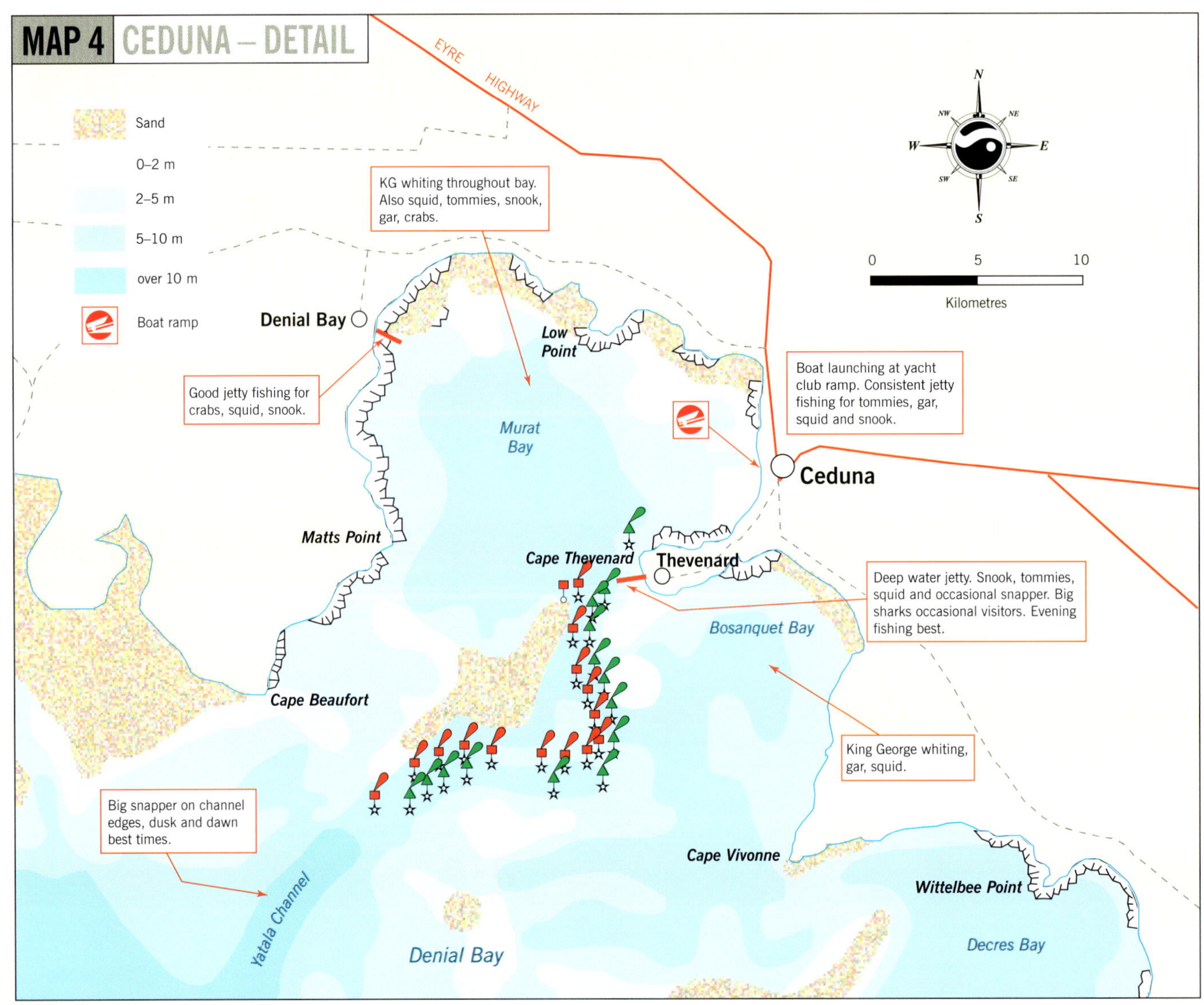

LEFT: The waters wide of Fowlers are reliable for school sized bluefin during the summer months

BELOW: A nice red snapper destined for the dinner table

smaller ones in Davenport Creek.

Davenport Creek itself teems with fish-life at times. It's a good spot to drop a net for blue swimmer crabs in the summertime and although you'll have to throw back some of the King George whiting, it's possible to grab a feed of legal-size ones from among the little guys. Salmon trout are available for most of the year, along with some nice garfish, flathead, tommy ruffs and the occasional flounder. Larger salmon enter from the sea spasmodically and generally pounce on any bait or lure they can find.

A small boat on the creek will open up fishing possibilities considerably. Trolling small lures will produce plenty of salmon trout, small to medium snook and larger tommies. Drop netting from small boats in the lower reaches also yields blue swimmers and is certainly a better option than crabbing from the shore.

MAP 4 CEDUNA

This is the last major settlement in South Australia for those heading west. It marks the beginning of the Eyre Highway and is often referred to as the gateway to the Nullarbor Plain. Ceduna is also a significant shipping and bulk handling port, with a long, deep water jetty at nearby Thevenard. The permanent population is 2,300 and the town offers a range of facilities for visitors. There are several caravan parks, modern motels and abundant holiday rental properties, so accommodation is rarely an issue.

There is plenty of productive land-based fishing around Ceduna, particularly beach and jetty, and species range from tommy ruffs and yellow eye mullet to flathead, snapper, snook and sharks. The Ceduna town jetty is very reliable for squid, gar and tommies, especially in the evenings. It's a popular place to wet a line and few anglers come home disappointed with their catch.

The Thevenard jetty, just a few kilometres to the south, is considerably deeper, as it handles ocean-going cargo ships on a regular basis. It, too, is good for snook at night time, tommies, gar, squid and the odd King George whiting. Big snapper are caught from the seaward end at times, but not consistently. Big sharks, mainly bronze whalers, can be hooked on big baits drifted out under balloons and there are occasional visits from great whites.

It was near Goat Island, just outside the entrance to Ceduna's Denial Bay, that the largest gamefish ever recorded was hooked back in 1959. The angler was renowned heavy tackle specialist, Alf Dean, and the fish was a white shark weighing 2,664 pounds. Dean's record has stood, unchallenged, for decades and now that white sharks are a protected species, it's a benchmark in gamefishing that is likely to remain forever.

A small boat can be used to fish inside Denial Bay in all but the worst weather and will provide access to productive King George whiting grounds. Most of the whiting are small to medium, but those who know the area well rarely miss out on a good feed. Big snapper enter Denial Bay from late spring through the summer months and specimens to 12 kilograms and more are caught along the edges of the shipping channel. Dusk and dawn are prime snapper fishing periods, but they are also hooked during the night.

Denial Bay teems with blue swimmer crabs throughout the summer months and these are netted both from boats and jetties. The Denial Bay jetty, which is now just one third of its original length, is a terrific family venue that produces crabs, squid, tommy ruffs and snook. It's just a 14 kilometre drive from Ceduna township and is therefore popular with both locals and tourists. This is one of the oldest and most historic piers in South Australia and was once the second longest. Oyster farms are scattered throughout the shallower sections of Denial Bay and producers are usually happy to sell fresh oysters to the general public.

For those towing a larger trailer boat to Ceduna or keen to engage the services of a local charter operator, the blue water fishing outside Denial Bay can be spectacular. There are snapper grounds stretching from the entrance of the bay southward and westward and although the majority of reds caught are six kilograms and under, they can be prolific at times. 'Bagging out' on these school snapper often takes less than half an hour and they can be a lot of fun on light tackle.

As you move further offshore into deeper water, bluefin tuna are a possibility during summertime as they migrate down the west coast toward Port Lincoln. Most of these fish are in the 10–20 kilogram class and put up a tremendous fight on light sportfishing tackle. Trolling skirted lures or 120 to 160 mm diving hard body lures is a reliable way of catching them, with frenzied seabird activity an indicator of feeding tuna schools. There are samson fish, yellowtail kingfish and some massive blue groper to be caught around the offshore islands and reefs, but you'll need the right equipment and some local knowledge to catch these consistently.

Blue groper are rarely targeted anywhere in South Australia, but are generally regarded as a welcome by-catch. They are tough, tenacious fighters and, as a bonus, make fantastic table fare. Many are hooked each year by those fishing offshore from Ceduna and a good majority are released. Groper are subject to a strict 'slot' size limit, with only fish of between 60 –100 centimetres long eligible to be kept.

CHAPTER 2
THE WEST COAST

A nice sunset over a west coast surf beach.

The stretch of coastline between Ceduna and Port Lincoln is rugged, spectacular and among the most productive in the state for angling of many types. Fronting the eastern shores of the Great Australian Bight, our West Coast varies enormously in geographical form. There are countless weather-worn headlands and cliffs, many kilometres of turbulent surf beach, a few sheltered bays and inlets and a host of offshore islands that see few visiting anglers each year. Apart from fresh water fishing, it has something for everyone.

Most of the coastal townships and ports are small, with some offering a good range of services and facilities and others offering little more than a pub and general store. This is a very popular coast with visiting anglers, both from within South Australia and interstate. Victorians, in particular, seem to have discovered exactly how good the surf and offshore fishing can be and now turn up in droves during the autumn and winter months.

Most of SA's West Coast is weather affected for a good part of the year. The influence of the Southern Ocean can be fickle and unrelenting and it's a good idea to plan extended fishing holidays during the periods of generally calm weather. It's often windy over the summer moths, with strong afternoon sea breezes seriously affecting offshore boating and hampering beach fishing. Autumn and early winter seem most stable and it's often possible to enjoy a week or more of cool, still conditions in April and May. This is the time to head offshore or plan to tackle any of the renowned salmon beaches.

Winter can offer windows of good weather, but there are frequent north-westerly gales during this period as well, so it can be a hit-or-miss time to visit. Spring is probably the most fickle season of all and although the air temperatures are generally pleasant enough, onshore winds blow regularly. October and November are often referred to by West Coast locals as 'Rocktober' and 'Blovember', indicating that plenty of breeze is to be expected.

CEDUNA TO ELLISTON

From mangrove-lined inlets to long stretches of sand and surf, this section of the West Coast is a true angling paradise.

MAP 5 Smoky Bay

Situated within a comfortable half hour southward drive from Ceduna, Smoky Bay is a delightful little settlement with a long jetty and, thanks to oyster farming, a thriving economy. Its permanent population is around 200 and it offers basic amenities, caravan park and good fishing, both offshore and land-based.

The bay is relatively protected from ocean swell by Eyre Island, which lies about 10 kilometres offshore. It is a vast and generally shallow bay that can present navigation issues around low tide for those unfamiliar with the area. Razor fish – those large bi-valve molluscs common in many South Australian bays and estuaries – are prolific in certain parts of Smoky Bay and these are collected both as seafood and bait for King George whiting.

Whiting are the most popular fish for small boat anglers and although those caught inside the bay are generally not large, most are above the legal minimum size and are well worth pursuing. Goolwa cockles, squid and razor fish are the most popular whiting baits and it's wise to keep your tackle light for best results.

There are snook, squid and plenty of nice garfish throughout Smoky Bay and big yellowtail kingfish put in an appearance from time to time. The jetty yields tommy ruffs, snook and some garfish at night time, but striped perch (trumpeters) can be a nuisance during the warmer months. These spiky, unpalatable fish arrive in plague proportions in late spring and can make life very difficult for those targeting more desirable species. Some nice silver trevally up to around 1kg in weight are caught regularly from the jetty. These fish will take small cubes of pilchard fished close to the bottom. If you do hook a nice trevally close to the pylons, you will have to direct the fish into clear water before your line gets severed on the barnacles.

There's a good, all-tide boat ramp in Smoky Bay and the caravan park is well appointed. Basic fishing tackle is available from service stations.

The ramp at Smoky Bay offers the closest launching point for Cannan Reef, which lies to the south-west of St Francis Island. It's a 72km run from the ramp at Smoky to access Cannan, so this is definitely big-boat territory. Some big kingfish and Samson fish are caught around the deeper edges of the reef system, and school-sized Bluefin tuna are fairly common out here in summer and early autumn. You will have to pick a good window of weather to access this offshore reef.

Back inshore, and around Point Brown south of Smoky Bay there is a huge variety of fish that can be caught from both the rocks and beaches such as blue groper, salmon, garfish, whiting, flathead, snook and tommies. Mulloway can be found in St Mary Bay around Easter, but require many hours of effort.

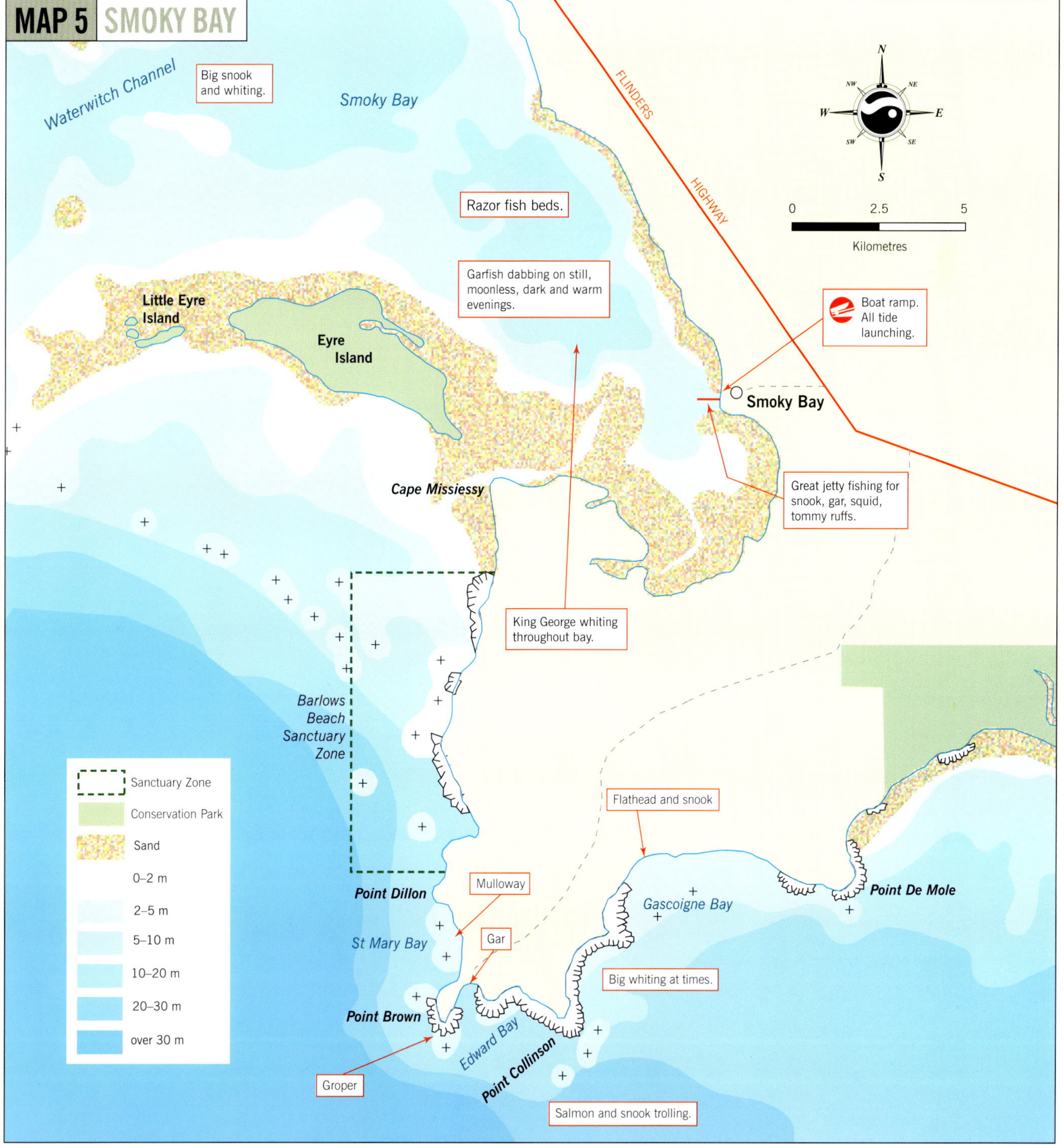

MAP 6 Acraman Creek

Just a 15 kilometre drive to the south of Smoky Bay, Acraman Creek is a small, but charming tidal inlet. It's reminiscent of Davenport Creek, near Ceduna, as it is lined with dense mangroves near the mouth and terminates in samphire flats further inland. Acraman is a very popular weekend venue for those living in Ceduna, Smoky and Streaky Bays, as it is easily accessed and provides some excellent fishing opportunities.

Salmon of various sizes are abundant throughout the creek system, with most in the 1–2 kilogram bracket. These can be trolled from a small boat or hooked from the shore on lures and fresh baits. Trevally, King George whiting and garfish are also present.Nice tommy ruffs, snook and mullet are also common in Acraman, along with blue swimmer crabs during the warmer months. There is small boat launching available, but a four wheel drive tow vehicle is necessary. This is a terrific venue for canoe and kayak fishing, as it is well protected from outside weather.

There's a shelter for picnics and barbecues adjacent to the launching site and camping is permitted in designated areas. About the only drawback when fishing Acraman Creek are the thousands of mosquitos, which invade on dusk and are relentless in their quest for human blood. A liberal coating of insect repellent is mandatory if you're there late in the day.

MAP 6 Streaky Bay

Discovered and named by Matthew Flinders in 1802, Streaky is now one of the West Coast's most popular holiday destinations with visiting anglers. It lies on the Flinders Highway and is roughly 730 kilometres by road from Adelaide and about 110 kilometres south of Ceduna. The population is around 1200, but this can swell to 3,000 or more during peak holiday times.

The township of Streaky Bay is nestled inside Blanche Port, which lies at the southern-most extremity of the bay. Most of Streaky is quite

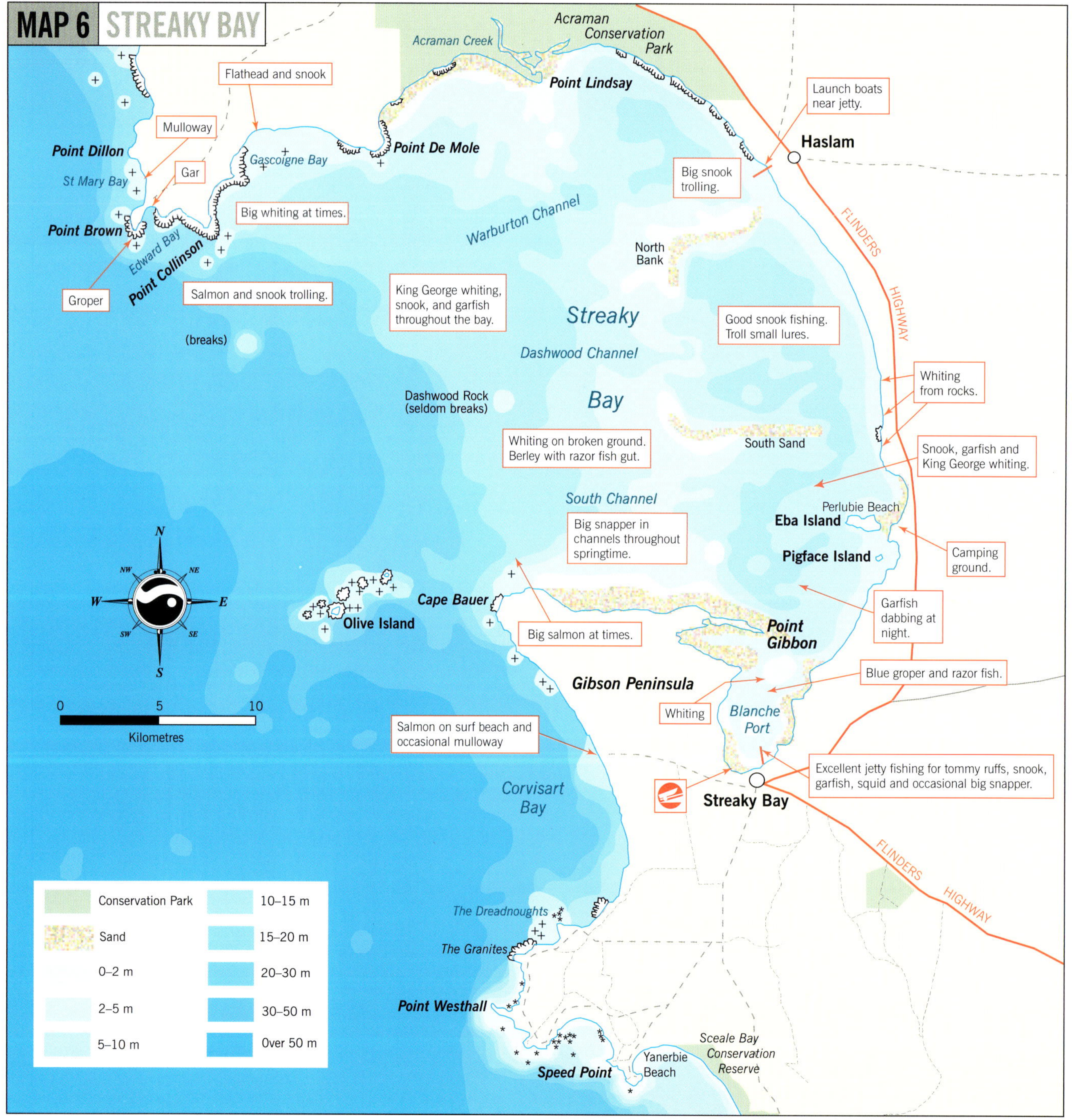

shallow, with tidal flats exposed at low tide and several recognised channels leading out toward the Great Australian Bight.

The bay is most famous for its King George whiting, which are available all year round in various concentrations. Catching a boat limit of whiting is generally easy, provided you have some knowledge of the area and are equipped with razor fish and berley. There are plenty of big snook, tommy ruffs, blue swimmer crabs, garfish and, in season, some big snapper.

It's practical to fish much of the bay from a five metre trailer boat, which can be launched from a good ramp located a short drive to the west of the town. The bay can chop up, however, particularly on summer afternoons, so it pays to be on the water early at this time of year (November in particular), and back by lunchtime to clean the catch.

Streaky Bay jetty produces most of the usual West Coast inshore fish varieties, along with big snapper in October. 25 pounders have been taken from the jetty by persistent anglers, with dawn and dusk easily the most productive periods. Big sharks are occasional visitors to Streaky Bay jetty and there have been several great whites seen at close quarters, so it's wise to take care. A mesh swimming enclosure is attached to the pier for those who like to take a dip.

There are a couple of productive surf beaches within easy driving distance that yield both salmon and mulloway. Probably the most famous of these is Paddy's Plains, which turns up mulloway of over 50 pounds annually, along with gummy sharks and the odd decent snapper. Streaky's Back Beach and Halley's Beach are worth a visit when sea conditions are favourable. The majority of mulloway caught along these beaches are school sized fish up to 10kg, but as mentioned before some big fish are caught every year. It's a good idea to fish around the peak of the high tide, with a medium size swell being an advantage. If the swell is too big, it tends to bring in clumps of weed along this coast, but when the swell is small, the fish tend to hang out wide and don't venture into these inshore gutters.

For those with larger boats, Streaky provides access to some truly wonderful offshore fishing. Southern bluefin tuna migrate past this area from December through until February annually and often venture within range of sportsfishers. The outside grounds are no place to be in that five metre half cab, however, and I'd suggest seven metres as a safe minimum vessel length if venturing out wide.

The islands of the Nuyts Archipelago can be accessed from Streaky Bay, but these are a long way offshore and a visit demands calm, predictable weather. Big blue groper, samson fish, yellowtail

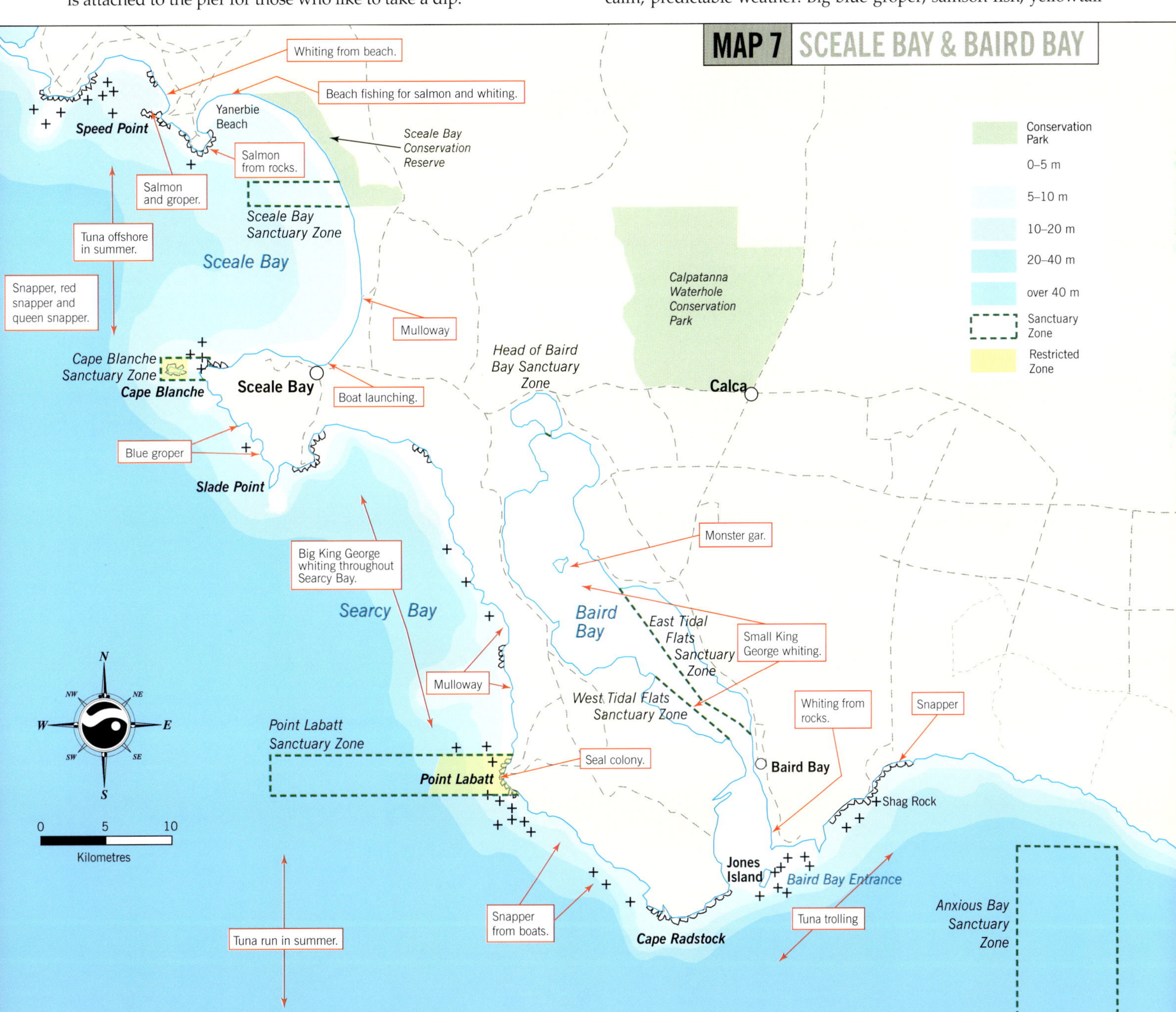

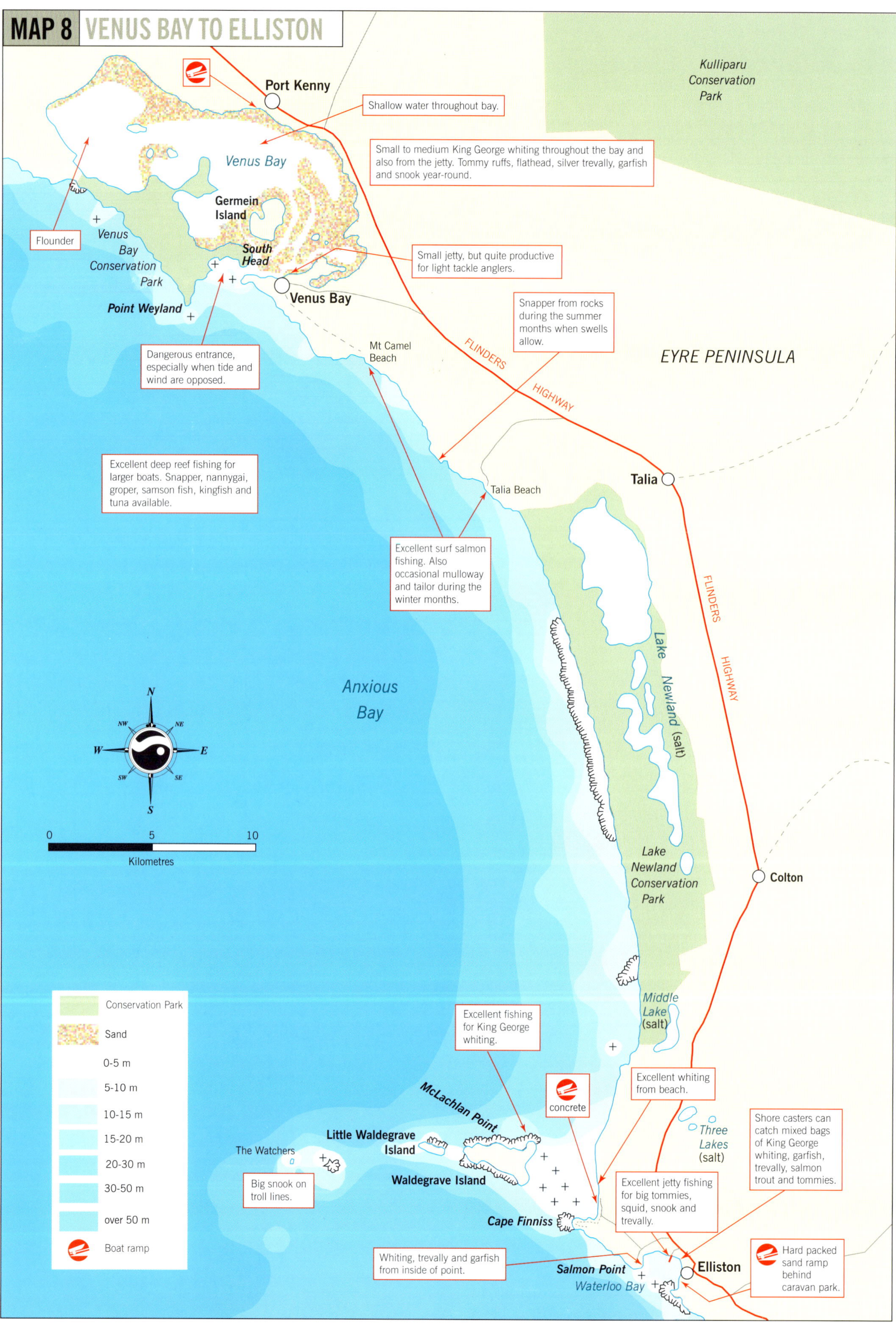

MAP 8 VENUS BAY TO ELLISTON
Port Kenny
Shallow water throughout bay.
Kulliparu Conservation Park
Small to medium King George whiting throughout the bay and also from the jetty. Tommy ruffs, flathead, silver trevally, garfish and snook year-round.
Venus Bay
Germein Island
Flounder
Venus Bay Conservation Park
South Head
Small jetty, but quite productive for light tackle anglers.
Venus Bay
Point Weyland
Snapper from rocks during the summer months when swells allow.
Dangerous entrance, especially when tide and wind are opposed.
Mt Camel Beach
FLINDERS HIGHWAY
EYRE PENINSULA
Excellent deep reef fishing for larger boats. Snapper, nannygai, groper, samson fish, kingfish and tuna available.
Talia Beach
Talia
Excellent surf salmon fishing. Also occasional mulloway and tailor during the winter months.
Lake Newland (salt)
Anxious Bay
N
NE
E
SE
S
SW
W
NW
0
5
10
Kilometres
Lake Newland Conservation Park
Colton
Conservation Park
Sand
0-5 m
5-10 m
10-15 m
15-20 m
20-30 m
30-50 m
over 50 m
Boat ramp
Middle Lake (salt)
Excellent fishing for King George whiting.
concrete
Excellent whiting from beach.
McLachlan Point
Three Lakes (salt)
Shore casters can catch mixed bags of King George whiting, garfish, trevally, salmon trout and tommies.
The Watchers
Little Waldegrave Island
Big snook on troll lines.
Waldegrave Island
Excellent jetty fishing for big tommies, squid, snook and trevally.
Cape Finniss
Whiting, trevally and garfish from inside of point.
Salmon Point
Waterloo Bay
Elliston
Hard packed sand ramp behind caravan park.

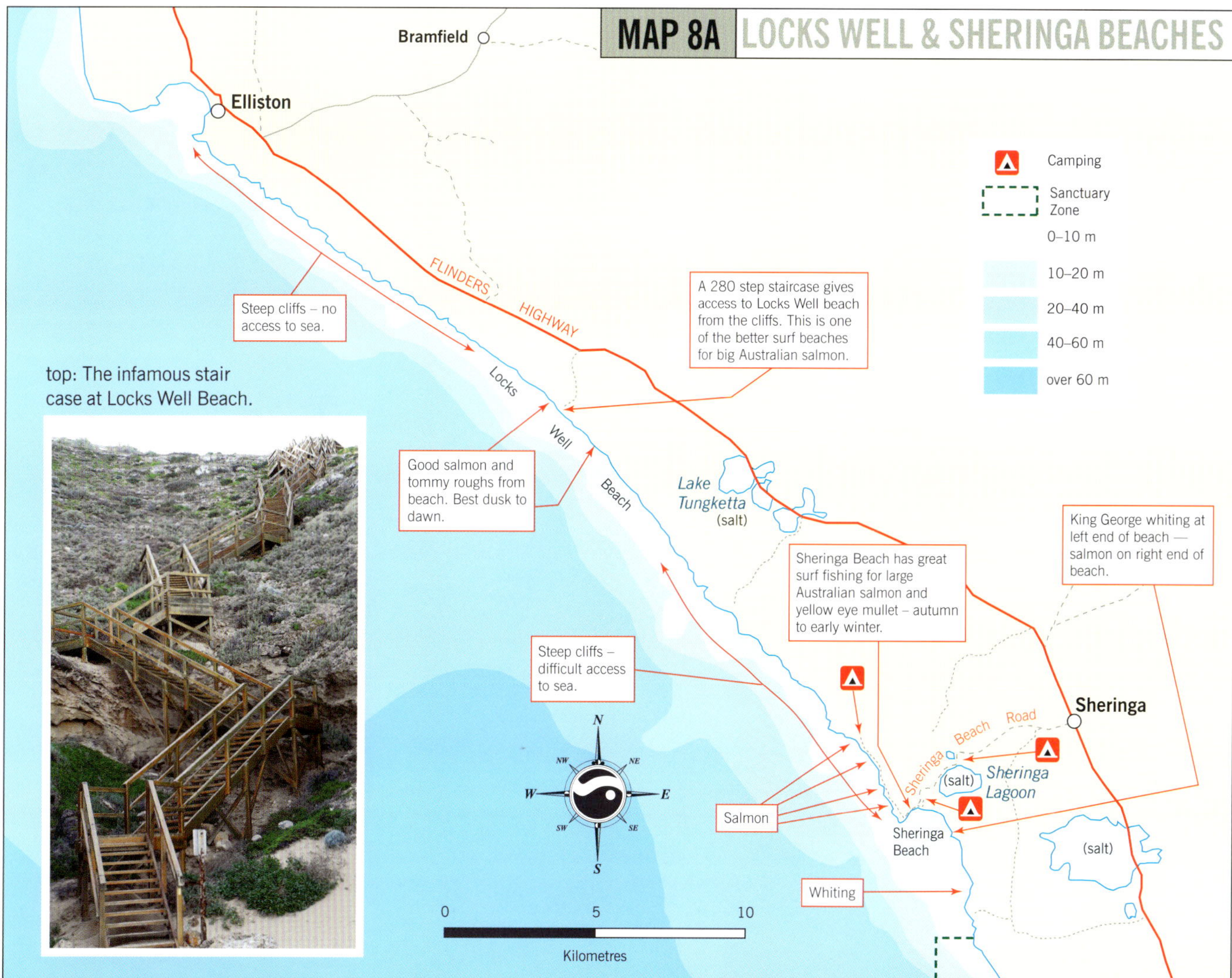

top: The infamous stair case at Locks Well Beach.

kings, snapper and sharks of several varieties are hooked regularly in this archipelago, particularly around St Francis, Masillon and Fenelon Islands. There are good overnight anchorages available, particularly at St Francis and Masillon Islands, and it is common to see several flybridge cruisers and similar large boats in these anchorages during the annual tuna run. This is prime white shark territory, as the islands all carry significant fur seal and sealion populations.

MAP 7 Sceale Bay

32 kilometres south of Streaky Bay lies one of the most naturally beautiful coastal bays in South Australia. Sceale Bay has a permanent population of just 30 or so and it's a great place to visit if you have a small boat and want ready access to the Southern Ocean. There's concrete ramp that will handle most trailer boats, a caravan park and basic camping area (no power available) and a general store which *may* be open on odd days in summer, but little else in the way of facilities.

There is some terrific offshore fishing available here when the weather is favourable, including trolling for bluefin tuna during summer time. Quite often the tuna schools pass within a few miles of Sceale Bay, enabling trailer boat sportfishers safe and easy access. There are also plenty of productive reef systems within striking range of Sceale Bay and these are generally good for big silver trevally, nannygai, snapper, blue morwong, samson fish and groper.

MAP 7 Baird Bay

Best known for its sealion population, Baird Bay is a vast and generally shallow inlet, separated from the Bight by Calca Peninsula. It's a small settlement that's home to one of the country's most renowned Eco-Tour operations. It's also a good spot for small boaties to try for King George whiting. Most of the whiting are small to medium and you will need to have a measuring device on board, but it's generally possible to grab a feed of legal-size fish. Winter time is the peak period for whiting in Bairds Bay, with good numbers of fish pushing into the shallow inlet from around May through until August.

Flathead, flounder, garfish, snook, salmon trout and tommy ruffs are also quite abundant inside Baird Bay. There are some good reef systems out in open water from Bairds Bay which fish well for snapper, nannygai and rock lobster, but navigating the entrance can be particularly dangerous, and isn't recommended in anything but perfect conditions.

MAP 8 Venus Bay

Venus is accessed off Flinders Highway via Port Kenny and the township is tiny, with a permanent population of just 20. The bay itself is vast and shallow, but it does provide ready access to the Southern Ocean. The Venus Bay heads can be treacherous at times, particularly under the influence of a strong run-out tide and opposing onshore winds. It's one of the few bar crossings here in South Australia, and can be unnerving, even for experienced crew. Large boats have come to grief here, so the entrance is best left to those with plenty of local knowledge and experience.

King George whiting abound throughout the entire Venus Bay system, but again they are generally small. Although whiting can be caught year round in this system, it is the winter months that fish more consistently. Silver trevally, squid, snook, garfish, flathead, tommy

MAP 9 INVESTIGATOR GROUP OF ISLANDS

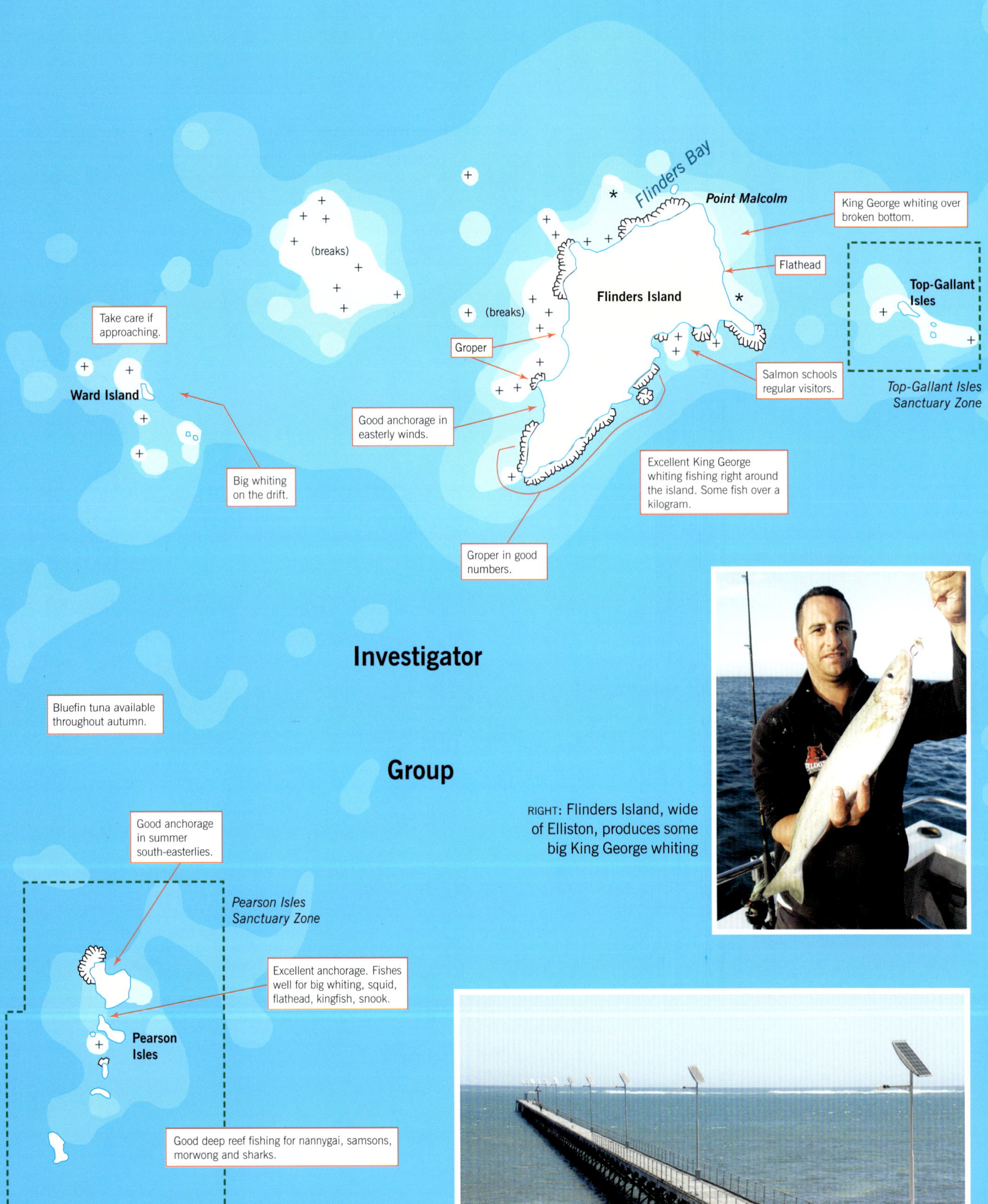

RIGHT: Flinders Island, wide of Elliston, produces some big King George whiting

RIGHT: Elliston jetty within Waterloo Bay.

BELOW: Beach fishing is what Elliston is famous for.

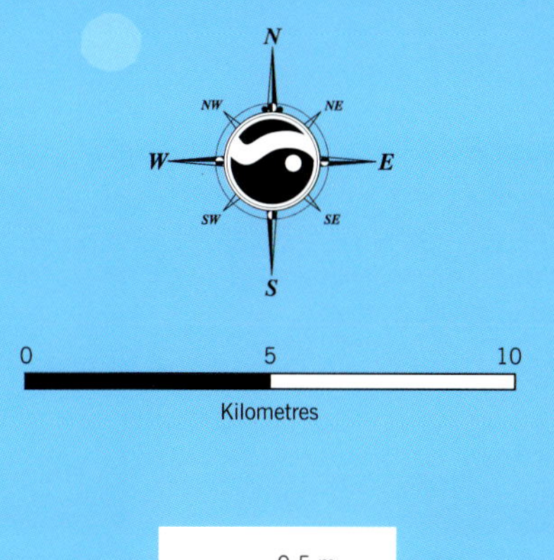

ruffs and salmon trout make up the remainder of the recreational catch and there are countless eagle rays for those after a bit of light tackle sport or flounder spearing at night. Some gummy sharks are caught throughout the bay during the night, so it's worthwhile soaking some fresh fillets baits in the channel if you like a feed of fresh flake. These aren't big gummies, averaging around the 3 to 5kg size.

The small jetty is a base to commercial fishing operators, mainly prawn and crayfishermen, but it's also popular with thousands of visiting anglers each year. Most of the species mentioned can be caught from the jetty at certain times of the year, but those with small boats will nearly always do best. Nearby Mount Camel Beach is a very reliable producer of big Australian salmon, as well as sharks and the occasional tailor.

MAP 8 ELLISTON

Named after teacher, Ellen Liston, who migrated to South Australia from England in 1850, Elliston is a thriving coastal community with a population of around 380. Originally a very important agricultural centre, the town relies heavily on tourism now for the wellbeing of its economy. As such, it is very well appointed, with terrific facilities, including two caravan parks, motel, supermarket and a range of privately owned accommodation options.

The Elliston jetty is one of the most consistent producers of quality table fish on the West Coast. It is usually reliable for squid, garfish, trevally and big tommy ruffs, with most of the better fishing coming from late afternoon into the night. The jetty is one of the town's major tourist drawcards and is well maintained for that purpose.

Aside from the jetty, some salmon trout and mullet are caught from the beach within Waterloo Bay, together with the occasional flathead. There is some good rock fishing on the northern fringe of the bay around Salmon Point, where tommies and garfish are caught in the top water using feeder floats, with King George caught from the sand holes underneath. There is a bit of rock and weed around this area, so expect to catch a few rock fish amongst the whiting. Salmon also patrol this area on a regular basis, so keep an eye out for passing fish.

Anxious Bay boasts a safe beach which is largely protected by Cape Finniss in the south and Waldegrave Island to west. It's a gentle sloping beach with scattered weed and the occasional patch of limestone. King George, garfish and tommies are caught by those wading the shallows.

Elliston is regularly used as a base for those keen on surf salmon fishing, as it is close to both Locks Well and Sheringa Beaches. At Locks Well there is a 120 metre, 280 step staircase leading down from cliff top to beach, which makes access a lot more convenient than was once the case. Locks has long been synonymous with great salmon fishing and, despite plenty of angling pressure, it continues to fish well. Salmon of all sizes are caught here, with plenty over the three kilogram mark and quite a few of 4-5 kilos. Dusk and dawn are prime times to be on the beach at Locks and salmon are taken on both lures and natural baits. This is one of several West Coast beaches that also produces a few enormous tommy ruffs in the surf.

Sheringa is a short drive south of Elliston and it, too, is a good spot for big salmon at times. There are two beaches at Sheringa and apart from salmon, it's also reliable for big yellow eye mullet in the autumn and early winter period. The Elliston Visitor Info Centre coordinates the Australian Salmon Fishing Championships, which runs annually and spans the three months of winter. June to August is the peak time for big salmon from the beaches around Elliston, with prevailing offshore northerly winds an advantage from many of these surf beaches.

MAP 9 THE INVESTIGATOR GROUP OF ISLANDS

Located well offshore from Elliston, this group of islands provides one of the most productive blue water recreational fisheries in South Australia. The two principal islands are Flinders and Pearson, both of which are home to some of the biggest King George whiting in the country. Whiting to better than 60 centimetres and 1.5 kilograms are taken from time to time, especially around Pearson from late afternoon into the evening.

Flinders Island has an area of some 9000 acres, 50 kilometres of coastline and 14 beaches, making it one of the largest islands in SA. It was once a thriving and privately owned sheep station, but now has been converted to attract visiting tourists. It has comfortable accommodation, as well as a well maintained airstrip for those who prefer to fly in.

The whiting fishing around Flinders, while perhaps not as consistent as it was back in the 'good old days', is still pretty good. Hooking kilogram-plus fish is common and catching whiting at less than 40 centimetres is unusual. Big tommy ruffs, Australian salmon of varying sizes, snook, big flathead, sharks and blue groper are found all around Flinders, many of which can be caught from rock and beach.

Pearson Island, located roughly 28 kilometres south-west of Flinders was once a popular location for long range charter and large recreational vessels, but has since been proclaimed a marine park sanctuary zone. There are essentially four islands that make up Pearson, the largest of which has two secure overnight anchorages for visiting boats.. Anchorage Cove is well protected in most of the winter winds from north-west around to south, while the smaller anchorage on the northern side is better in summer south-easterlies. Although Pearson can still be utilised as an overnight anchorage, fishing is prohibited. The island group can still be used as a base to access reef systems which lay outside of the sanctuary zone.

Pearson has a prolific population of blue groper, which were generally left alone by rec' fishers. It also sees visits from yellowtail kingfish, small to mid-sized samson fish, big snook, barracouta, salmon and small snapper. This again is white shark territory, as it hosts a healthy population of Australian sealions and smaller groups of New Zealand fur seals. Big flathead and some huge southern calamari were also regularly caught inside Anchorage Cove.

Outside both Flinders and Pearson Islands lay several significant deep water reef systems that consistently produce samson fish, yellowtail kings, blue groper, tuna, school sharks, nannygai and big silver trevally. This is definitely big boat territory and can only be reached in good weather, but the time and effort are nearly always rewarded with impressive catches.

Ward Island, directly west of Flinders, is a relatively small lump of granite in an isolated area and, as such, sees very few recreational anglers. It, too, is prime big whiting territory, particularly on the eastern side. There's a significant reef system adjacent to the north-eastern corner of Ward that can be quite nasty in heavy swell and is best given a wide berth on the approach.

ELLISTON TO PORT LINCOLN

With the exception of Coffin Bay, there is little boat launching as you head southward from Elliston. However, there is plenty of top shelf beach and rock fishing available.

MAP 10 POINT DRUMMOND

This rocky headland and Greens Bay offer some excellent land-based fishing for species such as salmon, sweep, silver drummer, trevally, snook and the occasional snapper. It can be swell affected and should only be fished when ocean conditions are favourable. Just to the north is Hall Bay, which fishes well from the shore for King George whiting, flathead, salmon and big yellow eye mullet.

Drummond Beach, to the south of the point, is a good one for salmon, but you'll need a reliable four wheel drive vehicle to get in and out safely. The sand is soft and some of the dunes are quite steep, so it's always wise to travel in company with a second vehicle in case of trouble.

Convention Beach, the next stretch of sand south of Drummond, is one of South Australia's premier salmon beaches, rivalling Locks Well for notoriety and probably more consistent. This beach got its name from a national fishing convention held back in the 1980s by the Australian Anglers Association. It produced hundreds of big salmon during that event and has gone on to produce thousands more in the ensuing decades. The beach is accessible by four wheel drive, with gutters spread along its length according to water movement and ocean swell.

There's a neat rock ledge at the very southern extremity of Convention Beach known locally as 'The Creek', as it's at the bottom of a steep ravine that flows well after heavy rain. This ledge can fish three or four anglers comfortably and is generally a great spot for big salmon and giant tommy ruffs. You'll need relatively heavy sidecast or threadline tackle here, as landing the fish involves a bit of a lift and some of the larger salmon can top four kilograms. This ledge has also seen the odd decent snapper, so a long handled gaff is a worthwhile inclusion.

Greenly Beach, Coles Point and The Frenchman all offer rock fishing possibilities for species like salmon, snook, flathead, King George whiting, sweep, drummer, silver trevally big tommy ruffs and the occasional snapper. This area is weather dependent and is best fished with a light offshore breeze.

MAP 11 COFFIN BAY

Protected from the wrath of the Southern Ocean by an imposing and magnificently rugged peninsula, Coffin Bay is one of our West Coast's true angling gems. It's a vast waterway fringed by limestone ledges, sand dunes and shallow tidal flats and carries about three times as much water as Sydney Harbor.

The bay was named by Matthew Flinders after his friend, Sir Isaac Coffin, and many of the local names in the local area can be traced back to Flinders and his crew. The Coffin Bay township, situated high up in the south-eastern corner of the inlet, is home to around 450 permanent residents, but this number increases up to five-fold during peak holiday times. There is a spacious and nicely appointed caravan park and abundant privately owned holiday rental properties, so accommodation options are plenty.

Coffin Bay has a modern, multi-lane launching ramp that will cater for trailer boats of virtually any size at all stages of the tide. This ramp is used regularly by oyster farmers, who tend their leases daily and produce some of the highest quality oysters in the world. Commercial fishing is extremely significant to the economy of Coffin Bay, particularly lobster trapping, abalone harvesting and, of course, those delectable oysters.

As far as the recreational angler is concerned, Coffin Bay has a lot to offer. Its adjacent surf beaches are among the best on Eyre Peninsula, its shallow water/light tackle fishing is superb and the nearby offshore action can be mind-blowing when Southern Ocean conditions permit. It is possible to spend a week holidaying in Coffin Bay and catch King George whiting, big Australian salmon, bluefin tuna and yellowtail kingfish; in few other locations statewide is such a combination available.

Those who trail small boats to Coffin can look forward to good catches of whiting, gar, silver trevally, snook, snapper, tommy ruffs, mullet and salmon trout. Most of the better fishing lies within 15 minutes of the boat ramp – even big snapper, which can also be caught from the rocks at locations such as The Ledge and Seal Corner.

Between mid September and November Coffin Bay sees an annual influx of big yellowtail kingfish, which are usually between 20-35 kilograms. These 'mega-kings' enter the bay in spawning condition and relentlessly hunt the local garfish and salmon trout. It's at this time that some truly amazing kingfish captures are made by anglers in small boats. Live baits suspended beneath balloons seem to produce

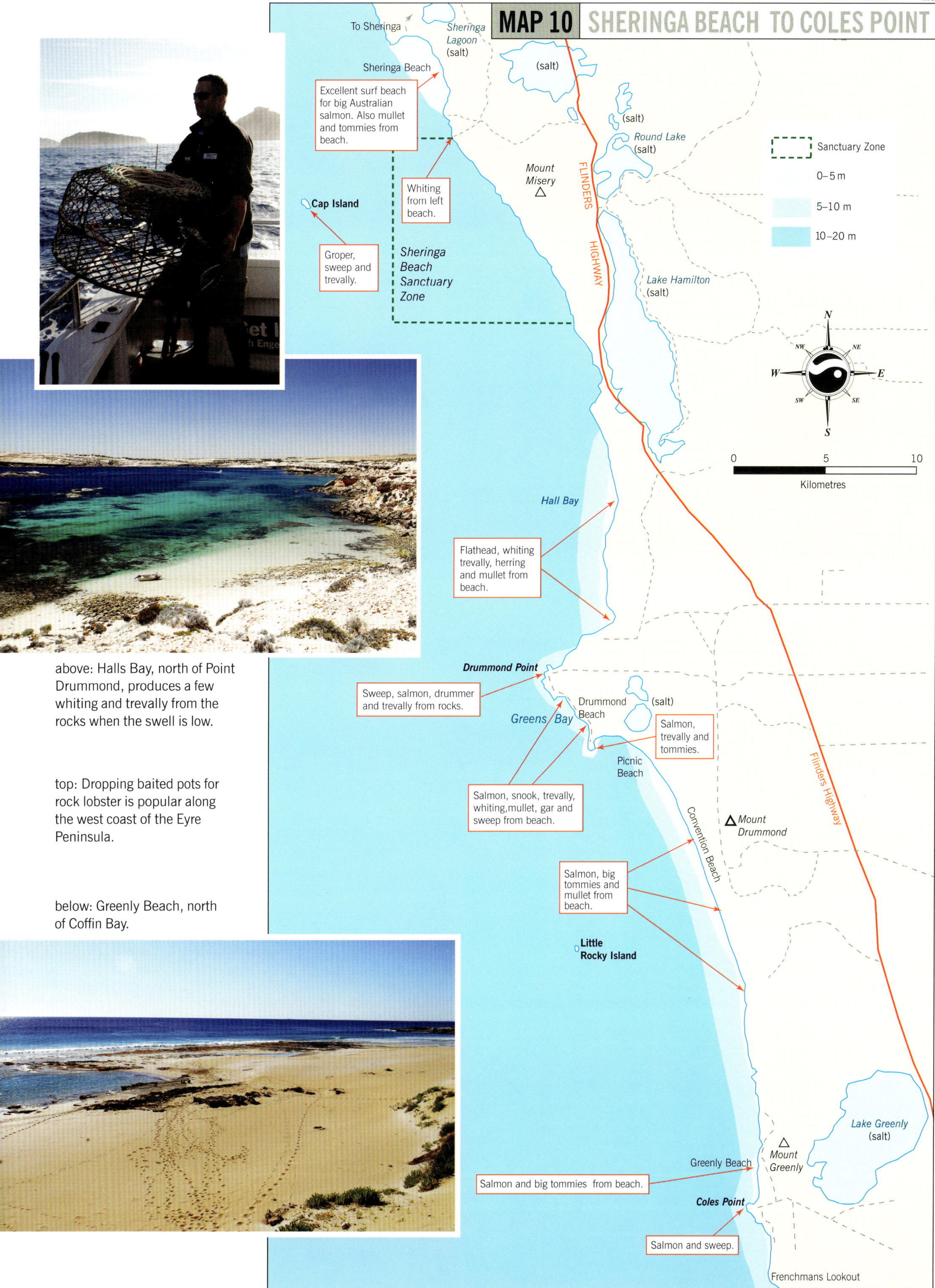

above: Halls Bay, north of Point Drummond, produces a few whiting and trevally from the rocks when the swell is low.

top: Dropping baited pots for rock lobster is popular along the west coast of the Eyre Peninsula.

below: Greenly Beach, north of Coffin Bay.

above: Samson fish are a popular target from the deep water reefs wide of Coffin Bay

above: Queen snapper (blue morwong) are gegularly caught on the reef systems wide of the Eyre Peninsula

most strikes, although the big kings are often taken on rigged dead garfish and lures as they hunt prey in the shallows.

Adjacent Kellidie Bay, which has an average water depth of around three metres, attracts kingies in large pods and catching these fish has been turned into an art form by several specialist anglers. Stalking feeding kingfish in water often as shallow as one metre demands skill and experience, as well as tackle that is up to the job. It's among the most specialised and spectacular fishing in the country.

There are several small islands within Coffin Bay that fish well for species like trevally and salmon trout and all are worth a try at various times. Small metal lures are effective on both varieties, as are natural baits like cockles, blue bait, pilchard pieces and squid. Garfish are widely distributed throughout the Coffin Bay system and will generally respond to baits fished in a steady berley trail. Gents (blowfly maggots) are regarded as the best garfish bait available and they will also catch tommy ruffs and salmon trout.

During the winter months gummy sharks are available throughout sections of the bay system, especially over the full moon. The gummies are quite active through the main channel at night, and in certain areas which 'bottleneck' the flow of water from one system to the next. Eagle rays can be a nuisance at times, but some lovely gummies up to 15kg are caught by persistent fishers. Fresh baits including salmon trout fillets and squid heads are effective.

The deeper water just outside Coffin Bay's Point Sir Isaac is well endowed with reefs and ledges that hold a mixture of nannygai, snapper and morwong. Big King George whiting are often hooked in this area as well, some of which are better than a kilogram each. Southern bluefin tuna pass Point Sir Isaac in the autumn, occasionally venturing within range of larger trailer boats.

Farm Beach, situated near the mouth of Coffin Bay on the eastern shore, is a legendary location for King George whiting. There's beach launching here, with tractors preferred by many as launch vehicles. Most of the whiting aren't large, but they are plentiful enough to support several commercial fishermen. There are also gar and snook in this area if the whiting aren't co-operative.

Coffin Bay Peninsula is an expansive piece of land and one that lures a few adventurous four wheel drivers who like to fish challenging locations. There are snapper to be had from the rocks on the eastern side of the peninsula and blue groper, sweep, salmon and sharks on the western side. This is remote and rugged territory and not for the unprepared. It's National Park, so both entry and camping permits are required.

Almonta Beach is a 25 minute drive through Coffin Bay National Park, and is one of the last stops for conventional car access. . This beach is a renowned producer of big salmon and is fishable without a four wheel drive, but reaching some of the better gutters can entail a lengthy walk at times. You'll come across emus and kangaroos as you drive into Almonta, so it pays to be alert on the road, especially around first and last light.

Gunyah Beach is far more difficult to get to, and involves plenty of sand driving. The entry track into Gunyah is about 7km before Almonta, with a signposted track veering to the left as you make your way through the national park. It, too, can be a salmon angler's paradise, but you'll need a capable four wheel drive and a bit of off-road experience. Quite often the sand is soft and unstable, making it necessary to deflate tyres and, most importantly, stick to the designated track. Many have come unstuck while attempting to fish Gunyah, so take care and seek local knowledge before heading off, particularly if you are unfamiliar with the area.

Gunyah is a bit more open to the southern swell than what Almonta is, and hence boasts deeper gutter formation. This in turn offers a bit more consistency in fishing. Gunyah fishes quite well around the full tide, with plenty of good salmon being caught from the surf; some of which hit the magic 10 pound mark. Gunyah is more suited to bait fishing, while Almonta is better for lure-fishing with its shallower water.

There is beach launching at Point Avoid, but again you will require a four wheel drive vehicle and need to make sure the ocean swell is down before contemplating a launch. Crayfish are abundant around the rock ledges along this part of the coast, but it is white shark territory and extreme care needs to be taken. Some recreational divers put their boats in off the beach at Point Avoid, then motor across to Point Whidbey to collect both crays and abalone. Provided conditions are suitable, it's generally not difficult to pick up a bag limit catch of both varieties.

MAP 13 & 13A SLEAFORD BAY

Situated in Lincoln National Park at the very foot of Eyre Peninsula, Sleaford Bay is totally open to the incessant pounding of the Southern Ocean, so fishing opportunities are somewhat limited. Sleaford Bay is a sanctuary zone restricting boat fishing, but shore based fishing is still allowed. It's a big bay with quite deep water not far offshore and regularly holds vast schools of Australian salmon. There are several beaches such as Wanna and Wisemans, and rock platforms around the northern side of Sleaford, the most renowned of which are Miller's Hole and the Salmon Hole. Miller's Hole is a rock platform that's around 12 metres off the water, which can be challenging when you're attempting to lift five kilograms of Australian salmon. Big salmon often invade this area in massive schools and when on the bite, the action can be fast and furious.

The Salmon Hole can be good, too, and because it's not quite as far above water level, the rock ledge is considerably easier to fish. A four wheel drive vehicle is mandatory for reliable access to all locations and a National Park Permit is required. Heavy sidecast gear is the most appropriate tackle.

Some big bronze whalers are regularly seen shadowing schools of salmon along this high-energy coastline, and provide heavy-tackle sport if you are able to get a bait out to them. Some of these bronzies are up around 9 to 10 feet in length and will punish anything but heavy tackle. There are a few smaller 4 to 6 ft models along this coast too, and are more of a manageable size for surf-casting tackle.

MAP 13A FISHERY BAY

Fishery Bay is located on the western shore of Sleaford Bay, near Cape Wiles. It's a 29 km drive south west of the township of Port Lincoln, half of which is over unsealed roads. Fishery Bay was the site of a whaling station back in the 19th century, with some remains and a plaque located on the eastern shore.

It's a picturesque bay guarded by prominent headlands on both sides, and it does collect a bit of swell on the points so it's popular with local surfers. When the swell is low, particularly during the summer months when the westerly groundswell is at its minimum, it is possible to launch smaller trailer boats up to around 5 metres from the sand at either end of the beach. You will need to have reasonable experience in launching and retrieving to ensure it is executed quickly to minimise the risk of a bogged vehicle or a wave over the rear of the boat.

Fishery Bay offers consistent reef fishing for nannygai, blue morwong, blue groper and school sharks on the deeper reefs a few miles offshore, with nearby Liguanea Island offering small to mid-sized yellowtail kingfish and school Bluefin tuna during the warmer months. Targeting southern rock lobster is popular from Fishery Bay, with a lot of productive rock ledges available on either side of the bay and extending out to nearby reef systems. Dropping baited pots is the most popular form of targeting rock lobster, but you will need an annual permit from PIRSA to be able to do so. Diving and using a snare is another effective means of catching rock lobster, but with regular great white shark sightings in the area every year, you need to enter the water with caution.

Land based fishing within the bay returns a mix of salmon trout and tommies from the beach, with the occasional school of bigger salmon venturing within casting range. The rocks on either side of the bay yield a few whiting from the sand holes along with a few silver trevally, but as usual when fishing close to reef, expect quite a few rock cod as by catch

MAP 13A THE CABBAGE PATCH

Located some 40 kilometres from the nearest landfall at Cape Wiles, the Cabbage Patch is a vast and intricate offshore reef system that comes out of very deep water. It's a Mecca for game and sport fishers during the annual summer/autumn bluefin tuna run and also produces yellowtail kings, samson fish, nannygai, silver trevally, blue groper and sharks of various breeds and sizes. Naturally, this is big boat territory only and often sees attention from Port Lincoln-based charter operators and members of various game fishing clubs.

The tuna often hang on the Cabbage Patch for weeks and even months at a time and generally vary between 10 –20 kilograms. They make great sport on light to medium tackle and are the subject of several organised and well patronised tournaments throughout the autumn. Both blue and mako sharks are regular visitors to the Cabbage Patch year-round, but particularly when the tuna action is at its peak.

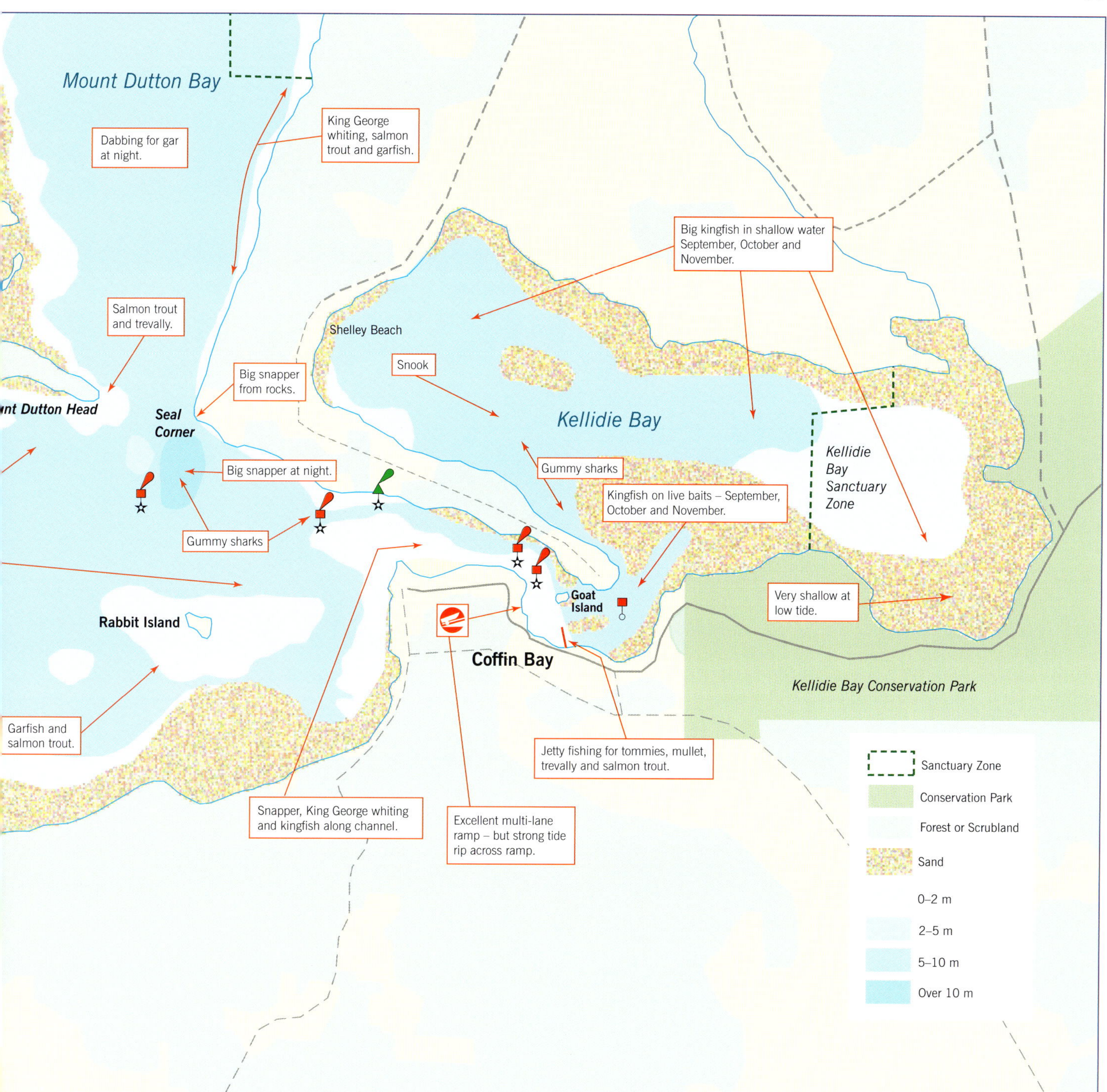

MAP 13A The Neptune Islands

North and South Neptune Islands have developed a global reputation as the home of great white sharks. Three charter operations specialise in taking groups of divers out to the Neptunes to view great whites from the safety of sturdy cages and this has become quite a lucrative business. As well as big sharks, however, the Neptune Islands have plenty of good fishing for those with the boats and experience to get there.

North Neptune Island has been zoned as a marine park sanctuary area, with no fishing allowed within a 5 km radius of the island. South Neptune and Low Rocks are still open to recreational fishing, although South Neptune is on the cusp of access for most trailer boats given it's an 85 km run one-way from Port Lincoln.

Big King George whiting are common in the shallower regions around these islands, as are big silver trevally, salmon and yellowtail kingfish of varying sizes. Bluefin tuna schools often pass within close range of the islands and nearby clusters of rocks, and can be caught trolling a spread of skirted or diving hard body lures. Some first rate reef fishing is available in the deeper water a short distance from these islands, with snapper, nannygai, blue morwong, plus gummy and school sharks regularly caught by those bottom bouncing baits in this area.

MAP 14 Thorny Passage

Matthew Flinders charted the coast and offshore islands south of Port Lincoln in 1802 and, tragically, lost several of his crew when their small boat capsized during a violent storm. He named the nearest landfall Cape Catastrophe and a nearby protected anchorage Memory Cove. Several islands are scattered throughout what Flinders called Thorny Passage, many of which bear the names of those he lost that fateful day.

Thistle Island is by far the largest of the Thorny Passage group. It has an area of some 4,000 hectares and a coastline over 40 kilometres long. It's the second largest island off the South Australian coast and has been sub-divided and sold off in 28 freehold titles. There are some 4,000 sheep grazing on Thistle, which can be accessed by both boat and plane.

The fishing around Thistle Island is nothing short of brilliant, particularly for large King George whiting. There are small to medium snapper, sharks, nannygai, morwong and occasional samson fish on the reefs to the south and west, but again this is big boat territory in all but the very best weather.

Both gummy and school sharks are caught throughout Thorny Passage and there are several 'lumps' that fish well for small to medium snapper. Memory Cove is one of the most reliable locations in this area for a feed of calamari and it also produces a good supply of King George whiting, snook and big tommy ruffs. It is possible to reach Memory Cove by four wheel drive vehicle from Port Lincoln. To do so you will need a key to access the Memory Cove Wilderness Area, with permit and key available from the Port Lincoln Visitor Info Centre. There are some wild and lightly fished rock ledges within the Wilderness Area for those who are fit and have a keen sense of adventure. A lot of the better rock ledges will require a lengthy hike, so appropriate footwear and adequate water and safety equipment is recommended.

A lot of these rock ledges drop into deep water, and it's not uncommon to be fishing in 20 m of water from the stones. Some nice nannygai, snapper, blue morwong, swallowtail and occasional harlequin fish can be caught from the rocks, with the occasional bust-off from bigger, unseen fish.

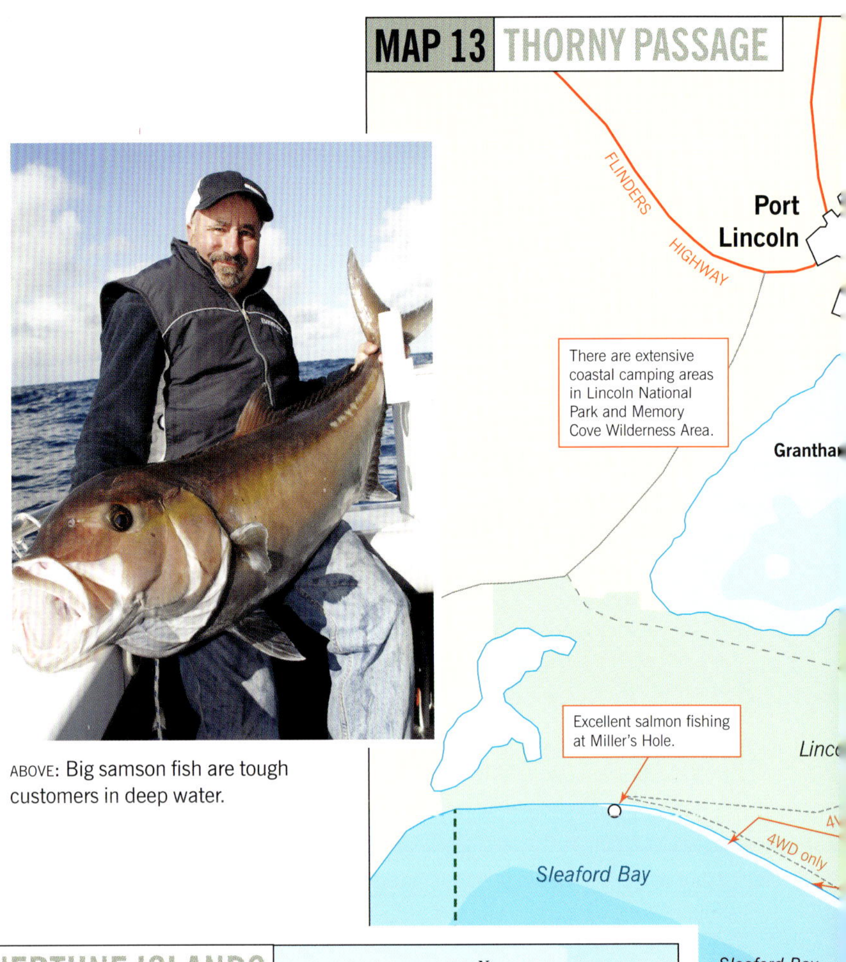

ABOVE: Big samson fish are tough customers in deep water.

MAP 13 THORNY PASSAGE
FLINDERS HIGHWAY
Port Lincoln
There are extensive coastal camping areas in Lincoln National Park and Memory Cove Wilderness Area.
Excellent salmon fishing at Miller's Hole.
4WD only
Sleaford Bay

Sleaford Bay Sanctuary Zone
Cape Tournef
Salmon

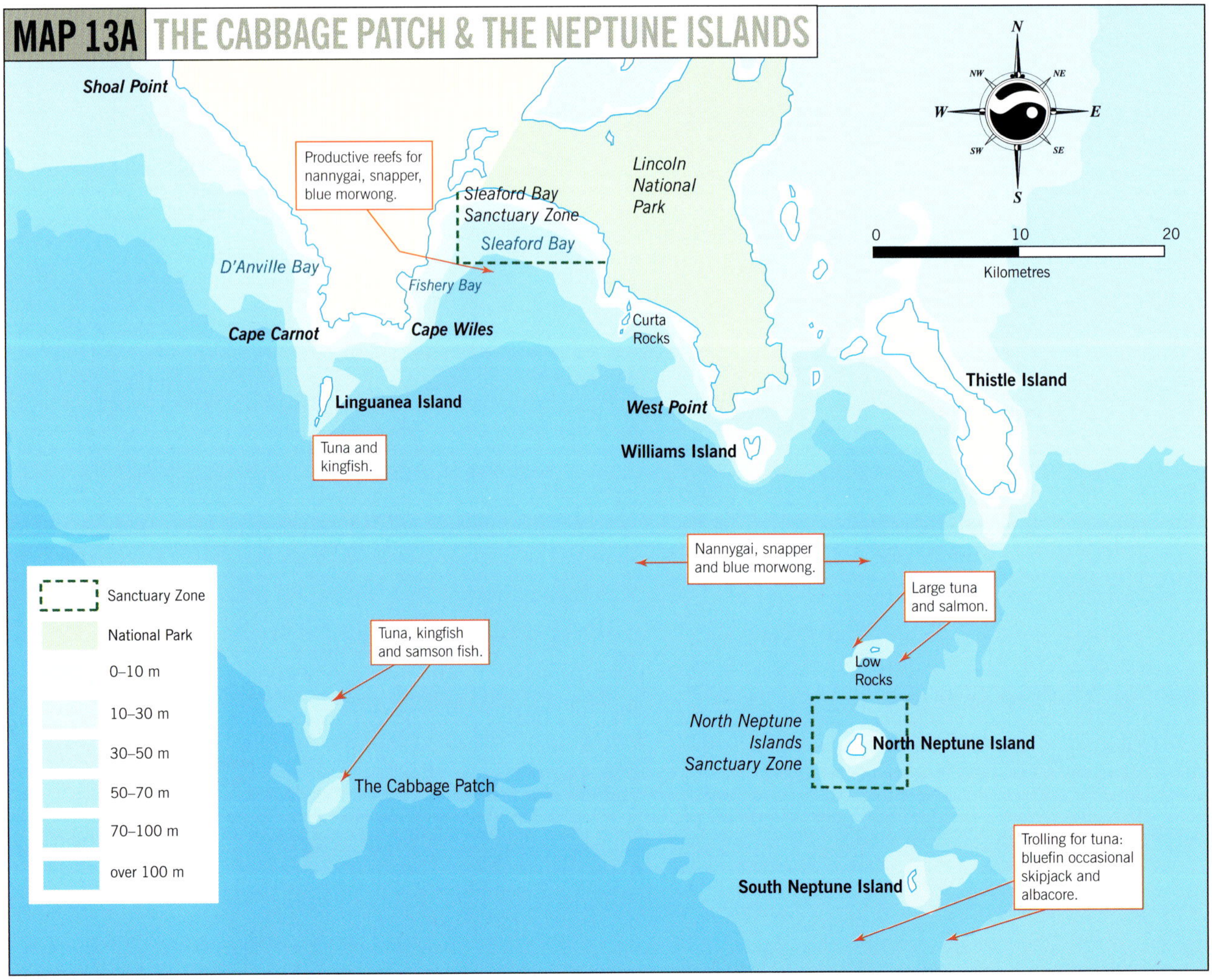
MAP 13A THE CABBAGE PATCH & THE NEPTUNE ISLANDS
Shoal Point
Productive reefs for nannygai, snapper, blue morwong.
Sleaford Bay Sanctuary Zone
Sleaford Bay
Lincoln National Park
D'Anville Bay
Fishery Bay
Cape Carnot
Cape Wiles
Curta Rocks
Linguanea Island
West Point
Thistle Island
Williams Island
Tuna and kingfish.
N
NW
NE
W
E
SW
SE
S
0
10
20
Kilometres
Nannygai, snapper and blue morwong.
Large tuna and salmon.
Low Rocks
Tuna, kingfish and samson fish.
North Neptune Islands Sanctuary Zone
North Neptune Island
The Cabbage Patch
Trolling for tuna: bluefin occasional skipjack and albacore.
South Neptune Island
Sanctuary Zone
National Park
0–10 m
10–30 m
30–50 m
50–70 m
70–100 m
over 100 m

Bass Shoal
Boston Island
e Hunte Shoal
Kirton Point
Hayden Point
Point Fanny
Donington Reef
Cape Donington
Bickers Islands
Engine Point
Fisherman Point
Surfleet Point
Port Lincoln Bay
Spalding Cove
Salmon and snook inshore.
Maclaren Point
Boat launching
Point Haselgrove
King George whiting, gar, squid.
onal Park
Taylors Landing
Owen Island
Taylor Island
almon from Vanna Beach.
Winter – King George whiting.
4WD only
Shag Cove
Grindal Island
Gummy sharks throughout Passage.
Doolan Shoal
Memory Cove anchorage.
Jussieu Bay
Harrison Shoal
Little Island
Lewis Island
Hopkins Island
Smith Island
Carrington Point
4WD only
Cape Catastrophe
West Point
Squid, whiting.
WARNING
Poisonous snakes on Williams Island.
Williams Island
Deep reef fishing for nannygai, snapper, morwong, sharks around Little, Lewis, Smith and Hopkins islands.
Deep reef fishing for samson fish, nannygai, snapper.
Bluefin tuna in this area throughout summer and autumn.
Thorny Passage
Jane Shoal
Nicolette Shoal
Stickney Island
Brigdet Shoal
Snook, squid, King George whiting, sharks.
Protection in southerly weather. Big boat territory only.
Dangerous Reef Sanctuary Zone
Dangerous Reef
Howard Rock (seldom breaks)
(breaks heavily)
Snapper
Simms Rock
Snapper
Porter Rock (breaks)
Snapper
King George whiting
Black Rock
Observatory Point
Thistle Island
Excellent King George whiting fishing.
King George whiting, snapper, salmon.
O'Laughlin Bay
Whalers Bay
Horny Point
Fossil Point
Thistle Island
Waterhouse Bay
Waterhouse Point
Albatross Island
South Rock
Sweep, snook, salmon, snapper.
Deep reef fishing for nannygai, snapper, morwong, sharks.
N
NE
E
SE
S
SW
W
NW
0
5
10
Kilometres
Sanctuary Zone
National Park
0–3 m
3–6 m
6–10 m
10–20 m
over 20 m

MAP 14 PORT LINCOLN

Originally gazetted as the site for South Australia's capital city, Port Lincoln is now a bustling town located on the shores of beautiful Boston Bay. Its population is around 15,000, making it by far the largest settlement on lower Eyre Peninsula, and this figure is growing steadily. Commercial fishing and aquaculture are vital components of Port Lincoln's economy and both are expanding at a rapid rate. The commercial wild catch consists mainly of southern rock lobster, abalone, prawns and scale fish, while the most significant aquaculture subjects are bluefin tuna, abalone and yellowtail kingfish.

The tuna farming industry, in particular, has injected billions of dollars into the local economy and is still growing at a steady rate. Circular fish pens are scattered over a large area to the east of Boston Island and as far north as Louth Bay. One spin-off of these farms is their propensity to attract and hold numbers of wild tuna, which swim outside the pens and are viable targets for recreational anglers. Provided they adhere to a recognised code of practice, small boat anglers are free to pursue these 'escapees', which brings tuna fishing within reach of practically anyone with the right tackle.

The land-based fishing options in and around Port Lincoln are both numerous and varied. Vast schools of yellowfin whiting turn up along the western shores of Boston Bay in winter time, with fish of over 30 centimetres quite common. These are great sport on ultra-light tackle and are highly regarded as table fish – almost as highly as their King George cousins.

Snapper move into Boston Bay during the spring and summer and

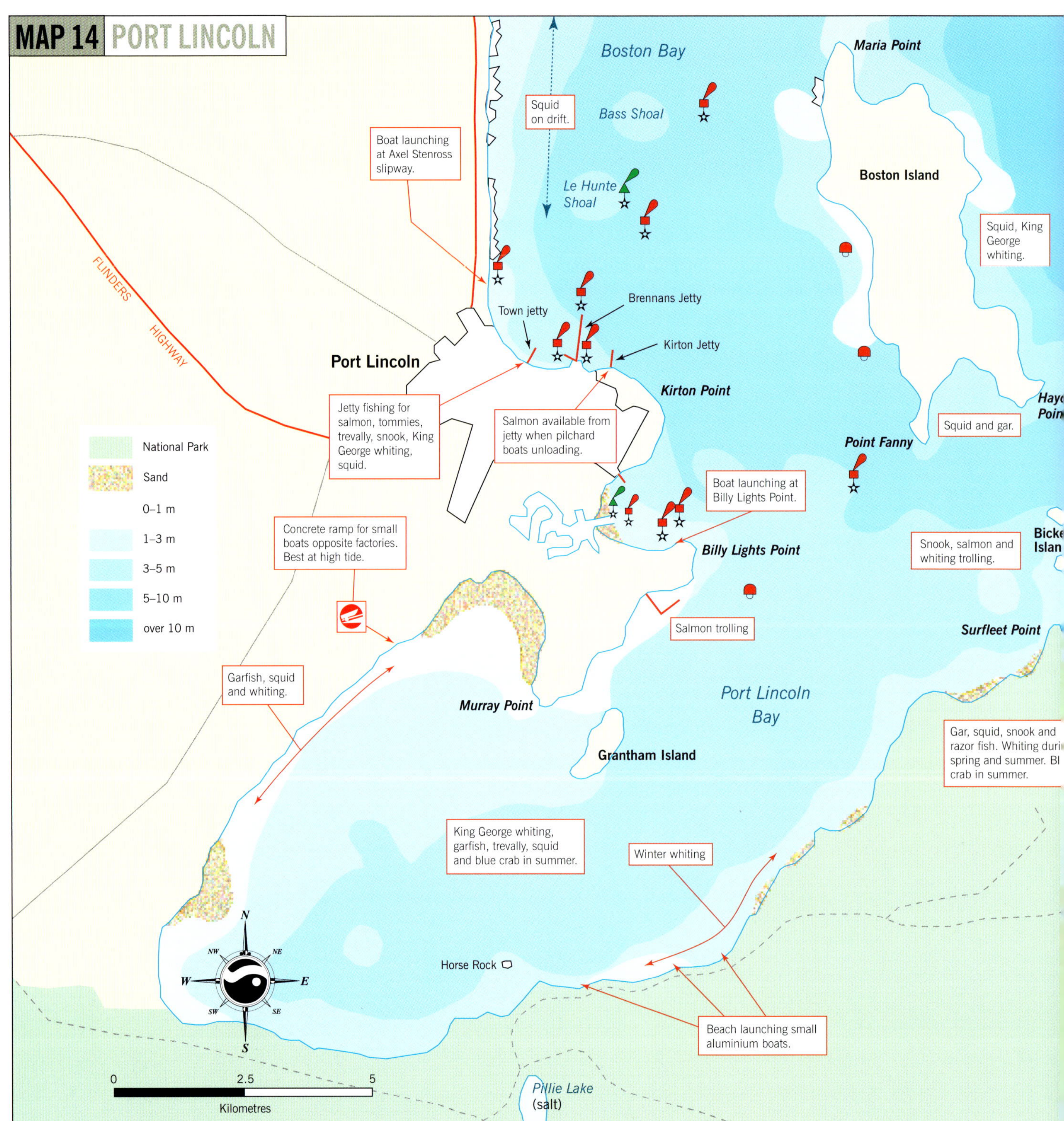

these vary from barely legal-size 'ruggers' to full blown 20 pounders. These larger fish are becoming increasingly harder to catch, but those who put in the time are often rewarded. There are also salmon to be hooked at a number of locations, including the long bulk loading jetty adjacent to the towering grain silos. These salmon are attracted by the offloading of pilchards from commercial craft moored at the jetty and often top two kilograms in weight. They are terrific sport from the pier, regularly drawing large numbers of anglers with an amazing array of tackle and techniques.

Lincoln's shorter town jetty is generally less crowded than the bulk loading pier, but can also produce good fishing. Yellowfin whiting and big yellow eye mullet are often hooked in the shallows, while calamari, tommy ruffs, snook and a few King George whiting come from the slightly deeper sections.

King George whiting can be expected in the waters surrounding Boston Island, along with squid, snook, trevally and more salmon. In recent years blue swimmer crabs have returned to the bay after an absence for quite some time. Most of the blueys are caught dropping hoop nets over tape weed meadows in the 4 to 6m depth range, and are at their peak from January to March. Some nice southern bluespot flathead move into the shallows of the bay during the cooler months, and can be caught on prawn style soft plastics or half-pilchards cast into likely looking areas. The bay is quite sheltered in all winds except strong northerlies and really is ideal for small boat owners. There is a multi-lane launching ramp at Billy Light's Point and another new facility adjacent to the Axel Stenross slipway, which is a better proposition at low tide for larger boats.

There is also a basic launching ramp near the tuna processing facilities on the northern shore of Proper Bay. This launch site does not have any boarding pontoons and is open to winds from the south. It can also be quite shallow on low tide, but suits smaller boats looking to assess Proper Bay. This expansive bay returns a mix of King George, tommies, garfish and squid, and is popular with local boaties.

Lincoln Cove Marina, located just south-east of the Port Lincoln town centre, is a world class facility for those with big boats. It is home to one of the largest commercial fishing fleets in the country and, as such, Port Lincoln is very well equipped with marine chandleries, stainless steel fabricators, boat repairers and similar businesses allied to the marine industry. It also has its own hotel, leisure centre and abundant holiday rental units.

There are plenty of big boat options outside Boston Bay, particularly for those targeting snapper and whiting. Locations such as Buffalo Reef and Rosalind Shoal are legendary for their snapper catches, but these are in open, exposed water and can only be fished in good weather.

There are several well equipped and experienced charter fishing operations based in Port Lincoln, some of which venture westward to fish Rocky and Greenly Islands. These remote granite outcrops are definitely in big boat only territory, but they produce large numbers of bluefin tuna in season, samson fish, sharks, blue groper and some of the biggest yellowtail kings in the country.

Davidson Rock
Small snapper at times.
Donington Reef
TIDE RIP
Sharks and salmon.
Cape Donington
Cape Colbert
Engine Point
Sweep, tommies and snook from Rocks.
Fisherman Point
ing Cove
Sweep, and flathead from beaches.
Maclaren Point
Point Haselgrove

LEFT: Blue groper are a tough fish, and are available around the islands and reef systems wide of the west coast.

Axel Stenross Boat Ramp in Port Lincoln.

Southern bluefin busting up on the surface.

CHAPTER 3

SPENCER GULF

Fishing for school mulloway from a beach in Spencer Gulf

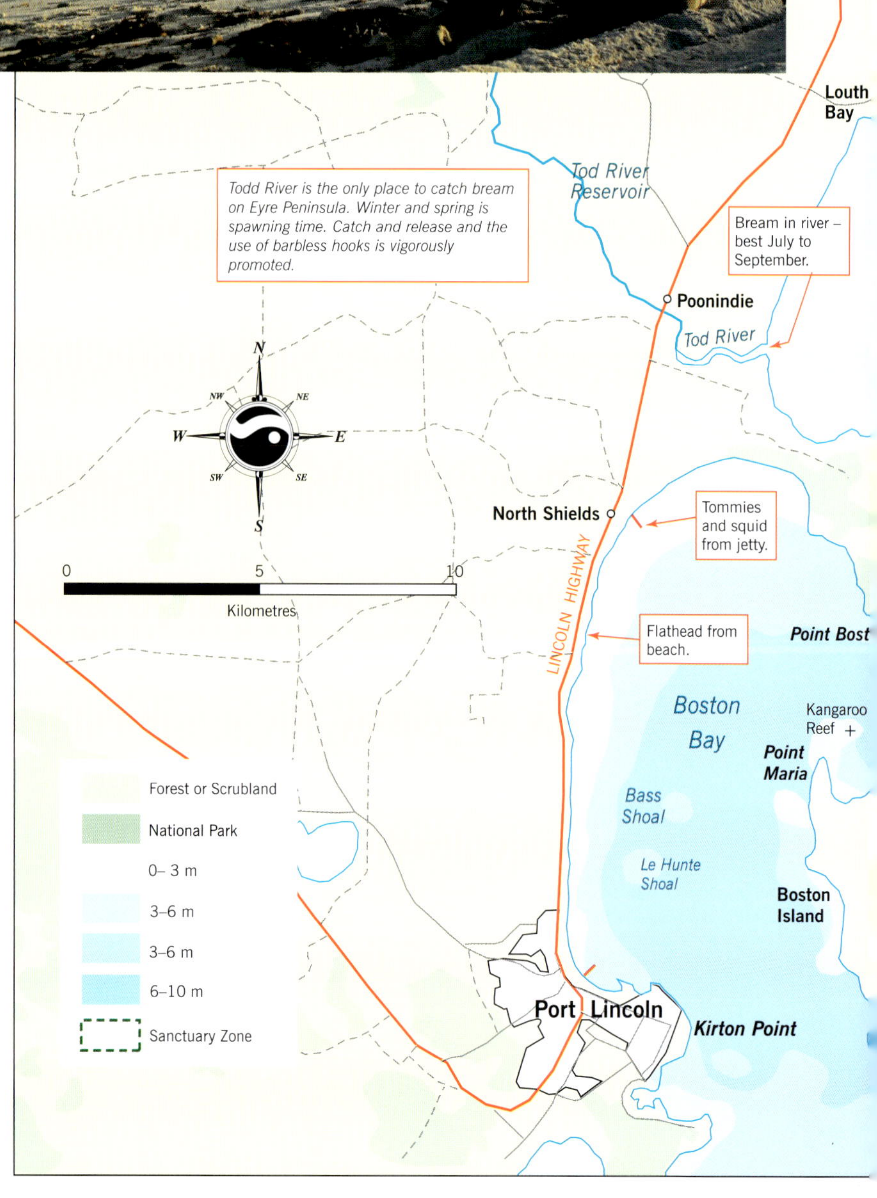

The larger of South Australia's two vast inlets from the Southern Ocean, Spencer Gulf is 322 kilometres long and 130 kilometres wide at the mouth. It is bounded by Eyre Peninsula to the west and Yorke Peninsula to the east. The Gulf was charted and named by Matthew Flinders in 1802 after Earl Spencer, an ancestor of the late Princess Diana. Flinders spent considerable time in this waterway and many of the location names can be directly linked to his family, friends or places in England that were dear to him.

On average, the water in Spencer Gulf is considerably deeper than that of Gulf St Vincent, which is situated further east. It is recognised as one of SA's very best fishing areas, both commercial and recreational. All up, there's close to 700 kilometres of coastline surrounding the Gulf, with most settlements small, but well served in terms of facilities. Two of SA's larger regional population centres, Whyalla and Port Augusta, are located at the top of Spencer Gulf.

Most types of fishing are available on and around the Gulf, from wading inshore sand flats to heavy tackle offshore for snapper, and practically everything in between. This area is generally regarded as the premier waterway in the country for big snapper and it's also home to vast schools of King George and yellowfin whiting. Great white sharks patrol its waters year-round and particularly so when the snapper are aggregating to spawn in the late spring and summer months. Contrary to their recognised offshore habitat, yellowtail kingfish are found throughout Spencer Gulf and some of them are monsters.

This is quite a special fishery with a rather unique tidal system and, some say, its own weather pattern.

PORT LINCOLN TO PORT AUGUSTA

The western shore of Spencer Gulf is quite sparsely populated, with several of the towns home to well under a thousand people. It's this coast that cops the brunt of strong summer south-easterly winds, but it is also THE place to catch that snapper of a lifetime.

MAP 15 LOUTH BAY

Just a short drive northward from Port Lincoln lies the tiny township of Louth Bay. There is good beach launching here off firm sand and excellent small boat fishing for King George whiting, squid, garfish and snook. The waters of the bay are generally shallow and, due to the town's small population, they see minimal fishing pressure. Gar dabbing at night time is both popular and highly productive. This involves the use of a small, manoeuvrable boat, a battery-powered spotlight and long-handled net and is best done on calm, moonless evenings.

The Louth Bay jetty is a cracker for squid, especially during the winter months when winds are predominantly offshore. Crystal clear water is mandatory for consistent squid fishing and also assists with catching good numbers of tommy ruffs, gar and snook.

A few snapper are hooked from the rock ledges to the east of the jetty at Louth, varying from just legal 'ruggers' up to double figure fish. The snapper seem to bite best when the winds are onshore and the water is stirred up. The most productive fishing periods are dawn, dusk and the first couple of hours of darkness.

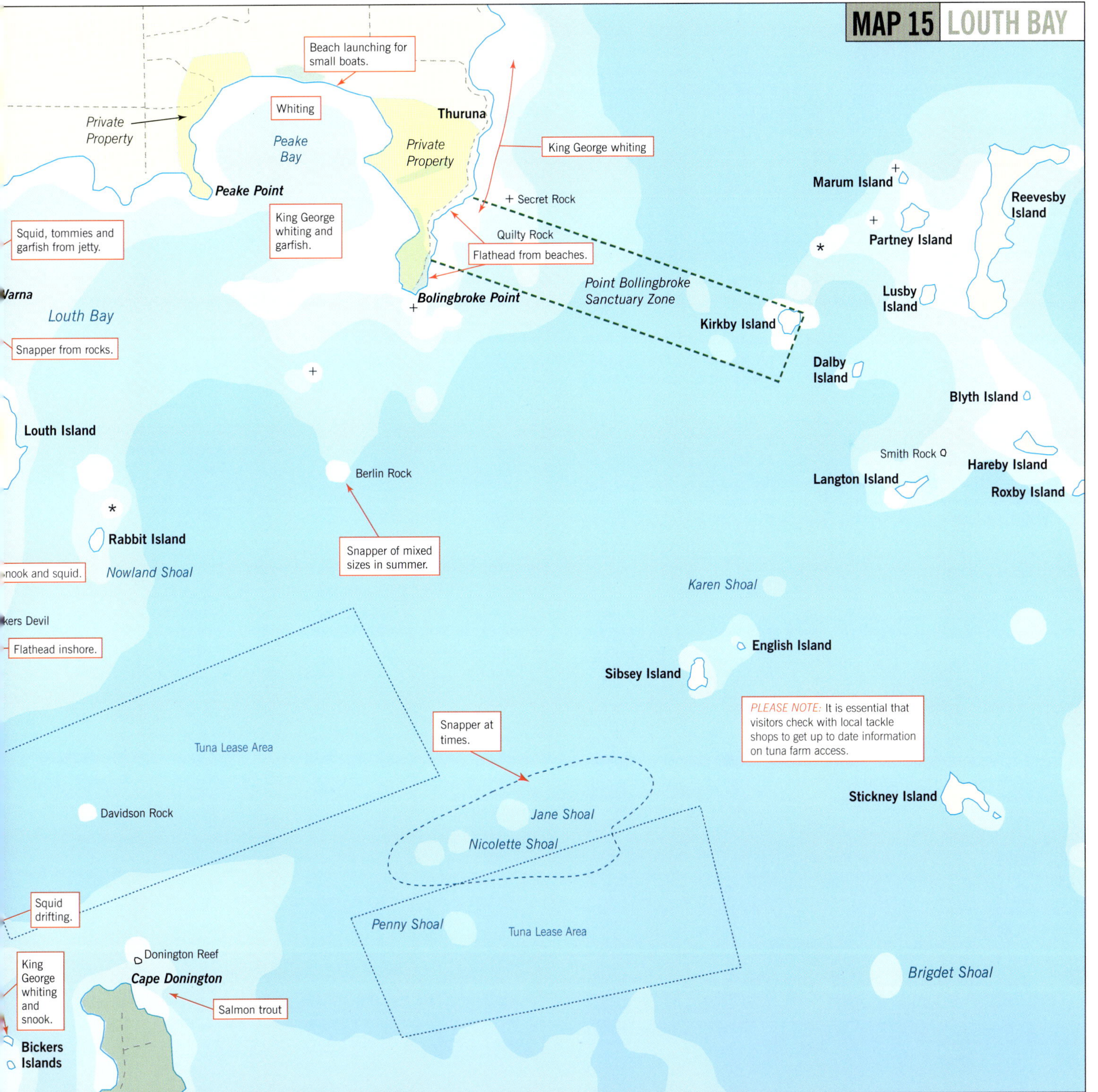

The Tod River near Poonindie produces some big bream at times, but catch and release is strongly encouraged.

MAP 15 THE TOD RIVER

This waterway, which begins as a fresh water stream in the ranges, is the only reliable producer of quality bream on Eyre Peninsula. The Tod flows to the sea beneath the Lincoln Highway and it's this section between highway and coast that produces the most consistent action. A lot of the land surrounding the Tod River estuary is either private farm property or reserved for local aboriginal people, so it is mandatory to gain permission from the appropriate owners before venturing in.

For most of its estuary section the Tod is quite shallow and, in some stretches, narrow enough to cast across. The tide from Spencer Gulf pushes well up into the higher reaches and mixes with fresh water inflow from Meadows Creek after significant rain. The best fishing occurs on the flood tide and particularly so if the water is running in late or early in the day. Although bream can be caught in different sections of the river year round, the peak of the population move into the river around April, and are regularly caught up until October.

Big bream are the main drawcard here and there have been fish in excess of three kilograms taken over the years. Kilogram-plus fish are quite common and these are caught on both lures and natural baits. Proven baits include live nippers (salt water yabbies), small crabs, shrimps and seaweed worms, but it's also possible to hook the bream on frozen green prawns, pilchard strips, mullet gut and even cockles at times.

It's lure fishing, however, that has proven most popular in the Tod in recent years and both hard-bodies and soft plastics are effective. Bream to over 50 centimetres have fallen to expertly fished lures and these are exceptional sport on ultra-light threadline tackle.

KG Whiting are a popular target within Spencer Gulf.

Most of the inshore reds in Spencer Gulf are pan sized fish but you do encounter some better fish from time to time.

School mulloway also patrol the lower reaches of the River and although rarely targeted, they are taken intermittently as by-catch on both lures and live baits. The majority are school fish of between 50–75 centimetres, but there are the odd larger models cruising around at times. The mulloway are particularly fond of live nippers and many of the bigger fish hooked on bream tackle break free. Most are taken within a kilometre of the River mouth.

Due to its fragile and rather unique nature, The Tod River is generally a catch and release fishery. As mentioned, there are no other streams or estuaries on Eyre Peninsula that hold consistent numbers of bream, so the population could be over exploited if those who fish there kill everything they catch. Putting the larger bream back is definitely wise and will ensure the future of the fishery.

MAP 15 THURUNA

Accessible via a good dirt road from Lincoln Highway, this delightful bay provides some surprising fishing, especially for yellow eye mullet in the autumn and squid in winter. The mullet are usually caught by casting with light tackle from the beach using mincemeat or worm baits. Bags of several dozen are possible when the main 'run' is on.

Some nice flathead are also caught from the main beach, and also the smaller beaches to the south of the camp. Autumn and Winter are the best months for these inshore southern bluespot, which can be caught by on soft plastic lures as well as baits. Whitebait, prawns and half pilchards are good baits to try.

The rocky ledges on the southern side of the bay can be particularly productive for squid when the water is clear and winds are either light or blowing offshore. Jigs set beneath styrene floats work well. It's wise to begin squidding around low tide, as access to some of the better ledges diminishes when the tide gets up.

There is beach launching for small boats at Thuruna and enough King George whiting, garfish and tommy ruffs offshore to make 'tinny' fishing well worthwhile.

MAP 16, 17 TUMBY BAY

Located about half an hour's drive north of Port Lincoln, Tumby has become one of SA's most popular holiday fishing locations. It's not a big town, but it offers plenty for visiting anglers and their families. The caravan park is spacious and well appointed, there's a multi-lane boat ramp and marina, and a long jetty for those without a boat.

The offshore fishing can be excellent, particularly among the islands of the Sir Joseph Banks Group, which are readily accessible from the Tumby Bay Marina. In all there are 17 islands in the group forming a relatively compact cluster about 50 kilometres north-east of Port Lincoln. Reevesby and Spilsby Islands are the largest and again, most were named by Matthew Flinders after people or places in his native England.

Reevesby Island is the closest to Tumby Bay and sees plenty of attention from local boaties when weather conditions are favourable. This island has a large lagoon that's protected from prevailing summer winds and is a popular overnight anchorage for yachties and trailer boat anglers. It is also possible to camp on the beach, which is particularly enjoyable during the warmer months. However, both death adders and tiger snakes inhabit Reevesby Island, so it's wise to stay on the beach and well away from the inland saltbush and native scrub.

The Banks Group is generally regarded as the best area in the state for King George whiting and it's not often that clued-in locals return from the islands without a bag limit catch. The fish are generally large and particularly so between Christmas and Easter time, when specimens of over 50 centimetres and a kilogram in weight are caught regularly. They are often taken in quite shallow water, which provides plenty of light tackle sport.

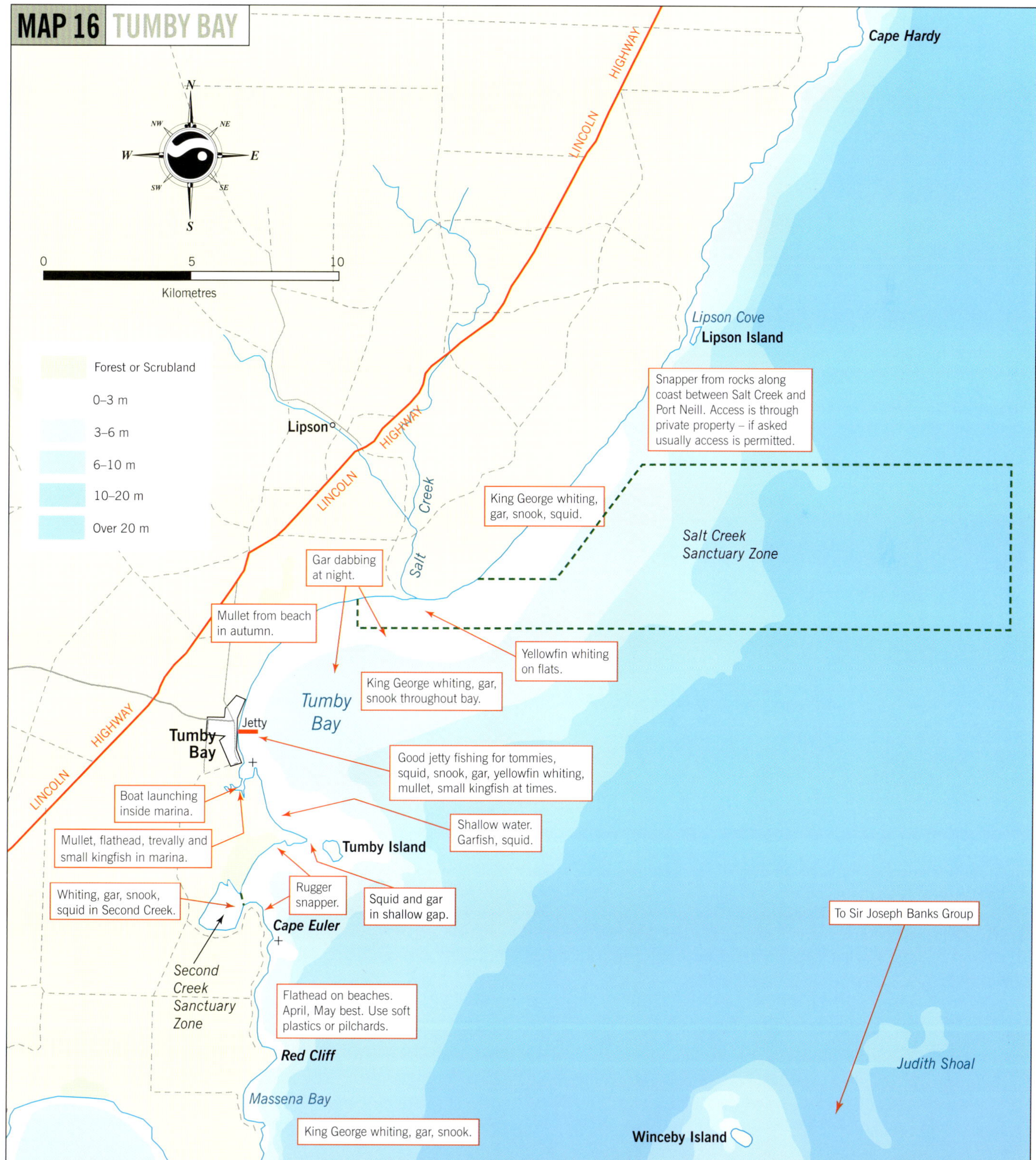

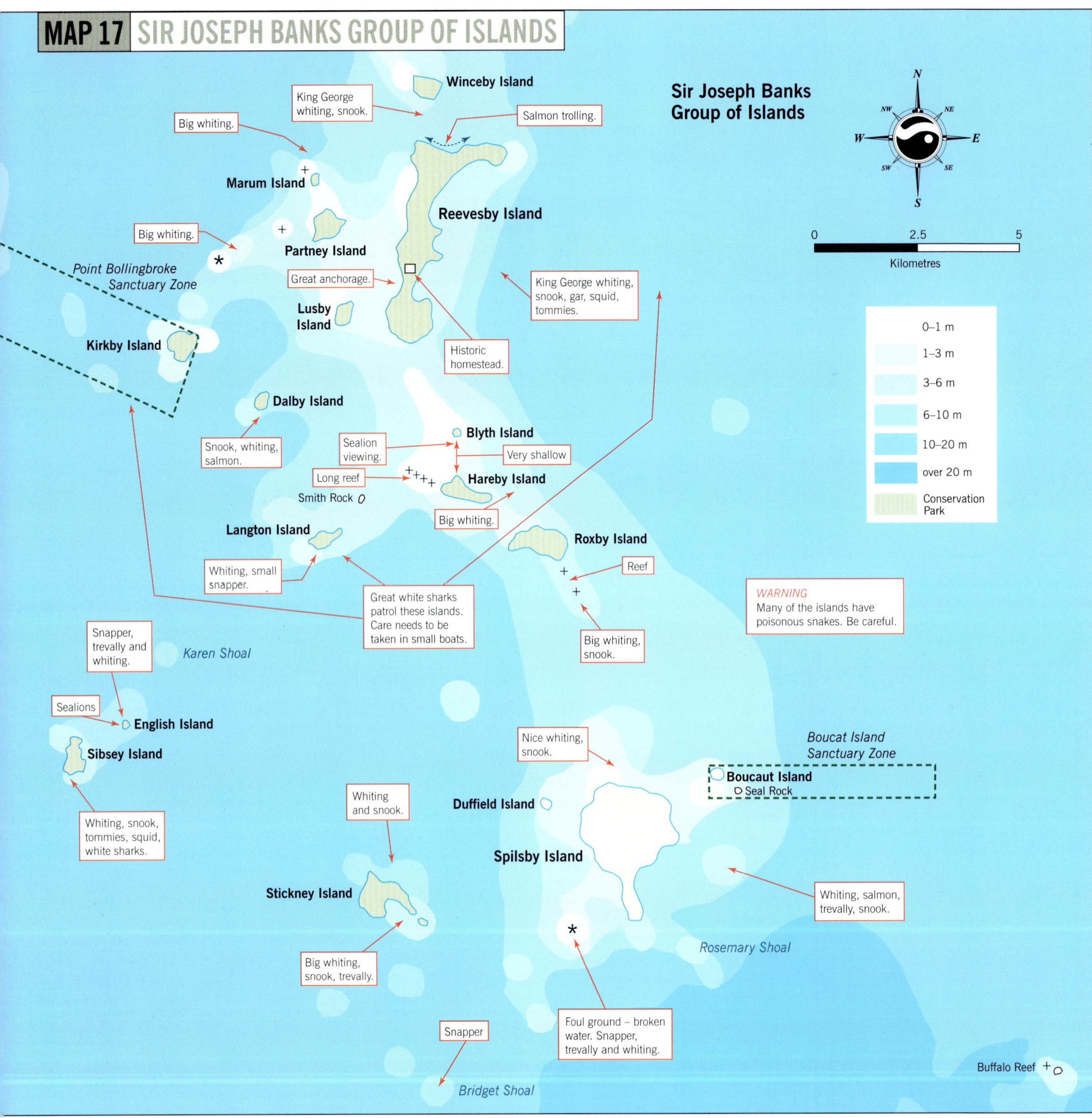

Other readily accessible fish species in the Sir Joseph Banks Group include tommy ruffs, garfish, snook, small snapper, squid and trevally. It's a bountiful area, but one that requires a bit of local knowledge, both for successful fishing and safe navigation. There are several reefs that are all but exposed at low tide and charging around without knowing their precise location could end up in disaster.

As mentioned, weather is the key to fishing a group of islands this far from the boat ramp. Fortunately, there's a Volunteer Marine Radio centre at Tumby Bay that provides up to date weather information for all boaties on lower Eyre Peninsula. There is a VHF radio repeater installed to provide exceptional range on channel 81, so as long as you have a VHF set on board, you will be able to receive weather news and maintain contact.

Tumby Bay jetty is very popular with visitors, particularly around peak holiday times. It generally fishes well year-round, with plenty of tommy ruffs in the evenings, a few garfish, squid, snook, a few yellowfin whiting in November to February only and mullet in the shallows. There is a fish cleaning facility at the base of the jetty and excellent overhead lighting for night fishing.

MAP 18 PORT NEILL

About 40 kilometres north of Tumby Bay, this little resort has a permanent population of just 250. It's well set up for visitors, with a neat caravan park, jetty and terrific multi-lane boat ramp with ample car parking and wash down facilities. King George whiting are the major drawcard for boat fishers, and these are available for

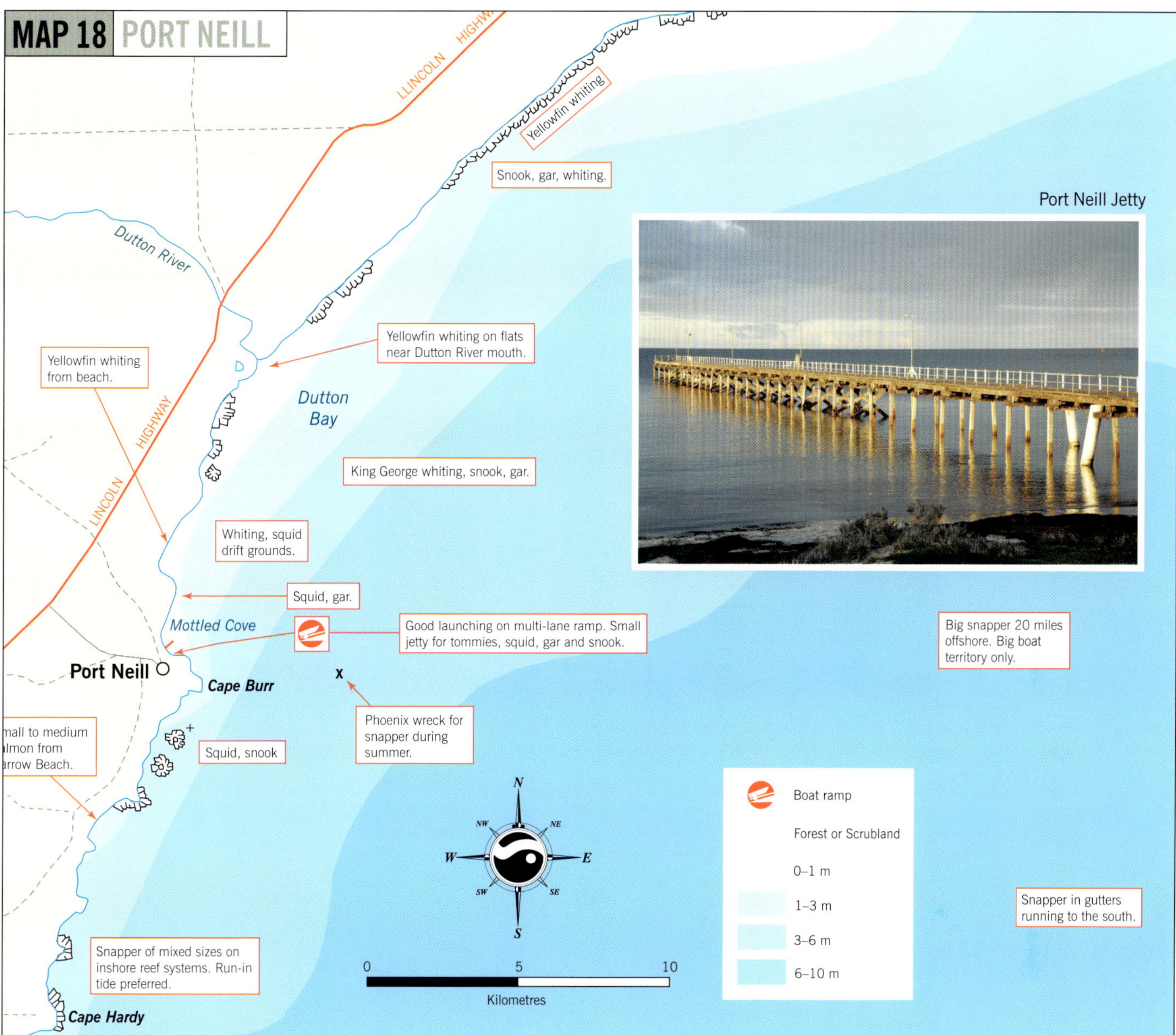

much of the year. The whiting grounds are scattered both north and south of the boat ramp and there are also plenty of gar, squid and snook in the same areas.

Port Neill is an under-rated snapper location. There are plenty of small, medium and large reds caught along the inshore reef systems from October through until Easter time, both on natural baits and soft plastic lures. The water is quite shallow and the larger fish put up a terrific fight on the right tackle. The wreck of the 'Phoenix', not far offshore from the Port Neill boat ramp, fishes well for snapper of mixed sizes in summer time and is accessible to small boats in good weather.

Those with larger craft will find excellent snapper grounds further offshore. Most of the more consistent areas lie around 20 miles east of the launching ramp, so you need to own a large boat and choose perfect weather for the trip. The water is around 25–30 metres deep and there is usually a strong tidal flow, so it generally calls for medium to heavy tackle. Most snapper on these offshore grounds are in the 50 to 70 cm size range, but there are still quite a few big reds up around the 20 lb mark for those who persist through the smaller fish.

Snapper are also available land based from a few rock ledges in between Port Neill township and Lipson Cove to the south. Casting baits such as squid heads or fish fillets over rubbly bottom after a strong blow can be productive, especially if the water is stirred-up and some reef is nearby. Surf casting tackle is recommended for this land based fishing.

Just to the north of Port Neill near the mouth of the Dutton River lies a series of inshore sand flats that produce big numbers of yellowfin whiting from October through until April. This is prime light tackle wading country and in good conditions it's usually possible to pull a personal bag limit of 20 whiting on one tide. Live seaweed worms or nippers (salt water yabbies) are the preferred baits, with peeled green prawns a reliable stand-by. Fresh yellowfin whiting are almost as good to eat as their King George cousins and are consequently very popular around Spencer Gulf.

Carrow Wells and Cowleys Beach lie three and ten kilometres respectively south of Port Neill along the North Coast Road. Both of these beaches return a few salmon trout and tommy ruffs during the winter months, with yellowfin whiting and mullet available during summer and autumn. The yellowfin are not normally around in as bigger numbers as seen on the shallower beaches to the north of town, but some nice fish are caught nevertheless.

MAP 19 ARNO BAY

One of the smaller settlements along this stretch of coastline, Arno has a permanent population of 400 or so, but this number increases

MAP 19 ARNO BAY

LEFT: The Estelle Star wreck offshore from Aro Bay receives a fair bit of fishing pressure these days and unfortunately does not yield as many fish as it used to.

LEFT: Big snapper is what Arno Bay has become famous for.

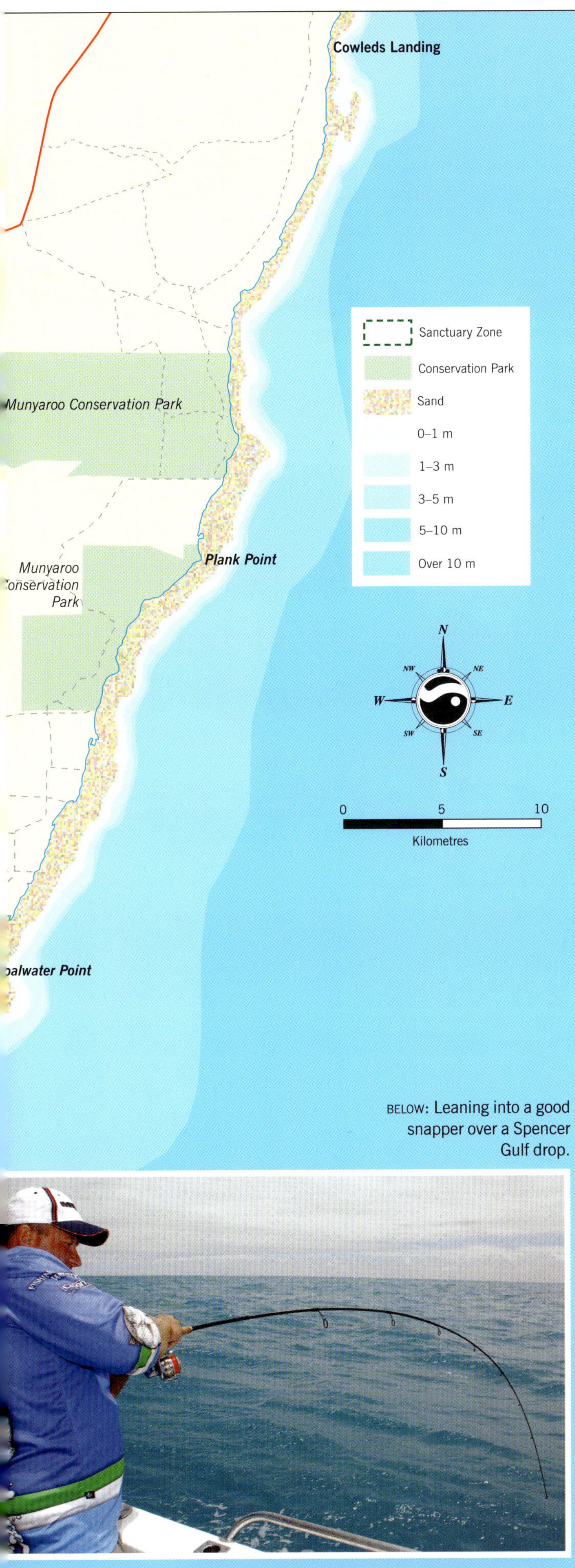

BELOW: Leaning into a good snapper over a Spencer Gulf drop.

dramatically during the holiday periods. For a little place, however, it has plenty to offer fisherfolk. The marina, located just a short drive north of the foreshore, is home to quite a few larger commercial boats, most of which are involved with local kingfish farms.

Accommodation options in Arno include the local caravan park and hotel, plus private accommodation options in holiday houses and shacks. There is a general store, beachside café, but that's about the extent of the amenities in town.

If towing your boat to Arno Bay, it's worthwhile remembering no fuel is available in the town, with the nearest fuel station located at Cleve, 26 km inland. There's a dual lane boat ramp with ample car parking, but the ramp can be affected by surge from outside when the wind is in the east. Exiting the marina demands some care, as there is heavy reef directly offshore and sticking to the clearly marked channel is imperative. There are also a lot of large, circular kingfish pens to the east, which can be difficult to see in low light.

Arno's inshore fishing revolves around the big three – King George whiting, garfish and squid. All are available in abundance for much of the year, although the better numbers of whiting show up in early autumn and are available until end of winter. These fish rarely achieve the same size as those further south off Tumby Bay, but they are still good ones of between 35–40 centimetres. Squidding over the inshore weed beds and broken ground rarely fails to produce a good feed, especially during the cooler months and when the water is clean. Snook and a few salmon are available, with March to May being the peak months for these species.

It's Arno Bay's deep water snapper fishing, however, which has seen the place leap to angling fame in recent times. The wreck of the Estelle Star, 30-odd kilometres offshore, is one of the best locations for truly big snapper in SA and now attracts many boats, both commercial and recreational. The wreck is scattered over a fair area these days, but seems to draw big snapper like a magnet from December through until the end of autumn. 40 pounders have been caught on the Estelle Star and countless others of better than 30 pounds. This wreck has received a lot of fishing pressure since its rise to fame, and unfortunately doesn't return the consistent numbers and size of fish that it once did. It still has bursts of activity, but this activity can be quite sporadic. There is a spatial snapper closure which sees the wreck being closed for three months annually from November first through to the end of January.

To the south-east of the wreck runs a series of deep gutters, which seem to act as highways to travelling snapper schools. This area is called the western gutter, and can hold good schools of snapper at the right time of year. It's unusual to see a 30 lb slob out here, but quite a few reds in the 10 to 20 lb size are caught around the natural limestone ledges along the gutter. There is also some good inshore snapper fishing available along Arno Bays coastline, both to the north and south of town, which sees quite a few fish caught from around inshore limestone bommies and ledges. Most of these grounds are under 10 m deep, and are pretty consistent with good tidal flow and stirred water. Most of the reds throughout these inshore grounds are in the 1 to 3 kg size, but a few better fish to 8 kg are occasionally caught.

Although it rarely makes angling headlines, Arno Bay offers some good beach fishing, particularly for small sharks and school mulloway. There are no surf beaches as such, but the beach near the Clean Seas fish farm and others nearby often turn up bronze whalers and jewies to 10 kilograms after periods of onshore wind and choppy seas. The best months for these Gulf mulloway are October/November, and again in April/May. The occasional nice tailor is also caught from these beaches, but these are the exception rather than the rule.

MAP 20 COWELL

With a population of nearly 900, Cowell is slightly larger than most of the settlements around it. It is located on the shores of the expansive Franklin Harbor and is equipped with an excellent launching ramp, long jetty and plenty of holiday accommodation options. The harbor is mangrove-lined for much of its perimeter and is recognised as a significant nursery area for species like gar, King George whiting and mullet.

Blue swimmer crabs are plentiful throughout Franklin Harbor, especially from Christmas time until April, when they tend to move outside into deeper water. They can be netted from the town jetty, but are easier to locate in numbers from a small boat and are generally large and full of meat. Drop nets baited with fish heads or squid seem to provide the best hauls of these succulent crustaceans.

King George whiting are scattered throughout the harbor over broken ground, but they are generally smaller than those caught outside in open water. During the summer months unwanted striped perch (trumpeters) invade the whiting grounds, making it hard to catch a decent feed of King George. Flathead, flounder, snook, salmon trout, garfish, mullet and tommy ruffs make up the remainder of the Franklin Harbor catch for boaties.

In the cooler months of July and August, vast schools of yellowfin whiting move on to the shallow flats at the northern end of the harbor and these are fun to catch while wading with light tackle. Seaweed worms are the primo bait and these can be excavated from beneath piles of rotting ribbon weed scattered along the shoreline. Digging worms is a bit of a messy business, but there can be no doubt they are the key to bag limit whiting catches.

Snapper fishermen often do well on the grounds immediately outside Franklin Harbor, but you'll need a larger boat to tackle the

ABOVE: School mulloway can be caught from a handful of beaches within Spencer Gulf when the conditions are right.

Lucky Bay

Good yellowfin whiting

Yellowfin whiting wading flats. Rising tide best. Use worms or nippers for bait. Plastics and poppers good also. Blue crabs also in this area.

Big snapper outside harbour on man-made 'drops'.

BELOW: Garfish are a popular target over shallow areas within Spencer Gulf.

deep water areas safely. Big reds are quite common from the Cowell entrance northward to Lucky Bay and some are found reasonably close to shore. There are dozens of holiday shacks along the Lucky Bay foreshore and plenty of keen anglers, so the local grounds cop a fair bit of pressure, but they seem to keep producing quality snapper and King George whiting.

MAP 21 WHYALLA

South Australia's second largest regional city, Whyalla has long been hailed as one of the country's very best locations for big snapper. It hosts the Australian Snapper Fishing Championship every year over the Easter weekend, an event that consistently turns up plenty of jumbo snapper and attracts hundreds of anglers and their families.

But Whyalla is about a lot more than snapper. Due to its size, population (23,000) and location, Whyalla boats top class facilities, including several nice caravan parks, comfortable motels, a large shopping centre, top class restaurants and, of course, a terrific marina and multi-lane boat ramp. It also has a short, but productive fishing jetty, specialist tackle store and marine dealership, so you can get virtually anything required for boating and fishing.

Although a few decent snapper are caught from the rocks, Whyalla's best snapper fishing is found offshore – often as far as 40 kilometres or more from the ramp. The reds vary in size from 'ruggers' of barely legal size (38cm) all the way up to big, bump-

ABOVE: The inshore snapper fishing along Spencer Gulfs western shoreline is pretty good, especially after a blow.

headed monsters of 15 kilograms and better. It's unusual for the winning fish in the annual snapper competition to weigh less than 14 kilos, so trophy specimens are still there to be had.

There are King George whiting offshore from Whyalla, but few are big ones. Most are just over the legal minimum size of 31 centimetres, but are still worth catching. There are yellowfin whiting as well, the majority of which are hooked from the local foreshore beach and also around the mangrove coast a little further south. Garfish, snook, squid, tommy ruffs and mullet are also available, along with good numbers of blue swimmer crabs in summer and autumn.

Point Lowly, at the tip of a rocky peninsula to the north-east of Whyalla, is a popular fishing spot for both shore-based anglers and boaties. There is a good boat ramp situated adjacent to the lighthouse and some excellent offshore fishing for big snapper, salmon, snook, garfish and squid. Big yellowtail kingfish roam around Point Lowly from November through until the end of summer, some of which top 30 kilograms. These are tough to land from the rocks, but several specialist local anglers have caught some beauties, generally using live squid or garfish for bait.

Those operating from small boats between the Point Lowly lighthouse and nearby Becky Point have a better chance of landing hooked kingfish, as they are able to get mobile quickly after hook-up and chase the fish before they are broken off on the reefy bottom. Naturally, hunting kingies around Point Lowly demands the right gear and the right techniques, as it does anywhere else in the state.

MAP 22 PORT AUGUSTA

Located right at the head of Spencer Gulf, this town of around 14,000 people offers a diverse range of fishing options and plenty of facilities and services. By road it is roughly half way between Adelaide and Port Lincoln and many who make the long westward trip choose to break it and stay in Port Augusta overnight. There are several caravan parks and plenty of motel and hotel accommodation alternatives.

These days Port Augusta is best known as Spencer Gulf's number one location for giant yellowtail kingfish. The kings usually start turning up at Port Augusta in June, with the smaller male fish arriving first and the much larger females following in July and August. These kings are all in spawning condition and vary in size from about 15 kilograms all the way up to 45 kg. There are few,

ABOVE: A yellowtail kingfish caught at Point Lowly, Whyalla.

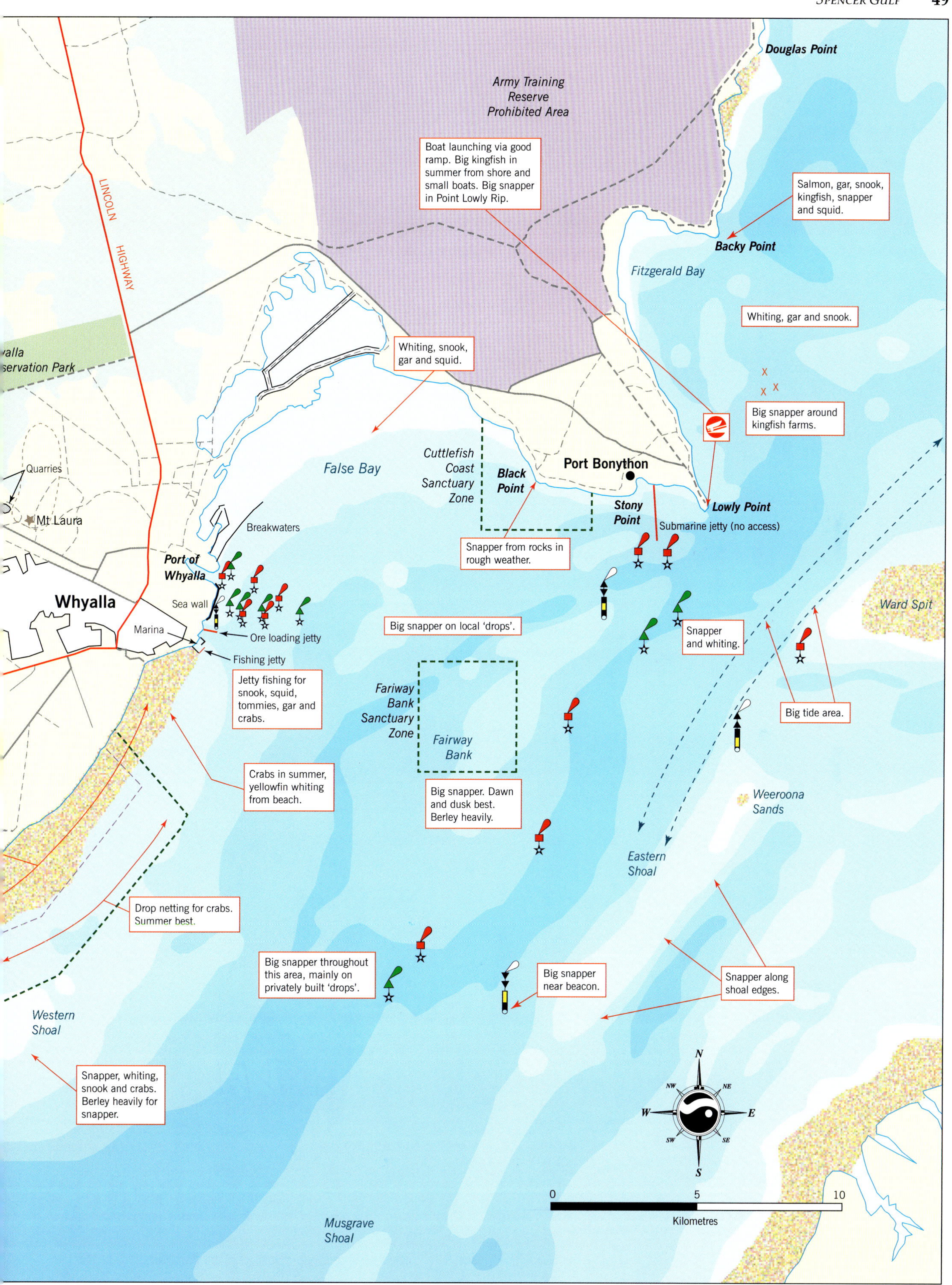

Douglas Point
Army Training Reserve Prohibited Area
Boat launching via good ramp. Big kingfish in summer from shore and small boats. Big snapper in Point Lowly Rip.
Salmon, gar, snook, kingfish, snapper and squid.
Backy Point
Fitzgerald Bay
Whiting, gar and snook.
LINCOLN HIGHWAY
Whiting, snook, gar and squid.
Big snapper around kingfish farms.
Quarries
Mt Laura
False Bay
Cuttlefish Coast Sanctuary Zone
Black Point
Port Bonython
Stony Point
Lowly Point
Submarine jetty (no access)
Breakwaters
Port of Whyalla
Whyalla
Sea wall
Marina
Ore loading jetty
Fishing jetty
Snapper from rocks in rough weather.
Big snapper on local 'drops'.
Snapper and whiting.
Ward Spit
Jetty fishing for snook, squid, tommies, gar and crabs.
Fariway Bank Sanctuary Zone
Fairway Bank
Big tide area.
Crabs in summer, yellowfin whiting from beach.
Big snapper. Dawn and dusk best. Berley heavily.
Weeroona Sands
Eastern Shoal
Drop netting for crabs. Summer best.
Big snapper throughout this area, mainly on privately built 'drops'.
Big snapper near beacon.
Snapper along shoal edges.
Western Shoal
Snapper, whiting, snook and crabs. Berley heavily for snapper.
N
NW
NE
W
E
SW
SE
S
0
5
10
Kilometres
Musgrave Shoal

MAP 22 PORT AUGUSTA

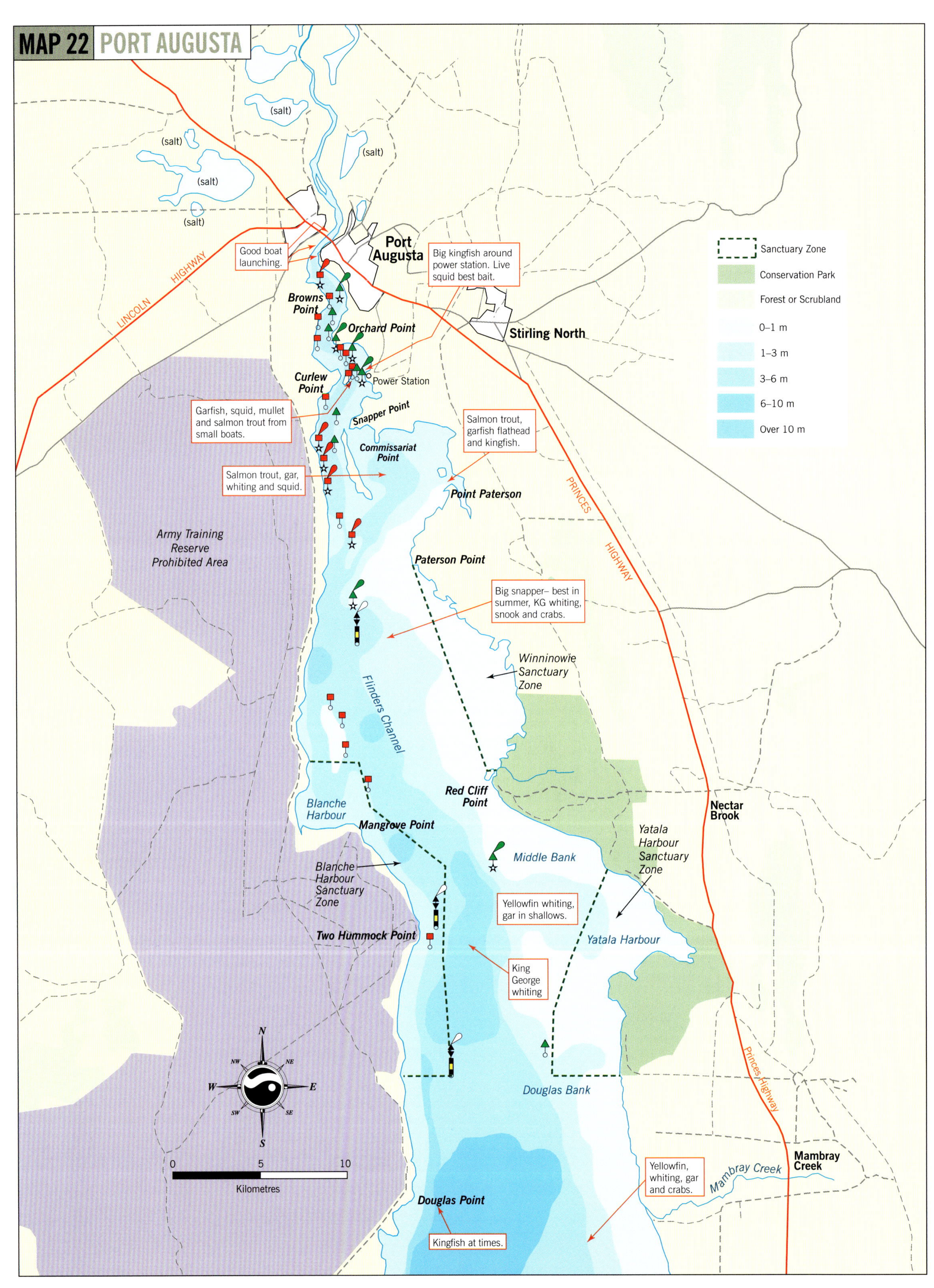

if any other locations in the country – and indeed the world – where hooking a genuine hundred pound kingfish within a stone's throw from shore is a distinct possibility most times out.

The majority of these giants are caught on live baits set under balloons or down riggers and the most productive fishing areas are immediately outside the two decommissioned power stations. Squid, garfish and salmon trout are usually the best baits and it's mandatory to use at least 50 pound tackle. It's possible to witness some aggressive surface feeding, and in this situation working a surface popper through the melee can bring spectacular results. As the water is quite shallow, bigger kingfish run long and hard after hook up and it's prudent to lift the anchor immediately and give chase.

Port Augusta at the top of Spencer Gulf is a known kingfish haunt. Brad Smith with a lovely fish.

Big snapper are taken frequently along the edges of the channel south of Port Augusta, but not in the same numbers as Whyalla or Arno Bay. There are also plenty of nice garfish, salmon, small to medium King George whiting and the occasional mulloway around the wharf and road bridge. This is also one of very few locations in SA where dolphin fish are occasional visitors. Most are quite small, but they are always a welcome bonus catch. Plenty of yellowfin whiting are caught around the mangrove lined shallows during winter, where they can be seen schooling in vast numbers.

Boat launching at Port Augusta is no problem. A dual lane ramp is located on the western side of the Gulf just after the main highway bridge and there is ample parking for both locals and visitors. Land-based fishing is confined to the wharf, the old road bridge and a short jetty on the western side.

PORT AUGUSTA TO MARION BAY

This side of Spencer Gulf begins with shallow, mangrove-lined flats at the northern extremity and concludes with spectacular rocky headlands and turbulent surf beaches in the south. Strictly speaking, Marion Bay is more correctly aligned with Investigator Strait, but as many who launch from this popular little resort travel around into Spencer Gulf to fish, it is convenient to use it as the southern boundary of this section.

Most of the same fish species found on Spencer Gulf's western coastline are also present to the east, but there are a few differences. Big mulloway and Australian salmon taken from the surf beaches are a prime example.

MAP 23 PORT GERMEIN

Located about 240 kilometres north of Adelaide on National Highway One, Port Germein is most famous for its extremely long jetty. At one stage this was the longest pier in the southern hemisphere at over 1.6 kilometres, but storm damage in recent times has shortened it somewhat and it now stands at around 1.2 kilometres. The jetty was once a very important grain loading facility for SA's mid-north, but it is no longer used for anything but recreational fishing.

The reason for Port Germein jetty's extreme length, of course, is the vast expanse of quite shallow water it traverses before reaching enough depth to berth major shipping. This section of the Gulf is generally shallower than the other side, particularly along the coastal fringe. The vast inshore flats are important nursery areas for all manner of fish and crustaceans and offer light tackle anglers plenty of opportunity.

Yellowfin whiting, mullet, flathead, blue swimmer crabs, garfish and salmon trout are all caught around Port Germein, particularly on the making tide. Most of these varieties can be hooked from the ageing jetty, as well as from the flats and adjacent mangrove creek systems.

Yellowtail kingfish make sporadic raids to the jetty, usually smashing up the tackle of unprepared anglers. Most of these fish are small, but still possess the speed and strength to break lines intended for garfish or whiting. In Spencer Gulf only it is legal (as at mid 2016) to catch and keep yellowtail kings of over 45 centimetres, with a personal bag limit of 10 and boat limit of 30. This is opposed to the regular limits which affect all other state waters. There is plenty of good snapper fishing offshore from Port Germein, but the only way to launch a boat is via tractor, due to the vastness of the inshore shallows. King George whiting, snook, squid and garfish are also in good numbers, but the area sees only a few boaties due to the launching difficulties.

MAP 23 PORT PIRIE

Pirie is one of South Australia's larger provincial towns with a population of just over 13,000. It's a major industrial centre and has the honour of possessing the tallest structure in the state – a 205 metre chimney belonging to Nyrstar, which is the world's largest lead smelter. Aside from heavy industry, however, Port Pirie is a bustling, vibrant town with some excellent fishing options.

Boat launching facilities are first class. A multi-lane, all tide ramp, located in the centre of town, sees plenty of traffic when conditions are good and a deep water channel provides ready access to Spencer Gulf. There is a specialist tackle store and a couple of marine dealers, all of which will gladly provide local fishing information to visiting anglers.

Some of the biggest bream in SA are caught in Port Pirie's harbor. 50 centimetre-plus specimens have been taken and most are released after capture. Small rubber tail lures seem to be most successful and also claim the occasional school mulloway. Those who target the mulloway with live baits are generally rewarded with fish up to seven or eight kilograms – not the monsters of our Far West Coast beaches, but nice fish on the right tackle. Trumpeters and mullet are the most readily available live baits and both seem to work well.

Outside the Port Pirie harbor lay several vast flats areas, tidal creeks

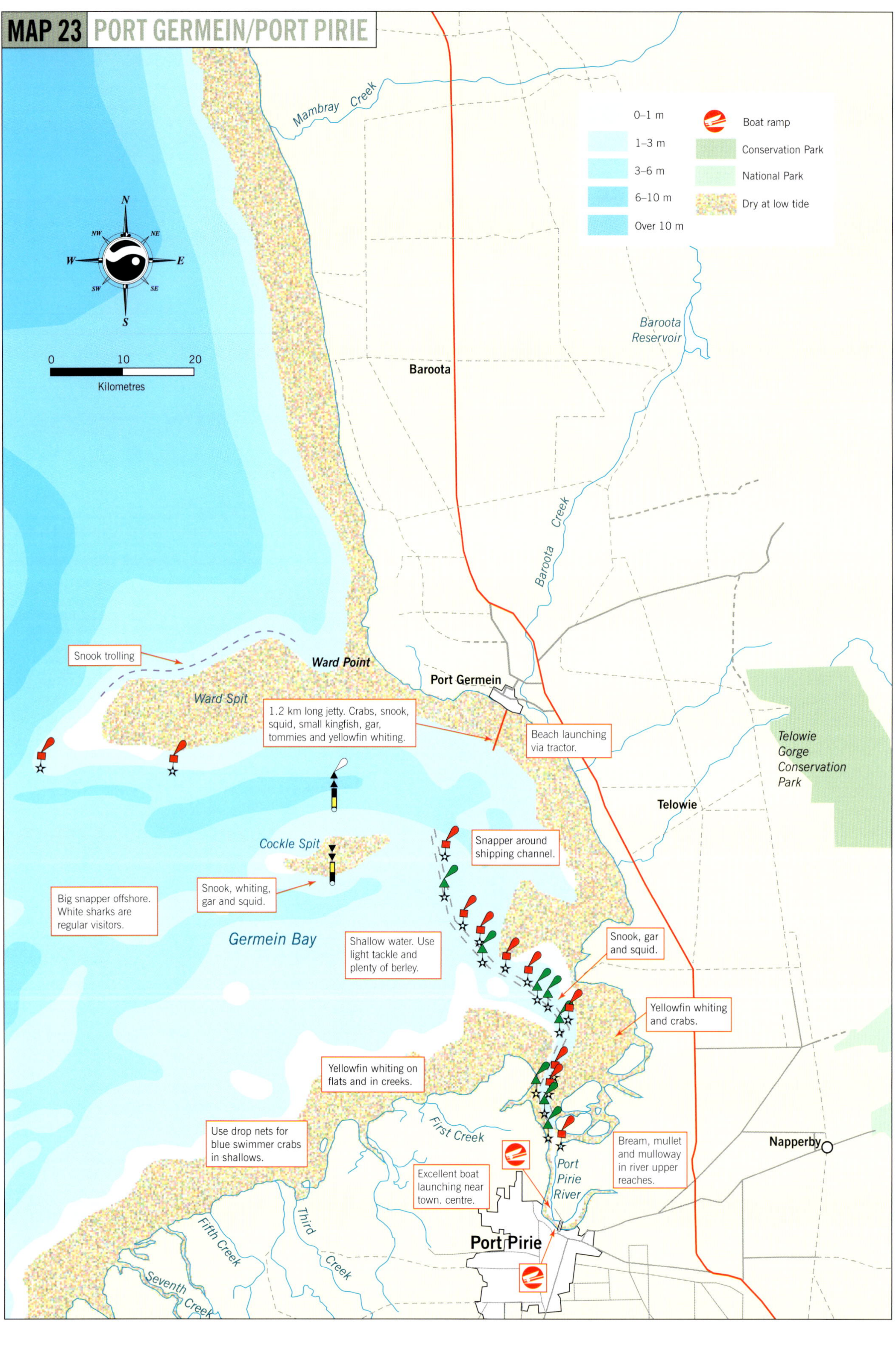
MAP 23 PORT GERMEIN/PORT PIRIE
0–1 m
1–3 m
3–6 m
6–10 m
Over 10 m
Boat ramp
Conservation Park
National Park
Dry at low tide
N
NE
E
SE
S
SW
W
NW
0
10
20
Kilometres
Mambray Creek
Baroota Reservoir
Baroota
Baroota Creek
Snook trolling
Ward Point
Ward Spit
Port Germein
1.2 km long jetty. Crabs, snook, squid, small kingfish, gar, tommies and yellowfin whiting.
Beach launching via tractor.
Telowie Gorge Conservation Park
Telowie
Cockle Spit
Snapper around shipping channel.
Big snapper offshore. White sharks are regular visitors.
Snook, whiting, gar and squid.
Germein Bay
Shallow water. Use light tackle and plenty of berley.
Snook, gar and squid.
Yellowfin whiting and crabs.
Yellowfin whiting on flats and in creeks.
Use drop nets for blue swimmer crabs in shallows.
First Creek
Napperby
Bream, mullet and mulloway in river upper reaches.
Excellent boat launching near town. centre.
Port Pirie River
Third Creek
Fifth Creek
Seventh Creek
Port Pirie

Spida Everett with a nice snapper caught wide of Port Broughton.

and deeper water for the snapper angler. Yellowfin whiting are prolific at times, especially in and around the mangrove creeks and most are good size. These fish are commercially netted, sometimes in their tonnes, which understandably upsets the local recreational anglers.

King George whiting, garfish and snook are also quite common around the inshore ribbon weed grounds and over broken bottom. Cockle Spit is one of Port Pirie's better known small boat grounds and this area can teem with snook during the warmer months. There are also plenty of squid to be hooked off Pirie, particularly in the cooler months.

As is the case across the Gulf at Whyalla, there are several man-made snapper 'drops' outside of Port Pirie. These are constructed of old car bodies, building refuse and sometimes derelict boats. Nowadays it's illegal to construct artificial reefs of this nature, but they are undoubtedly effective at aggregating school fish like snapper and King George whiting. Most of these 'drops' were built many years ago and have subsequently disintegrated to some degree, but they continue to produce good fish for those who know their precise whereabouts.

Great white sharks of frightening proportions are regular visitors to Port Pirie's snapper grounds when the seasonal aggregation of spawning reds is in full swing. One of the largest sharks ever caught in South Australia came from Pirie back in the 1990s. It was hooked accidentally on a professional snapper long line and measured close to 17 feet from nose to tail. Consequently, those fishing from small boats in this region should always be mindful of a possible big shark visit.

MAP 24 Port Broughton

The trend of shallow coastal water continues as you head southward to the delightful township of Port Broughton and its little 'satellite' settlement of Fisherman's Bay. A meandering channel provides access to Spencer Gulf from the Port Broughton boat ramp, which has been upgraded and is now first class.

Around 1500 people live in and around Broughton and it is indeed well served in terms of facilities, holiday accommodation and fishing options. The long jetty runs over quite shallow water for much of its length and terminates with a 'T' section that is used for mooring and unloading by commercial fishermen. The jetty yields good numbers of nice yellowfin whiting during the cooler months, with most of the better catches coming in the evenings. These are taken on marine worms, nippers and pieces of peeled green prawn. Those who enjoy blue swimmer crabs can usually net a good feed around Port Broughton when they are running in summer and early autumn. There are plenty of garfish around during the same period and some squid if you know where to look for them. Most of the King George whiting caught at Port Broughton are small to medium and, as is the case right along this section of Spencer Gulf, trumpeters are a major headache when the water is warm. These inedible, spiky pests can be a whiting specialist's nightmare and when they are at their worst, fishing becomes impossible.

Port Broughton's offshore snapper fishing is legendary. Most of the bigger reds are caught a long way out into the Gulf, so a big, seaworthy boat and a good weather forecast are mandatory. By far the most famous of all Broughton's offshore snapper grounds is the

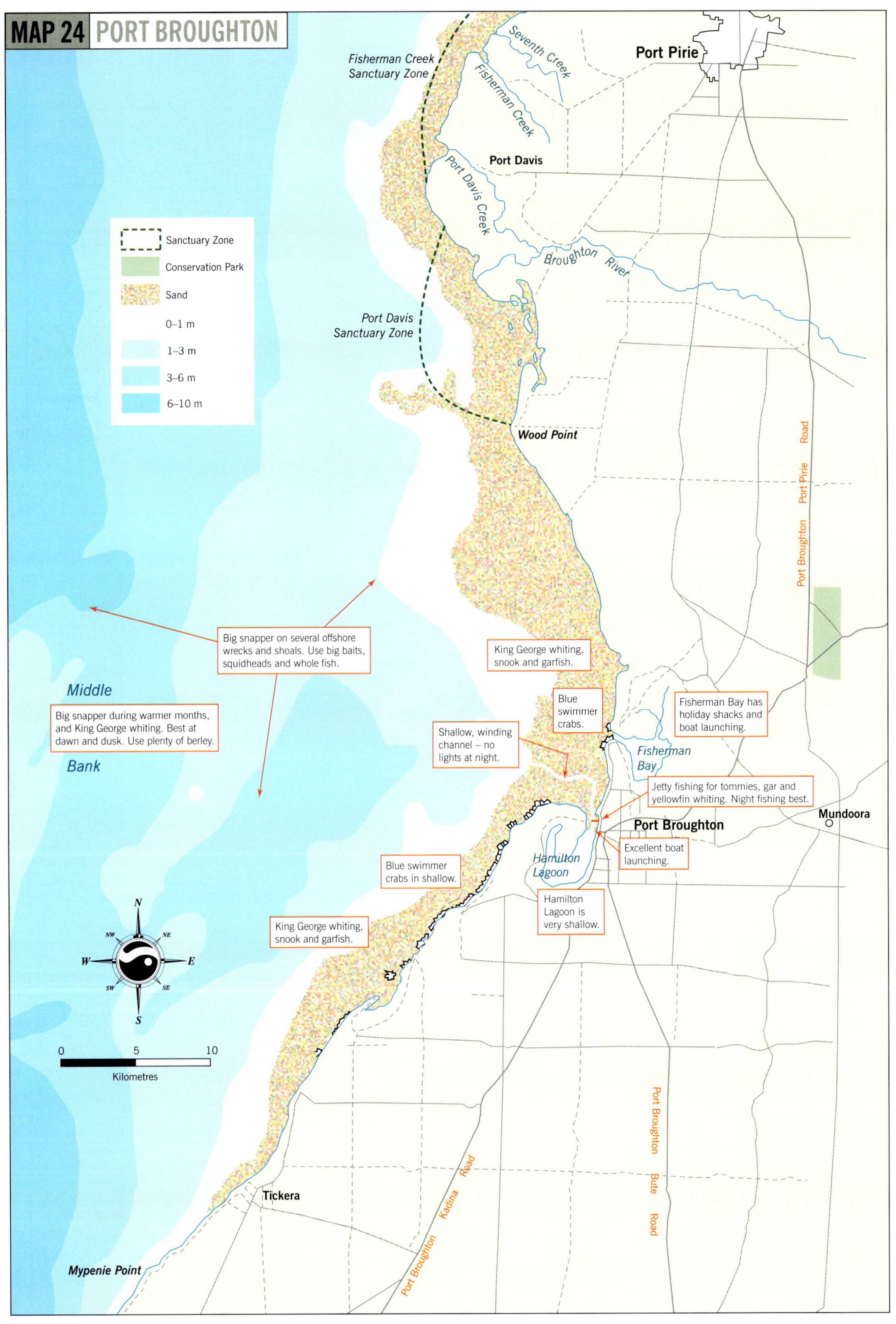
MAP 24 PORT BROUGHTON
Sanctuary Zone
Conservation Park
Sand
0–1 m
1–3 m
3–6 m
6–10 m
Fisherman Creek Sanctuary Zone
Seventh Creek
Fisherman Creek
Port Pirie
Port Davis
Port Davis Creek
Broughton River
Port Davis Sanctuary Zone
Wood Point
Port Broughton Port Pirie Road
Big snapper on several offshore wrecks and shoals. Use big baits, squidheads and whole fish.
King George whiting, snook and garfish.
Middle Bank
Big snapper during warmer months, and King George whiting. Best at dawn and dusk. Use plenty of berley.
Blue swimmer crabs.
Fisherman Bay has holiday shacks and boat launching.
Shallow, winding channel – no lights at night.
Fisherman Bay
Jetty fishing for tommies, gar and yellowfin whiting. Night fishing best.
Mundoora
Port Broughton
Excellent boat launching.
Hamilton Lagoon
Blue swimmer crabs in shallow.
Hamilton Lagoon is very shallow.
King George whiting, snook and garfish.
N
NE
E
SE
S
SW
W
NW
0
5
10
Kilometres
Port Broughton Bute Road
Tickera
Port Broughton Kadina Road
Mypenie Point

There are numerous artificial reefs out wide of Port Broughton.

wreck of the Illusion. The old boat sits in around 20 metres of water and is subject to strong tidal flow, so it's big sinkers, big baits and big fish!

Plank Shoal, further out still, is another well known and heavily fished snapper ground. It's popular with professional fishermen, charter operators and a few recreationals with large trailer boats. When the snapper are 'on' at Plank Shoal, it's possible to catch a boat limit in double quick time; in fact, you often spend a lot more time travelling out to the grounds than actually pulling fish! While a lot of these fish are in the schooling size of 6 to 8kg, plenty of big slobs of 12kg and better are caught from this area every year. This area has seen its fair share of fishing pressure over recent years, and as a result these truly big fish are becoming harder to locate.

The Port Broughton channel is relatively narrow and winding, which causes few problems in daylight, but can be a little unnerving for those returning from snapper fishing after sunset. The channel marker poles have reflectors, but no lights, so you'll need a spotlight or powerful torch to navigate safely in the dark.

MAP 25 WALLAROO

One of the most significant bulk handling ports around Spencer Gulf, Wallaroo is a Mecca for trailer boat fishers year-round. The bay can be fished from a small boat in reasonable weather for garfish, squid, King George whiting, snook and tommy ruffs, while those with larger craft can venture offshore for snapper of all sizes.

Boat launching at Wallaroo is about as good as it gets in South Australia. There is a first class multi-lane, all-tide ramp with spacious car park, which is often full when the weekend weather is good and the big snapper are on the bite. This is a far cry from the old ramp, which was essentially a four wheel drive proposition only.

The Wallaroo bulk loading jetty is open to recreational anglers and provides access to good fishing at times. In the shallow section it's reliable for yellowfin whiting, squid, blue swimmer crabs and mullet. It's not unusual to see dozens of crabbers on a warm Saturday or Sunday and most take home a good feed. Fresh fish heads are prime crab bait.

The yellowfin whiting can be a bit fickle and are nowhere near as consistent or reliable as at Port Broughton. Ultra light tackle and baits of seaweed worm, tube worm or beach worm are preferred and you'll need patience if there are a lot of people fishing the same area. Yellow eye mullet will take the same baits on the same tackle, so a mixed bag is a definite possibility.

Snapper of mixed sizes are the fish most people associate with Wallaroo jetty and the majority come from the middle of the pier towards the end. Best time is definitely after heavy weather from the north-west, but they can be taken at any time by those with the right gear. Fishing for snapper by casting baits back under the jetty has become quite popular, but this isn't for the ill prepared or faint hearted. The technique involves baiting up on heavy tackle (usually 80 pound!) and throwing back beneath the pier between the pylons. If a decent snapper picks up the bait, it's hook up, hang on and try to steer the fish clear of the sub-surface structure. Some snapper are landed, but a lot are lost!

Despite the fact that Wallaroo jetty is long, broad and sturdy, vehicles are not permitted. It's also against regulations to camp on the jetty for extended fishing, which is quite unusual in the overall scheme of SA coastal piers. Some regulars have home-made jetty trollies, which they load up with rods, reels, tackle and bait and wheel out to their chosen fishing location.

The Wallaroo jetty does close periodically for grain vessel berthing and bulk loading. For up to date information log on to *www.portmis.flindersports.com.au* to check accessibility of this structure for recreational fishing.

The relatively new Wallaroo Marina has quickly emerged as a worthwhile fishing venue, particularly for those with kayaks. There are some lovely bream to be caught, mainly on lures, as well as salmon trout, mullet and the occasional school mulloway. Like most new marina developments around our coastline, this one is lined with upmarket housing and the privately owned boarding and mooring pontoons have quickly formed cosy habitats for resident bream.

MAP 25 MOONTA BAY

Although not generally associated with great fishing, Moonta Bay is a very popular holiday resort with its own jetty. It is possible to catch squid, garfish, tommy ruffs, mullet and snook from the jetty, with blue swimmer crabs an option when the inshore water is warm.

MAP 25 PORT HUGHES

Just a stone's throw further south, Port Hughes has gone from being a sleepy little village with an 'iffy' boat ramp, general store and very little else, to one of the busiest launching sites on Spencer Gulf. It's about a two hour drive from Adelaide and attracts plenty of weekend boaties when the fish are on and the weather is fine. The launching ramp is now top class, with an enormous car park, but the entrance to the small marina still silts up over time and can be tricky to negotiate on exceptionally low tides.

Once outside the marina, fishing options are many and varied. Those with small boats can usually pick up a mixed bag of King George whiting, garfish, squid and snook without venturing out too wide. There are plenty of grounds within five or six miles of the ramp that are fishable in a 4.5-5 metre runabout when the weather is reasonable and most are reliable for all four of the above species.

Those with larger boats and some local knowledge regularly head further out, where the deep water grounds offer first class action on big whiting, snapper of all sizes, sharks and big snook. Those who head south to Cape Elizabeth often find XOS whiting,

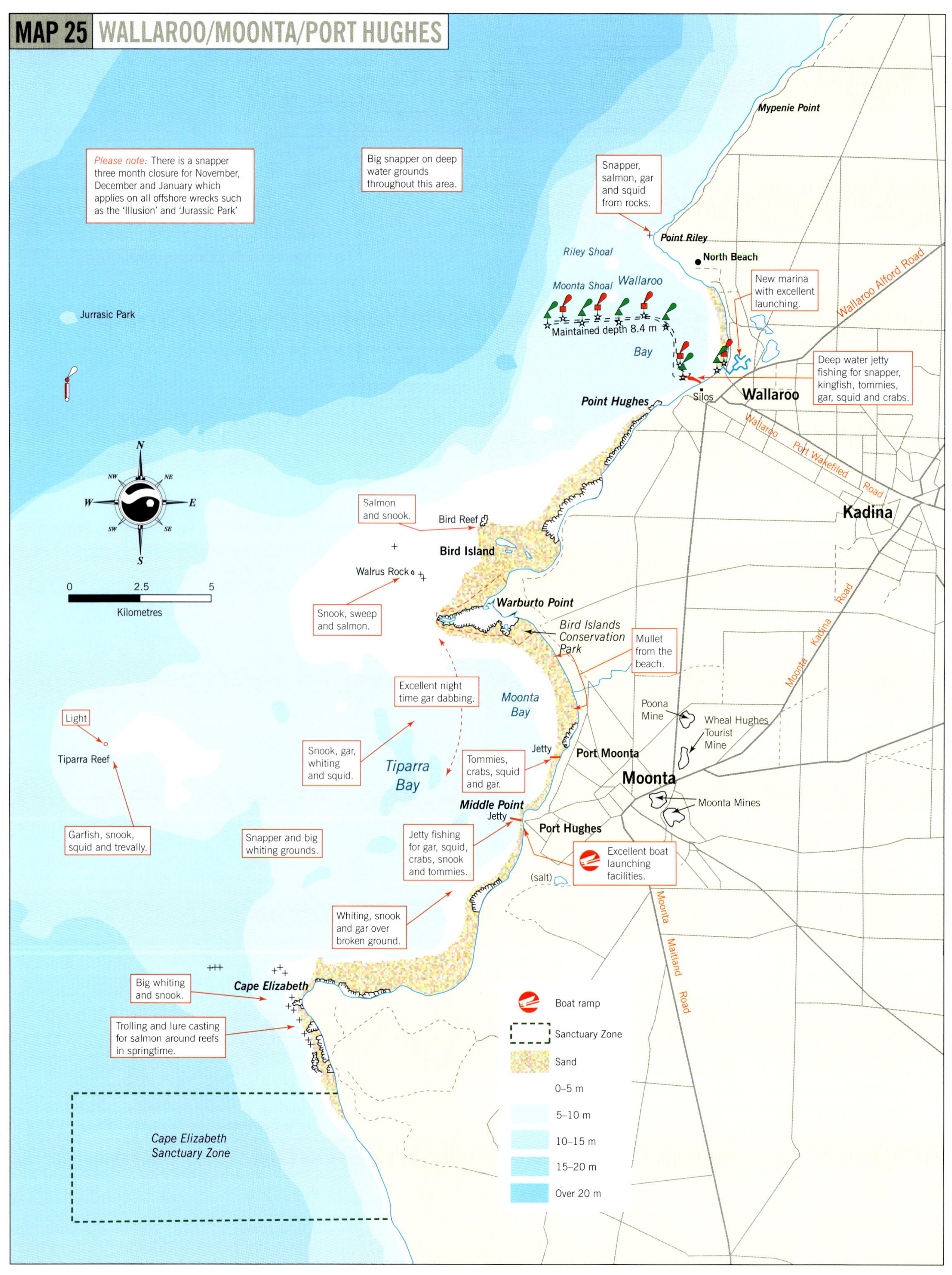
MAP 25 WALLAROO/MOONTA/PORT HUGHES
Please note: There is a snapper three month closure for November, December and January which applies on all offshore wrecks such as the 'Illusion' and 'Jurassic Park'
Big snapper on deep water grounds throughout this area.
Snapper, salmon, gar and squid from rocks.
Mypenie Point
Point Riley
North Beach
Riley Shoal
Moonta Shoal
Wallaroo
New marina with excellent launching.
Wallaroo Alford Road
Maintained depth 8.4 m
Bay
Deep water jetty fishing for snapper, kingfish, tommies, gar, squid and crabs.
Jurrasic Park
Point Hughes
Silos
Wallaroo
Wallaroo Port Wakefiled Road
Kadina
N
NW
NE
W
E
SW
SE
S
0 2.5 5
Kilometres
Salmon and snook.
Bird Reef
Bird Island
Walrus Rock
Snook, sweep and salmon.
Warburto Point
Bird Islands Conservation Park
Mullet from the beach.
Road
Moonta Kadina
Excellent night time gar dabbing.
Moonta Bay
Poona Mine
Wheal Hughes Tourist Mine
Light
Tiparra Reef
Snook, gar, whiting and squid.
Tiparra Bay
Tommies, crabs, squid and gar.
Jetty
Port Moonta
Moonta
Moonta Mines
Middle Point
Jetty
Port Hughes
Garfish, snook, squid and trevally.
Snapper and big whiting grounds.
Jetty fishing for gar, squid, crabs, snook and tommies.
Excellent boat launching facilities.
(salt)
Moonta Maitland Road
Whiting, snook and gar over broken ground.
Big whiting and snook.
Cape Elizabeth
Trolling and lure casting for salmon around reefs in springtime.
Boat ramp
Sanctuary Zone
Sand
0–5 m
5–10 m
10–15 m
15–20 m
Over 20 m
Cape Elizabeth Sanctuary Zone

Flathead like this one caught around the bottom of the Eyre Peninsula can also be caught in the shallows of Yorke Peninsula

with some fish pushing a kilogram each. There are some giant snook in this area as well and, during late winter/ early spring, nice Australian salmon. These salmon usually vary between 2-3 kilograms and can be taken on minnow lures, rubber tails or whole pilchards on ganged hooks. They are great fighters over reefy territory and a lot of fun on light tackle. Small to mid-sized bronze whalers are caught during the warmer months in this area too. Floating a whole mackerel or a fillet of salmon or trevally out on a wire trace under a balloon is a good way to hook-up to these energetic inshore whalers.

The steamer channel is out in the middle of Spencer Gulf and can only be accessed in the right weather. This is where most of the big snapper are caught and the best fishing occurs around tide changes. Big baits like squid heads, whole tommy ruffs and slimy mackerel are the go for the steamer channel reds, many of which top 25 pounds.

Tiparra Reef, about 10 miles to the west of Port Hughes, is a terrific location for big garfish, squid and snook. The gar are very reliable, especially when the weather is calm and warm. All you need is some light tackle, gents (blowfly maggots) for bait and a steady surface berley stream with plenty of tuna oil for smell. Most of the gar are big ones and are well worth the boat ride to catch.

Port Hughes jetty is a long one and quite high off the water. It draws tourists in big numbers over the high season and most are happy with what they catch. Tommy ruffs are the most readily available species and these vary in size from 'throw backs' to much better specimens of around 25 centimetres. Garfish are also a common jetty catch and can be taken on the same baits and floating rigs as the tommies.

Squid are prolific at times around the Hughes jetty, especially when the wind is light and the water is clear, but they are highly sought after and there is usually plenty of competition among visiting anglers. Blue swimmers are available as well and are usually at their best early in the New Year until Easter time. These are caught in standard drop nets on the usual baits of fish heads and squid.

MAP 26 Balgowan

This tiny settlement has a well stocked store, nice caravan park and a single lane boat ramp. It's nowhere near as popular as Port Hughes, but offers access to many of the same offshore fishing locations. The Balgowan ramp doesn't have floating boarding pontoons like many of the

MAP 26 BALGOWAN TO POINT TURTON

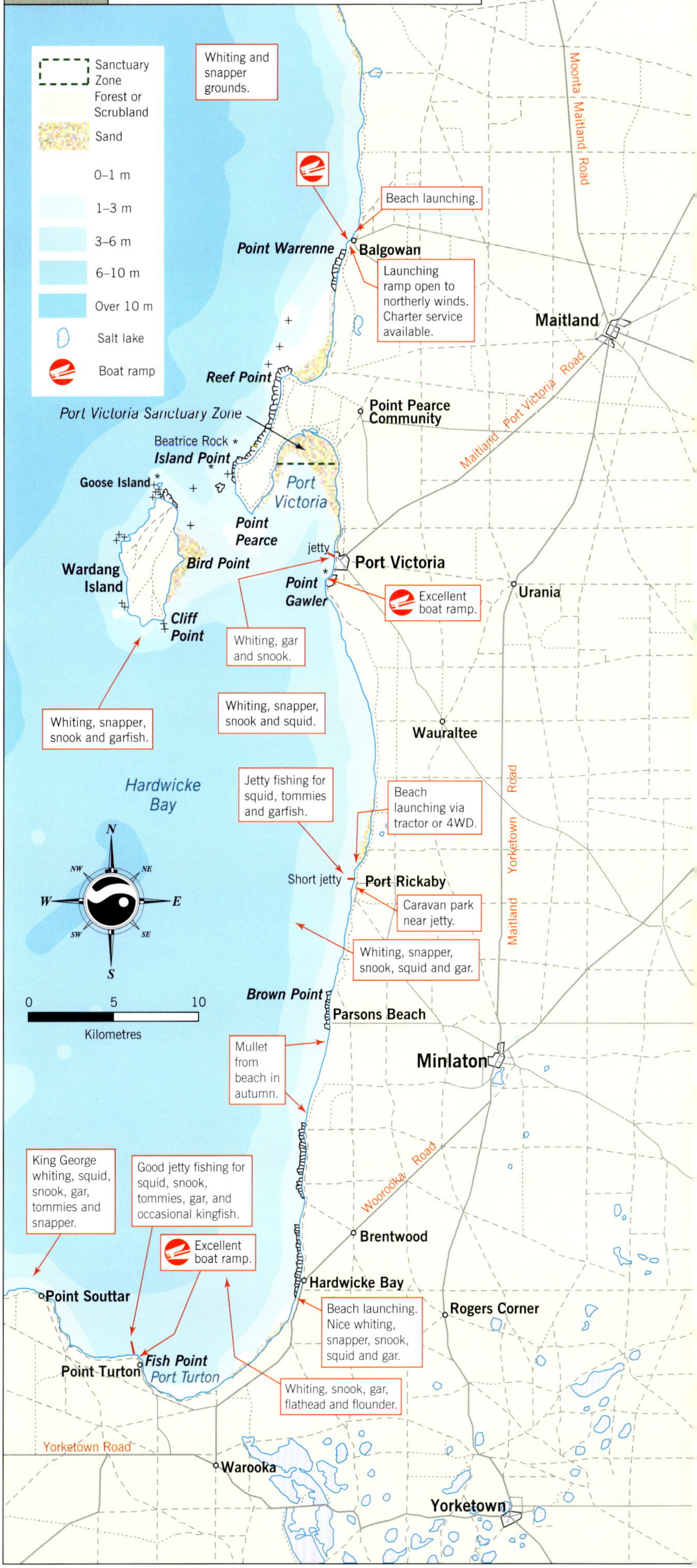

Sanctuary Zone
Forest or Scrubland
Sand
0–1 m
1–3 m
3–6 m
6–10 m
Over 10 m
Salt lake
Boat ramp

Whiting and snapper grounds.
Beach launching.
Launching ramp open to northerly winds. Charter service available.
Excellent boat ramp.
Whiting, gar and snook.
Whiting, snapper, snook and squid.
Whiting, snapper, snook and garfish.
Jetty fishing for squid, tommies and garfish.
Beach launching via tractor or 4WD.
Caravan park near jetty.
Whiting, snapper, snook, squid and gar.
Mullet from beach in autumn.
King George whiting, squid, snook, gar, tommies and snapper.
Good jetty fishing for squid, snook, tommies, gar, and occasional kingfish.
Excellent boat ramp.
Beach launching. Nice whiting, snapper, snook, squid and gar.
Whiting, snook, gar, flathead and flounder.

Point Warrenne
Balgowan
Maitland
Moonta Maitland Road
Reef Point
Point Pearce Community
Port Victoria Sanctuary Zone
Beatrice Rock
Island Point
Goose Island
Port Victoria
Maitland Port Victoria Road
Point Pearce
Wardang Island
Bird Point
jetty
Port Victoria
Point Gawler
Urania
Cliff Point
Wauraltee
Hardwicke Bay
Short jetty
Port Rickaby
Maitland Yorketown Road
Brown Point
Parsons Beach
Minlaton
Wooroka Road
Brentwood
Point Souttar
Hardwicke Bay
Rogers Corner
Fish Point
Point Turton
Port Turton
Yorketown Road
Warooka
Yorketown

N
NE
E
SE
S
SW
W
NW

0 5 10
Kilometres

LEFT: King George are the number one target in a lot of Spencer Gulf locations

others around Spencer Gulf and is open to winds from the north and north-west, so it does have its drawbacks. Many professional fishermen and keen local anglers prefer to launch their boats from the hard sandy beach to the east of the ramp, but a tractor or similar heavy duty tow vehicle is necessary.

There are good snapper and King George whiting grounds offshore and plenty of squid, garfish and snook in closer. A local charter operator is available to take visiting anglers out in a big, fast and seaworthy boat and is a sensible option for those unfamiliar with the area.

MAP 26 PORT VICTORIA

This is another Spencer Gulf resort that has seen a significant upgrade of most facilities and is now well equipped for visiting anglers. It has an all-tide boat ramp, an experienced local fishing charter operation, long jetty and plenty of accommodation options.

The Port Victoria jetty is one of the best in this area for catching snook at night time. These aren't the metre-long fish trolled out wide, but are usually half of that length and still a lot of fun to catch on light gear. The usual technique is to rig two or three hooks close together and bait up with a whole small fish like a blue bait or anchovy. This is lightly weighted and cast around the illuminated area beneath the jetty lights. Snook are aggressive predators and usually pounce on baits like this or small minnow lures.

The offshore fishing in this location can be excellent. Nice King George whiting are caught both inside and outside the bay, as well as around Wardang Island, which lies a few miles to the west. Snapper of all sizes are also abundant during the spring and summer months, but these are a little harder to pin down if you're unfamiliar with the offshore grounds. Quite often whiting and 'rugger' snapper are taken on the same reefs, providing their captors with a very tasty mixed bag. School sharks and smaller bronze whalers can be found in good numbers around some of the offshore broken bottom at times. If you manage to hook a school shark, it's worthwhile persisting for more as invariably there will be others nearby given their schooling nature.

MAP 26 PORT RICKABY

Although it's quite small, Port Rickaby has a top class caravan park and good facilities for visiting anglers. There is no boat ramp, but it is possible to launch smaller trailer boats from firm sand via four wheel drive tow vehicle. There is good fishing to be had offshore, particularly for King George whiting, snapper and snook.

The short jetty has no overhead lighting for night fishing and the most commonly caught varieties are squid, tommy ruffs and gar. Black ink stains right along the jetty indicate the popularity of calamari and indeed most who visit the pier do so with squid jigs on either hand lines or light rods.

MAP 26 HARDWICKE BAY

Again, there is no fancy launching ramp in this location and most who fish here rely on beach launching from a couple of sites. You'll need either a tractor or substantial four wheel drive and launching should only be attempted when the swell is down. There is some excellent King George whiting fishing in the bay, with many of the fish over 40 centimetres long. Snook, gar, squid and a few snapper are taken as well.

MAP 26 POINT TURTON

Few locations around the Spencer Gulf coast have gone ahead in recent times as much as Turton. It is served by a terrific all weather marina with dual lane launching ramp, floating boarding pontoons and fish cleaning station. Reaching Point Turton involves a two and a half hour drive from Adelaide and there are plenty of holiday accommodation options. The Turton Caravan Park is one of the best on Yorke Peninsula and its proximity to both jetty and marina make it a very attractive option.

All the usual inshore fish varieties are on tap, including King George whiting, gar, snook, squid, tommy ruffs and some nice flathead. Further offshore those with big boats find snapper year round, but most of the larger reds come during the spring/summer season. Some of these grounds are 15 miles or more from the ramp, so it's fine weather fishing only.

The L-shaped jetty is predictably popular with caravan park visitors and also weekenders from Adelaide. It's a good pier for garfish, squid and tommies, but

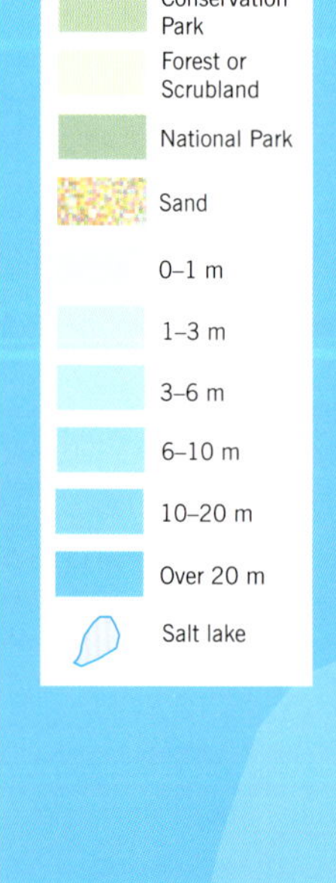

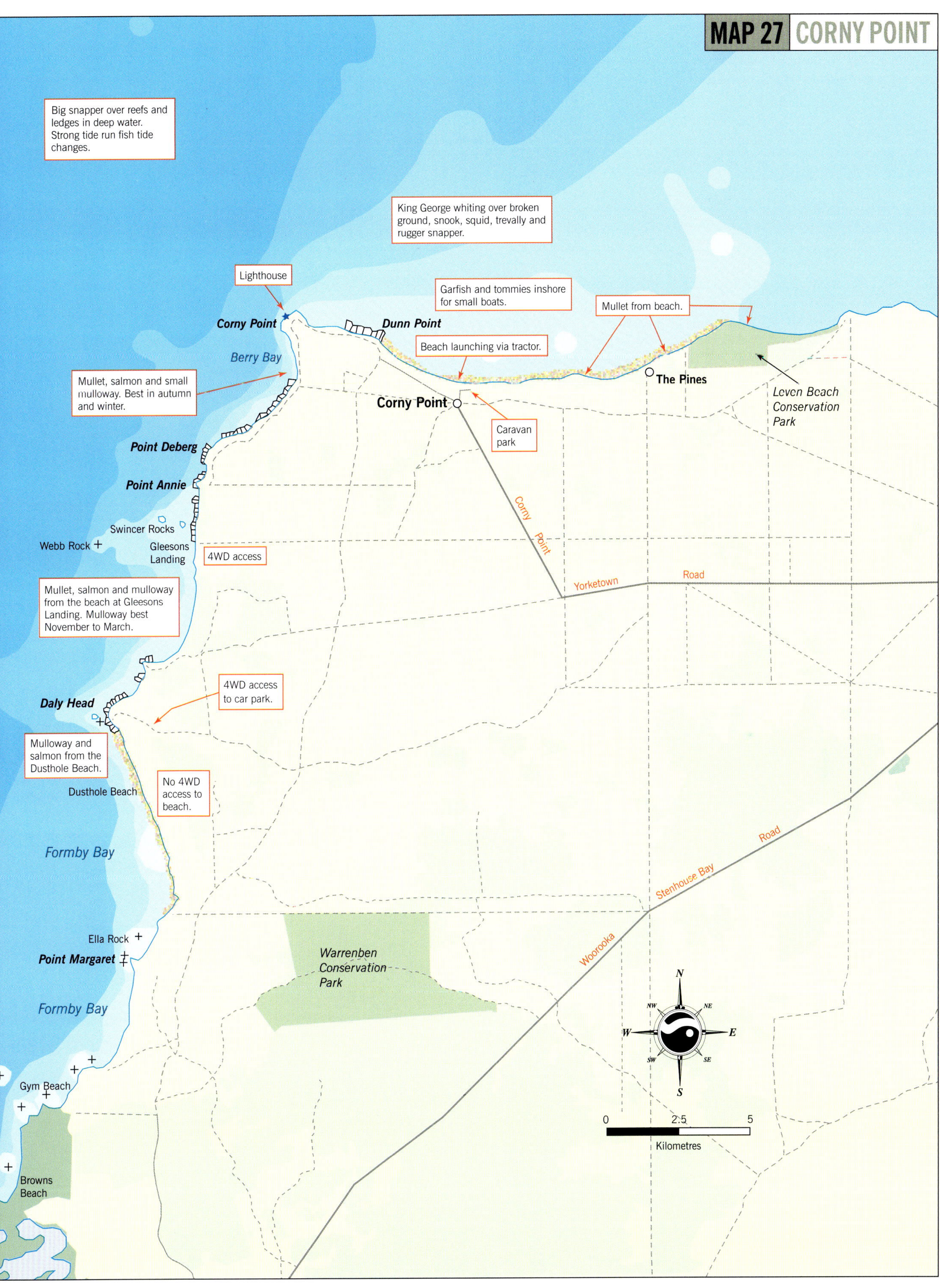

MAP 27 CORNY POINT
Big snapper over reefs and ledges in deep water. Strong tide run fish tide changes.
King George whiting over broken ground, snook, squid, trevally and rugger snapper.
Lighthouse
Garfish and tommies inshore for small boats.
Mullet from beach.
Corny Point
Dunn Point
Beach launching via tractor.
Berry Bay
Mullet, salmon and small mulloway. Best in autumn and winter.
The Pines
Corny Point
Leven Beach Conservation Park
Caravan park
Point Deberg
Point Annie
Corny Point
Swincer Rocks
Webb Rock
Gleesons Landing
4WD access
Yorketown
Road
Mullet, salmon and mulloway from the beach at Gleesons Landing. Mulloway best November to March.
4WD access to car park.
Daly Head
Mulloway and salmon from the Dusthole Beach.
Dusthole Beach
No 4WD access to beach.
Formby Bay
Road
Stenhouse Bay
Ella Rock
Point Margaret
Warrenben Conservation Park
Woorooka
Formby Bay
N
NW
NE
W
E
SW
SE
S
0
2.5
5
Kilometres
Gym Beach
Browns Beach

occasionally sees invasions of small kingfish, which are probably escapees from fish farms on the opposite side of Spencer Gulf. Fishing room on the jetty is often at a premium during holiday periods, particularly in good weather.

MAP 27 CORNY POINT

Corny has no boat ramp, no jetty and relatively few facilities, but it is still a very popular fishing venue for a number of reasons. First up, it is close to some of the best snapper and whiting action in eastern Spencer Gulf and secondly, because it is an excellent base for a weekend's surf fishing.

You'll need access to a tractor to launch from the tidal flat or you can hire the services of the caravan park proprietor, who will put your own boat in and out for a modest fee. It's because of this difficulty of launch and retrieve that boating traffic is light around Corny Point and it shows in very consistent catches of quality fish. There are excellent snapper grounds north-west of the lighthouse and many of the summer reds are monsters, some pushing the magic 20lb markKing George whiting from the grounds a little closer to shore are generally larger than those found further north and it's not unusual to pull a 50 centimetre specimen or two from among a bag limit catch. These grounds are generally broken hard bottom, so there will be a bit of by catch mixed in with the whiting. Many of the better whiting grounds off Corny Point fish well on the drift when winds are light and the by-catch often includes trevally, rugger snapper, flathead and snook.

Calm weather means garfish and squid, especially in the shallower areas over ribbon weed beds. Big gar are common during

Some big yelloweye mullet are caught from the surf around the bottom of Yorke and Eyre Peninsulas, especially during autumn.

MAP 28 WEDGE ISLAND

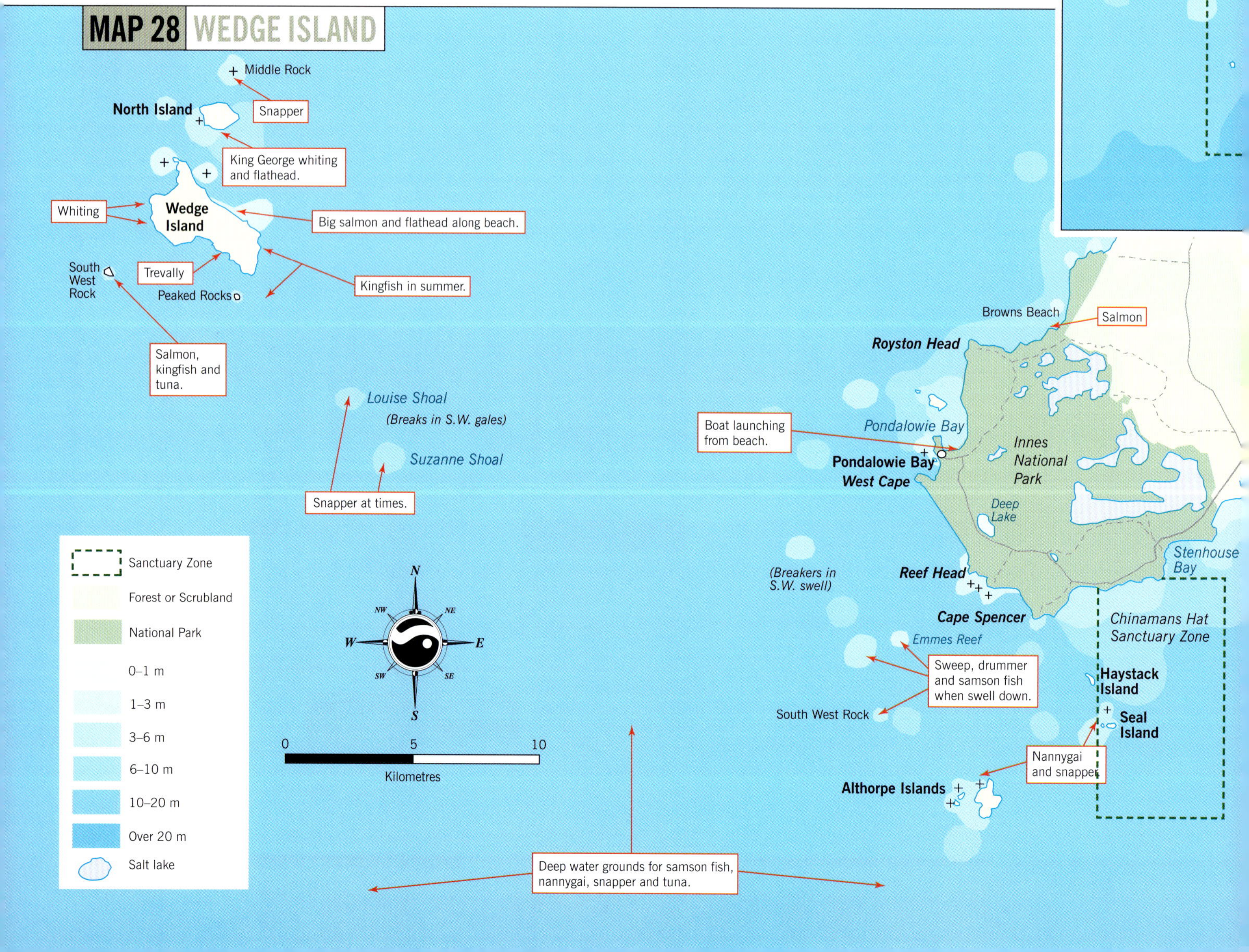

Middle Rock
Snapper
North Island
King George whiting and flathead.
Whiting
Wedge Island
Big salmon and flathead along beach.
South West Rock
Trevally
Peaked Rocks
Kingfish in summer.
Salmon, kingfish and tuna.
Louise Shoal
(Breaks in S.W. gales)
Suzanne Shoal
Snapper at times.
Camping permits available.
Stenhouse Ba
Cape Spencer
Packman Shoal
Haystack Island
Seal Island
Browns Beach
Salmon
Royston Head
Boat launching from beach.
Pondalowie Bay
Pondalowie Bay West Cape
Innes National Park
Deep Lake
Stenhouse Bay
(Breakers in S.W. swell)
Reef Head
Cape Spencer
Emmes Reef
Chinamans Hat Sanctuary Zone
Haystack Island
Seal Island
Sweep, drummer and samson fish when swell down.
South West Rock
Nannygai and snapper
Althorpe Islands
Deep water grounds for samson fish, nannygai, snapper and tuna.

Sanctuary Zone
Forest or Scrubland
National Park
0–1 m
1–3 m
3–6 m
6–10 m
10–20 m
Over 20 m
Salt lake

N NE E SE S SW W NW

0 5 10
Kilometres

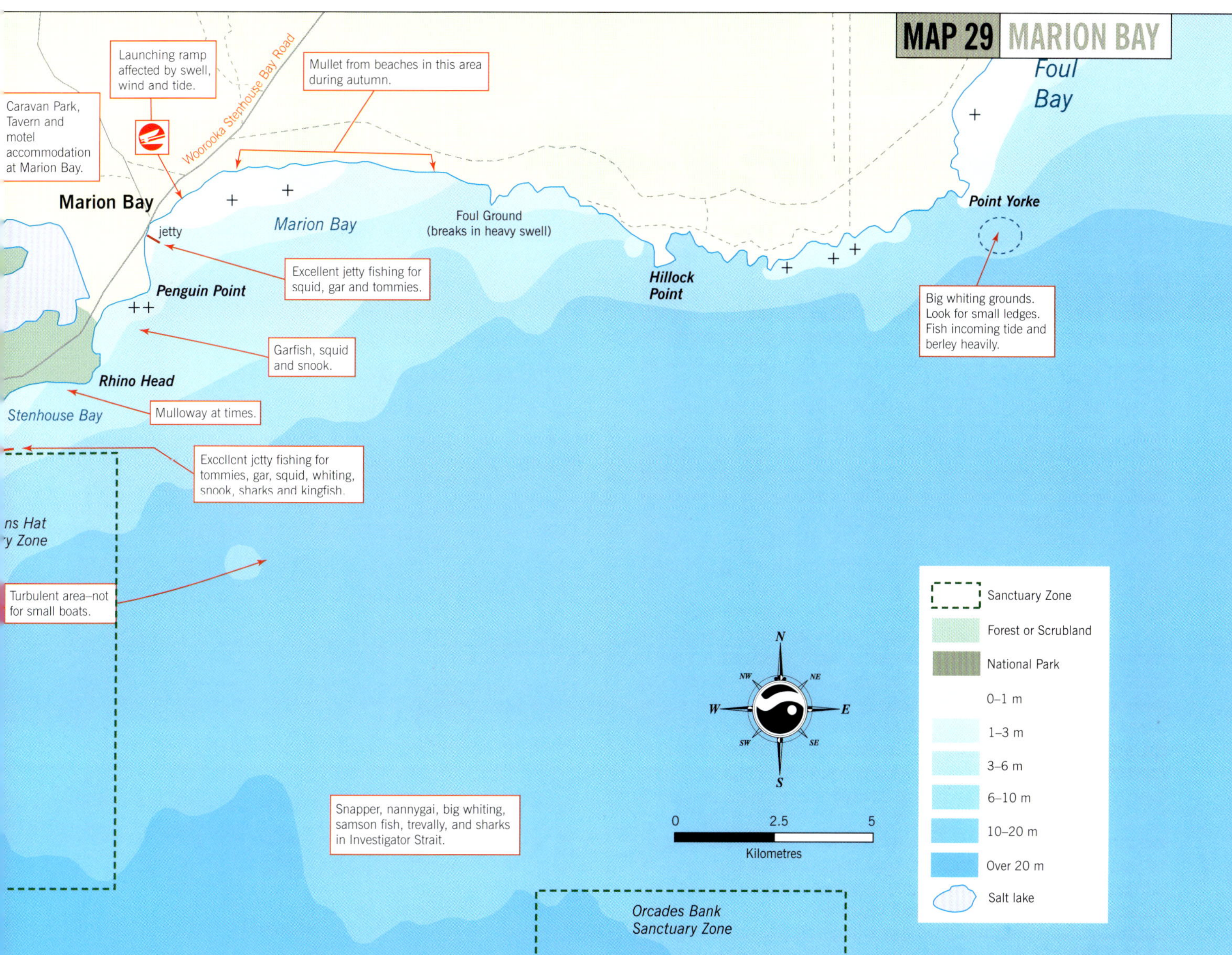

the spring and summer and there are often some big tommy ruffs mixed in with them. Calamari are usually reliable, particularly when the water is clear, and these are most often taken from small boats on the drift.

Although the surf beaches to the south of Corny Point aren't generally as productive as those on the West and Far West Coasts, enough nice mulloway, Australian salmon and mullet are caught annually to make them a worthwhile proposition. Gleesons Landing is one such beach and one that yields a lot more decent mulloway than most locals care to let on. Dusk through until a couple of hours after dark is prime time at Gleesons, particularly if this period coincides with a tide change.

The Dusthole Beach, near Daly Heads, is another magnificent surf beach that manages conveniently to stay out of the limelight. It's a big salmon proposition during winter and spring and a good bet for mulloway when things warm up. Fishing the Dusthole usually involves a lengthy walk to reach the deeper surf gutters, which often deters all but the keenest anglers, but mulloway to 30 kilograms are taken here each summer, along with sharks, rays and the occasional big flathead. Look to fish around the peak of the high tide, especially when there is a medium swell running. Offshore north to north east winds are preferred.

MAP 28 Pondalowie Bay

Popular with beach launchers, Pondalowie provides access to some terrific offshore fishing. Big snapper, nannygai, morwong, King George whiting, samson fish, yellowtail kings, Bluefin tuna and harlequin fish are often hooked on the reefs to the west of Pondalowie, but you'll need good weather and low swell to launch safely and fish well offshore. There is a charter service operating in this area for those without the right boat or enough local knowledge to fish safely in unfamiliar waters.

Mullet swarm into Pondalowie Bay around Easter time each year, providing plenty of light tackle fun from the beach. These bite best on a rising tide early or late in the day and seaweed worms are top bait. A few King George and flathead are also caught together with plenty of smaller salmon trout from the beach. The occasional school of larger salmon also ventures into the bay providing plenty of light tackle fun.

MAP 28 Wedge Island

One of the largest islands in Spencer Gulf, Wedge gets its name from its distinctive shape, tapering from towering cliffs on the southern side to a very productive beach at the northern end. Wedge Island has its own airstrip and several privately owned holiday houses overlooking a protected bay and nearby North Island. Many of these properties are truly upmarket and some can be rented on a short term basis.

Yellowtail kingfish, ranging from little guys of under five kilograms to bruisers in the 20 kilo-plus category, are available around Wedge at different times of the year. Most are hooked on the island's eastern side by trolling deep diving minnow lures, but they

Marion Bay Jetty

can also be found among the heavy reef to the west. This is difficult territory to fight any big fish and many are lost in this area as they dive into and around the reefs and bommies.

The beach on Wedge's northern side is a beauty for big Australian salmon and flathead. Quite often the salmon are trolled just 20 metres offshore and they can sometimes top five kilograms. The flathead are generally large, too. Plenty of big southern bluepot in the 60 to 80cm bracket are caught each year, particularly in late autumn when they aggregate to spawn. These are taken on rubber tail lures or fresh baits like pilchards and garfish fillets and, due to their size, most are returned to the water after a quick photo.

Big King George whiting are common between Wedge and North Islands and it's not unusual to pull a boat limit of fish between 45-50 centimetres in double quick time. Relatively few boats fish this area, so pressure is light. Only a couple of charter boats from Marion Bay operate regularly around Wedge, resulting in little competition and high productivity.

MAP 28 BROWNS BEACH

Outside of places like Locks Well, Sheringa and Convention Beaches on the West Coast, Browns is probably the most famous salmon beach in South Australia. It's accessible via Innes National Park, so you need an entry permit to fish or camp, but it does produce nice salmon on a consistent basis and attracts thousands of anglers annually.

The beach at Browns is fronted by a low reef that forms a lagoon of sorts. The salmon usually enter on a rising tide and then spread into the deeper gutters to feed. Many salmon are caught on metal lures, but it's always wise to have some fresh pilchards on hand if the fish are a bit finicky. Dusk, dawn and the first couple of hours of darkness are usually the most productive time to try your luck and as well as salmon, it is often possible to catch big tommies and yellow eye mullet.

It's a bit of a walk from the Browns car park to the far end of the beach and most seem to fish the nearer gutters, especially if the sand is soft and the going is difficult. It is possible to catch salmon from this beach year-round, but it is more consistent in winter and spring.

MAP 29 STENHOUSE BAY

Situated at the entrance to Innes National Park, Stenhouse has a long and generally productive jetty that yields gar, tommies, squid, snook, whiting and the occasional nice snapper. There are no lights for night fishing and it is a fair walk back up the hill to the car park after a full day – hopefully with a good bag of fish! Nearby Chinamans Beach is a reliable location for yelloweye mullet during the autumn months.

MAP 29 MARION BAY

Boat launching at Marion is very much a hit or miss proposition, as the ramp is just a single slab of concrete open to wind, swell, seaweed and tide. This is still a very popular launching point, however, as it provides access to Investigator Strait and much of lower Spencer Gulf. In fact, it's the only place to launch on lower Yorke Peninsula except for Pondalowie Bay, which can also be dicey.

Marion Bay jetty is legendary for the big squid it produces, as well as tommy ruffs, gar and mullet. Autumn sees a huge influx of mullet anglers, who pull these tasty little fish from the beach in their thousands while the 'run' is on.

Marion Bay is nicely equipped for visiting anglers, with a top class caravan park, motel, tavern and abundant private holiday accommodation options. There are also several professional fishing charter operators, most of whom fish Investigator Strait, Kangaroo Island's North Coast, Wedge Island and lower Spencer Gulf reef systems.

CHAPTER 4
ST VINCENT'S GULF

Ardrossan jetty is a popular venue for land base fishing.

Although considerably smaller than Spencer Gulf to the west, St Vincent's Gulf is still an expansive body of water. It is around 145 kilometres long and 75 kilometres wide at the mouth, with water depth increasing from north to south. With Adelaide and suburbs situated on its eastern shoreline, this Gulf sees a lot more traffic than Spencer and the fishing pressure is consequently far greater.

Despite this, however, St Vincent's Gulf still produces plenty for both commercial operators and recreational anglers. There are countless options, ranging from jetties, rock ledges, beaches and tidal flats for those land-based, to deep water shoals, wrecks and reefs offshore. It's a diverse fishery and one that offers something for just about everyone.

As is the case with most other parts of South Australia, St Vincent's Gulf has a rather unique tide cycle, which culminates with a 'dodge' tide every fortnight. During this period, which lasts for 36 hours or so, there is virtually no tidal flow at all and most fish varieties go off the bite. Only in a handful of other locations in the world, such as Torres Strait and the Gulf of Mexico, does the dodge tide phenomenon occur.

The western shore of St Vincent's Gulf is punctuated by small settlements, most of which are home to less than a thousand people. These now rely heavily on tourism and much of this revolves around recreational fishing. The eastern shore is considerably different; most towns are set back away from the coast, which is dominated by shallow tidal flats, mangrove forests and creeks. Very little is readily accessible and it doesn't attract anywhere near the number of anglers as the Yorke Peninsula coast.

TROUBRIDGE POINT TO PORT WAKEFIELD

Possibly the most popular stretch of coastline in the state for weekend 'get-away' fishing trips, Yorke Peninsula's eastern shore offers countless options. The furthest point southward is less than three hours' drive from Adelaide and there is easy access to practically the entire coast.

MAP 30 Troubridge Point

Rock fishermen often visit this rugged location at the 'heel' of Yorke Peninsula and although the fishing can be a bit hit or miss, it's generally worth a shot when the weather is right. Troubridge is just 10 kilometres or so from Edithburgh, so it's not far to travel to check conditions before organising a trip. It is also right at the intersection of St Vincent's Gulf and Investigator Strait, with a towering lighthouse to alert passing ships.

Salmon of various sizes, big snook and the occasional snapper are the main catch from the rocks, with sweep, tommy ruffs, garfish and leatherjackets also common. The salmon and snook are generally hooked on whole pilchard baits fished beneath a float, but are sometimes taken on metal or rubber tail lures.

MAP 30 Edithburgh

With a permanent population of around 450, Edithburgh is one of the oldest settlements around lower St Vincent's Gulf. It was once an important grain port, but loading has long since transferred to

Port Giles, a little further north, and the Edithburgh jetty is now maintained solely for recreational use. It is a very popular jetty and although not overly long, it stretches into about seven metres of water at the seaward end.

Squid, garfish and tommy ruffs are by far the most popular fish varieties at Edithburgh and it's not uncommon on a fine summer weekend to find 50 or more people fishing for them. The jetty is adjacent to the town centre and within walking distance of hotels and accommodation houses, so access is about as easy as it gets.

Most of the better fishing from the jetty occurs from late afternoon through into the evening, particularly for tommies, which are nearly always bigger and more plentiful after dark. Black ink stains on the jetty indicate the most productive areas for calamari and it's often possible to pull a decent snapper from the end if you set a big bait on the right tackle.

Boat launching at Edithburgh is no problem. A small, but well protected harbor adjacent to the caravan park boasts a multi-lane ramp with boarding pontoons and spacious car park. Trailer boats of all sizes can be launched at any stage of the tide and from here it's just a short ride to some of Edithburgh's inshore whiting and snook grounds. The whiting inside the bay are generally good ones, as are the snook, and for some variety there are garfish and squid available when the water is calm and clear.

Those with big boats often venture out to Marion Reef and Tapley Shoal to try their luck for snapper of mixed sizes and larger King George whiting. Tapley Shoal, in particular, has become

extremely popular with charter boats and recreationals alike and with good reason. During the summer months it fishes very well, but it is a strong tide area and can only be fished around tide changes with relatively heavy tackle.

MAP30 Coobowie

Located on the shores of a very shallow coastal inlet just a short drive northward from Edithburgh, this delightful little settlement offers limited access to offshore fishing. The surrounding flats all but dry out at low tide, but they do provide good fishing for wading anglers as the water flows back in. Flathead, yellowfin whiting, garfish and the occasional flounder are caught with light tackle.

Coobowie has a nice caravan park, but no boat launching. It is well located for jetty anglers between Port Giles and Edithburgh.

MAP30 Port Giles

At 617 metres, the Port Giles bulk loading jetty is one of the longest in South Australia. It stretches into 15 metres of water and was once renowned as the best jetty in the state for big snapper. The big reds have slowed down somewhat since the 'good old days' of the 1970s, when it was almost a foregone conclusion to catch several per session. 25 pounders were common, as were King George whiting, silver trevally, snook and copious amounts of squid. It's still a good jetty to fish, but not like it used to be.

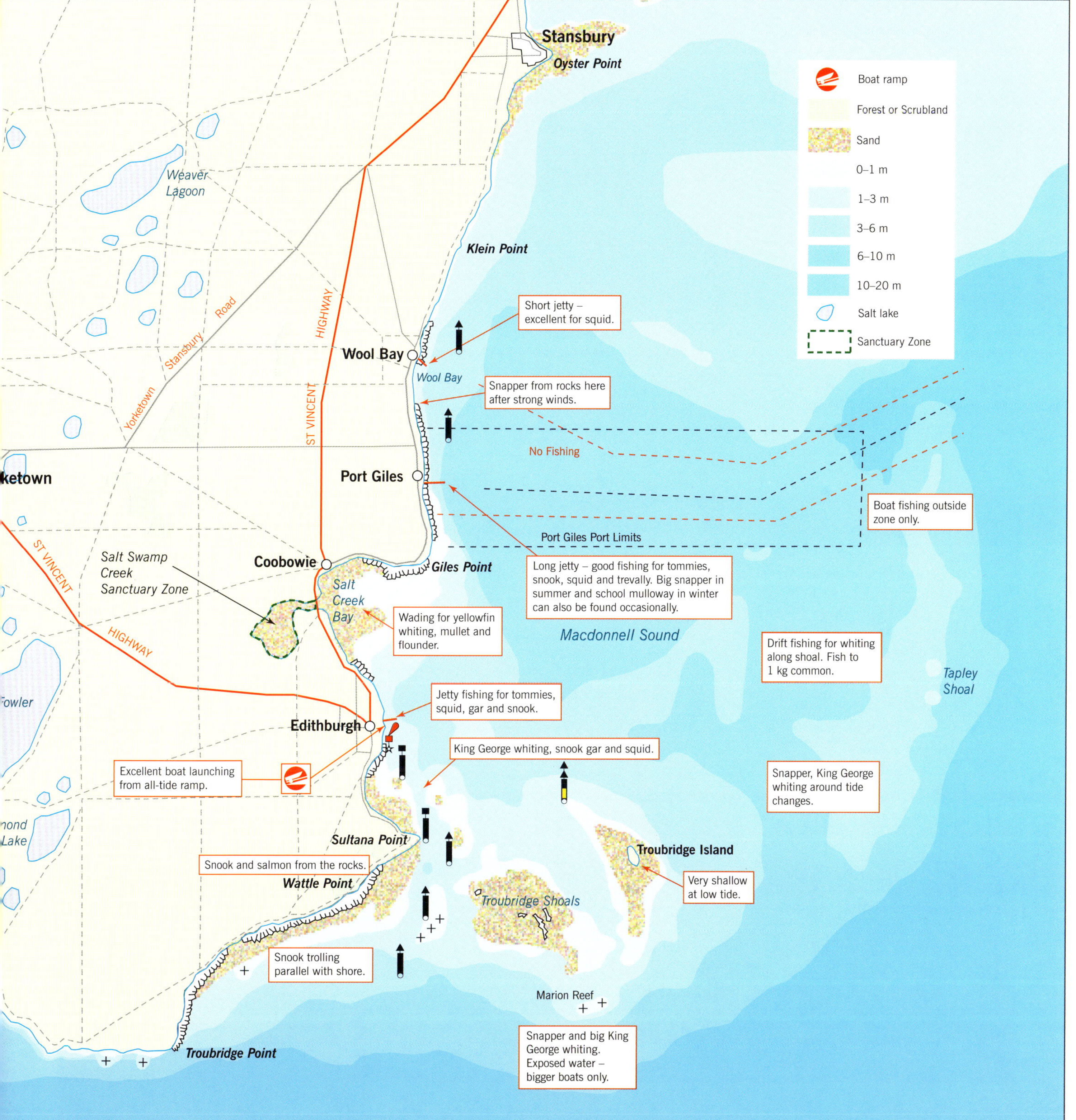

The jetty is closed to the public during working hours and, due to theft and vandalism, has sustained periods of total closure over the years. It is off limits now when a grain ship is being loaded and isn't anywhere near as popular these days due to these access issues.

MAP 30 Wool Bay

Wool Bay was once the site of an active lime kiln and quarry, but today it's little more than a small township of 250 people with a short jetty. At low tide there is only a couple of metres of water at the jetty's end, but that doesn't deter visiting anglers. Squid are the main targets and at times they are plentiful. Bag limit catches (15 per person) are often made when the water is calm and clear, along with snook, tommies and gar.

There is a basic boat ramp at Wool Bay, but it's not recommended for larger craft and you'll need a four wheel drive tow vehicle. The offshore fishing is generally good for whiting, squid, gar, snook and the occasional snapper.

MAP 31 Stansbury

Often considered as Yorke Peninsula's most charming seaside town, Stansbury is certainly popular during weekends and holiday periods. It offers great facilities, including a multi-lane/all tide boat ramp, neat caravan park, plenty of private rental accommodation and a very productive jetty. It is within a comfortable two and a half hour drive of Adelaide, which puts it well within range of weekend anglers and their families.

The Stansbury jetty is a good one for light tackle fishing, particularly around dusk and into the evening, when tommy ruffs, snook, garfish and squid are most active. In autumn there are usually plenty of nice mullet to be caught and there are blue swimmer crabs for drop netters in the summer months. This is one of the St Vincent's Gulf jetties that also produces nice King George whiting for those who persist at the seaward end.

Raking blue swimmers is a popular activity when the crabs are in residence from November through until Easter time. Stansbury's back beach is a productive place to try and most of the 'blueys' are big and full of meat. The gear you'll need for this style of crabbing includes a special rake (available from most tackle stores), a floating tub and old sneakers to protect your feet from those menacing claws!

Snapper, whiting, snook and squid attract visiting boaties to Stansbury and most of the better fishing occurs with ten kilometres of the launching ramp. Boat limit hauls of nice King George whiting are common, particularly in autumn and early winter when weather conditions are stable and predictable.

There are some nice hammerheads and smaller bronze whalers on offer during the warmer months of the year for those who enjoy a bit of light tackle sport fishing. Setting a bait under balloon is a popular way of connecting to these feisty summer visitors, with the smaller sharks offering quite good table fair if bled and iced immediately.

MAP 31 Port Vincent

Located just under 200 kilometres from Adelaide, Port Vincent has a population of around 500 people – a figure which can treble at peak holiday times. It has no jetty, but is the site of the largest marina complex on the western shores of St Vincent's Gulf. As Port Vincent is almost directly across the Gulf from Adelaide, this new facility is enormously popular with yachties and those with larger cruisers and sees plenty of weekend traffic. It has 90 permanent berths and is well equipped to handle boats of any size.

There is an excellent all-tide launching ramp inside the marina with a vast car park. It's a busy place in good weather, as the fishing offshore can be excellent. King George whiting are the major

Stansbury Jetty

MAP 31 STANSBURY – PORT VINCENT – PORT JULIA

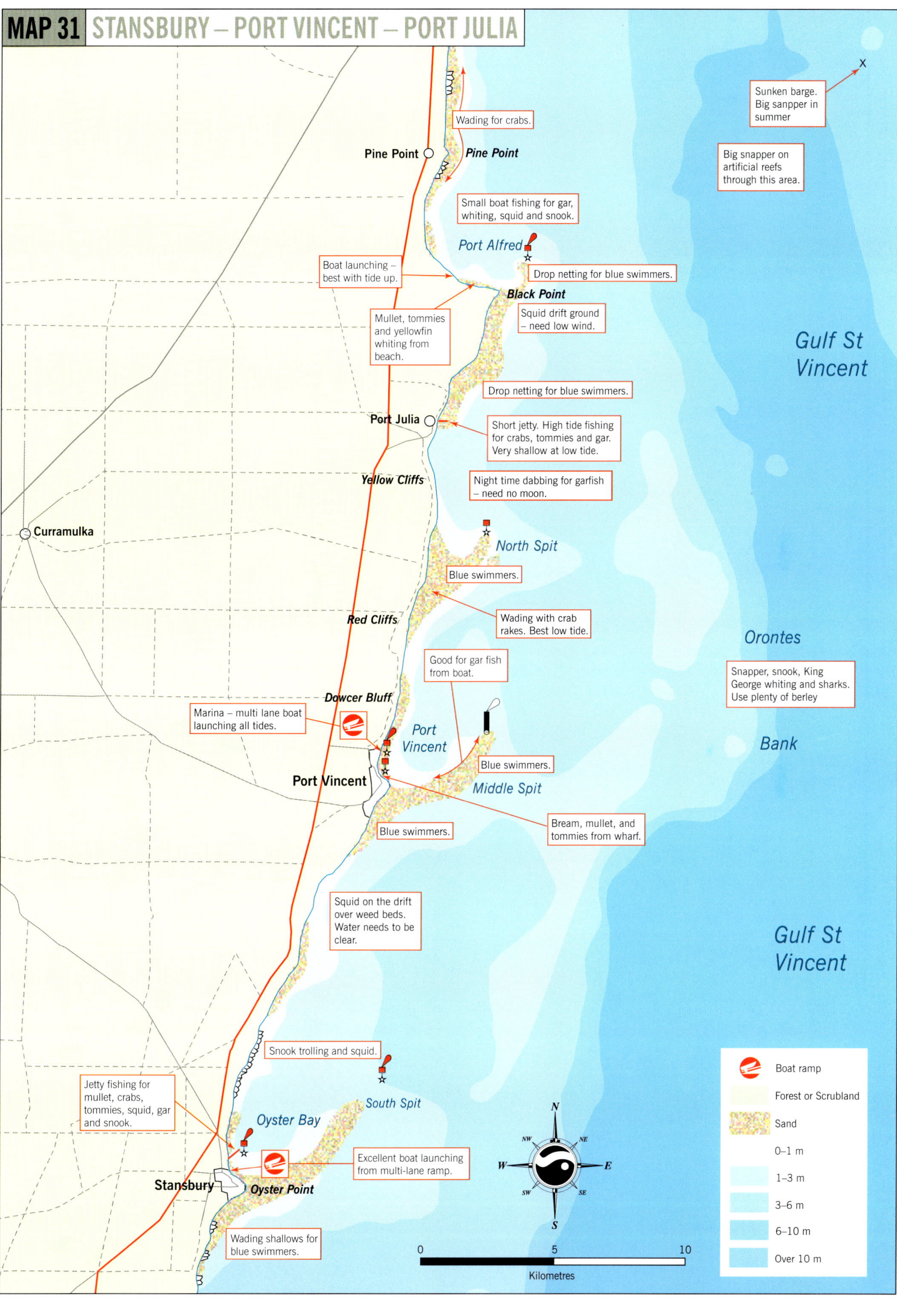

Bronze whalers are common throughout Gulf waters during the warmer months.

drawcard and these can vary in size from just legal (31centimetres) up to 45 centimetres or more. Boat limit catches of 12 whiting per person are often easy to achieve and most are caught quite close to shore.

The Orontes Bank, a long, undulating shoal, roughly 18 kilometres offshore from Port Vincent, is one of St Vincent's Gulf's most productive natural fishing grounds. It's a 40 kilometre run across the Gulf from Adelaide, so it only attracts big boat owners from that side and is far easier to access from the Vincent Marina.

Big whiting are taken along the edges of the shoal, usually by drift fishing in calm weather, and there are some big snapper hooked during summer and autumn. Snook, slimy mackerel and garfish are often abundant and great white sharks occasionally patrol the Orontes Bank when there's plenty of food around.

Like most coastal towns along this stretch of St Vincent's Gulf coast, Port Vincent can be a great location for blue swimmer crabs. They can be raked on the inshore flats when the tide is down or drop netted offshore from small boats. December through until March is the best crabbing period.

The old Port Vincent wharf still sees a few anglers at times, although it's nowhere near as popular these days as it once was. Bream are hooked here occasionally, along with yellow eye mullet and tommy ruffs, but only when the tide is well up.

MAP 31 Port Julia

This small inlet is popular with weekend anglers from Adelaide. There's a short jetty that is really only fishable at high tide, but produces tommy ruffs and gar in the evenings and a few squid and blue swimmer crabs during daylight hours. There is launching for small boats and some good fishing offshore for crabs, gar, snook and King George whiting. Julia Reef lies to the left of the jetty and occasionally produces big snapper on dusk in winter.

MAP 31 Black Point

As far as holiday coastal real estate goes, there are few locations in South Australia that have leapt ahead in value like Black Point. Beachside shacks that may have been worth next to nothing 20 years ago are now bringing frightening amounts of money for developers. Black Point is a truly delightful place to spend a weekend or longer, particularly in summer time when the prevailing winds are offshore and the water in the sweeping bay is calm.

The bay between Black Point and nearby Pine Point is relatively shallow, making it ideal for species like garfish, blue swimmer crabs, flathead, King George whiting, tommy ruffs and mullet. It's an ideal area for small boats and it is not unusual to see everything from flybridge cruisers to aluminium dinghies fishing on the same grounds for the same fish varieties.

Blue swimmer crabs are prolific around Black Point in summer time, with February through until early March usually the peak crabbing period. The crabs can be taken by wading flats or offshore with drop nets, with the latter generally more reliable. Best net baits are whiting heads and squid, although practically any fish off cuts will do the job. The most popular crabbing location is along the edge of the large sand spit, just a couple of kilometres from the beach.

There is some first class snapper fishing offshore from Black Point, with December, January and February the peak months. The majority of these are caught on man-made 'drops' constructed from old car bodies, building refuse, bundled car tyres and old boats. These accumulate marine growth over a period of time and form habitats for crustaceans and small fish, which, in turn, attract larger predators like snapper. The creators of these artificial reefs usually guard their location strenuously and often won't fish them while other boats are around.

Black Point's boat ramp isn't one of the best around St Vincent's Gulf; in fact, it's regarded as quite poor by local standards. The concrete section is often high and dry on the lower tides and the ramp is totally open to winds from north-east round to north-west. Many who have holiday houses on the beach at Black Point will usually launch their boats on a high tide and then leave them in the water on established moorings overnight until they pack up to head home.

Beach fishing here can be quite rewarding, particularly with the tide well up in the late afternoon. Yellow eye mullet are easy to catch during the autumn, yellowfin whiting can be expected in the summer time and there are tommy ruffs and salmon trout year-round.

MAP 32 Ardrossan

With a population of around 1,100, Ardrossan is one of the larger settlements on the western shore of St Vincent's Gulf. It's located roughly an hour and a half's drive from Adelaide and is once again very popular as a weekend venue for those keen to escape the capital city and take home a good feed of fish. Interestingly, it was named after a sea port in Scotland and has a long history as an important grain loading centre.

There are two jetties at Ardrossan; one that's extremely long (900 metres) and off limits to recreational angling, and a second that is maintained solely for the use of anglers and divers. The town jetty is just over 400 metres long, with around six metres of water at the end at high tide. It's usually busy on weekends and during holiday periods and often produces a good mixed bag of table fish for those who are prepared to persist.

Most of the 'usuals' are caught from the Ardrossan town jetty, including tommy ruffs, garfish, squid, mullet, snook and blue swimmer crabs. An occasional bonus comes in the form of school mulloway, some of which don't quite make the legal minimum size of 75 centimetres, but there are sometimes a few larger specimens taken. These fish will take well-presented dead baits fished on the bottom, but live baits bring the best results. Live salmon trout, mullet, herring, trumpeters and squid are all gun baits for school mulloway.

Crabbing from the jetty is an iconic activity and one that has been popular for decades. When the 'blueys' are on, it is often possible to net a couple of dozen in a session and most are good size. These crabs can be raked on the flats adjacent to the jetty as well, but a low tide is necessary.

Ardrossan is equipped with a first rate boat ramp. It features double lanes, floating boarding pontoons and a spacious car park and is protected by strategically positioned breakwaters. Trailer boats of all sizes are launched here and while most head along the coast to fish for whiting, gar, snook and squid, there are some reliable snapper grounds further out into the Gulf.

One of these is the wreck of an old hopper barge that lies in around 20 metres of water and roughly 15 kilometres offshore. This barge was towed to the area back in 1984 and deliberately sunk to form a substantial artificial reef. It began producing snapper of

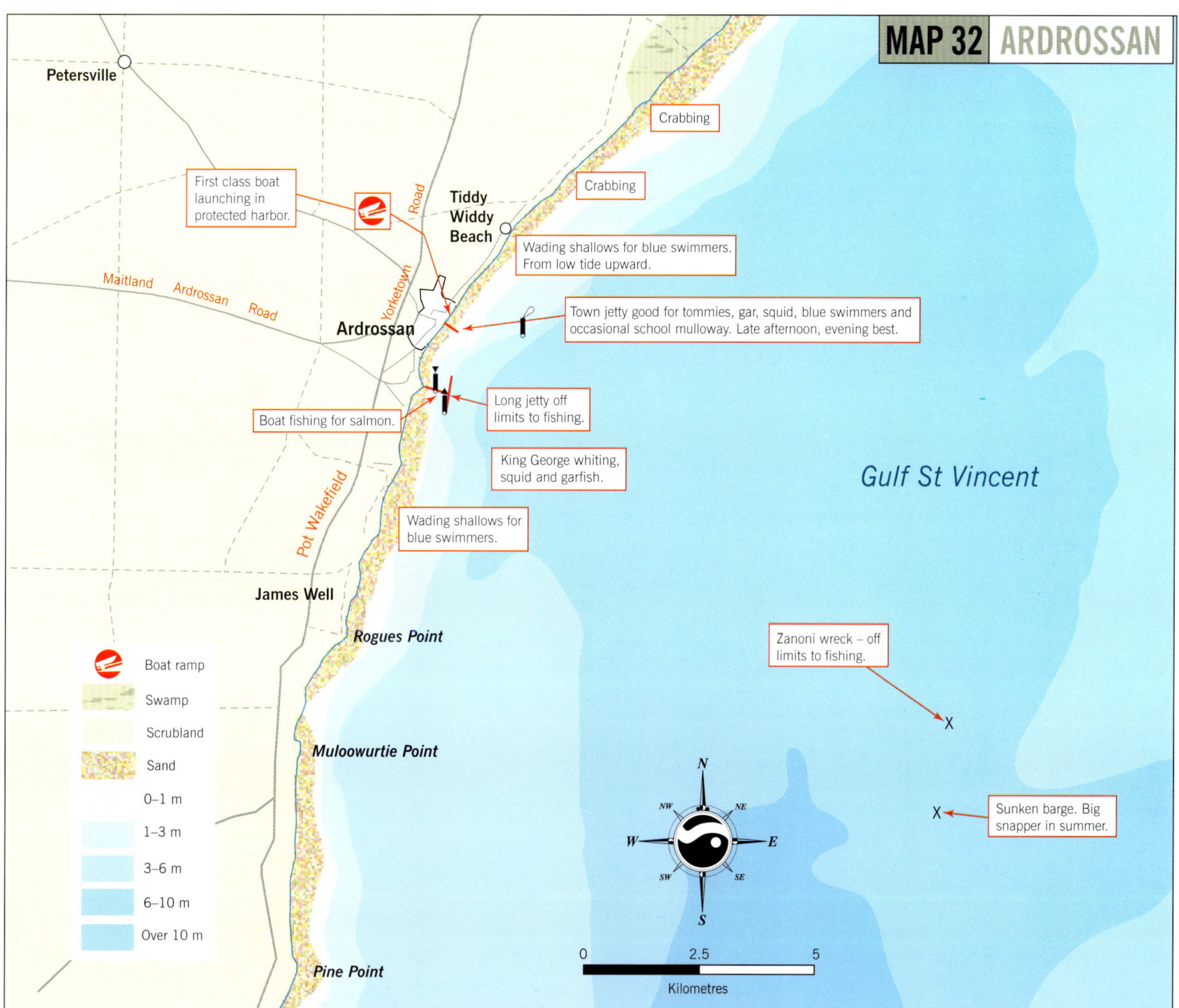

Big snapper are available out from Ardrossan.

all sizes in just a couple of years and has been very consistent ever since. The barge attracts plenty of boats from Adelaide when the weather is good, but it's an 80 kilometre round trip and is more safely accessed from Ardrossan.

The wreck of the Zanoni, an old ship that sunk 16 kilometres east of Ardrossan in 1867, was once a prolific producer of snapper and the occasional big mulloway. However, it was declared an historic shipwreck site some time ago and was made off limits to fishing. To compensate anglers, the State Government sank the hopper barge mentioned above and it seems that the entire project has been extremely successful.

When the summer snapper migration is in full swing, vast schools of mature fish make their way up St Vincent's Gulf to spawn and often settle on these wrecks for weeks at a time. The schools are attended regularly by great white sharks, and it's always sensible to keep this in the back of your mind, particularly when gaffing big snapper from small boats.

The snapper fishing out from Ardrossan has been pretty consistent for a number of years now, and rivals some of the bigger name locations in SA for snapper fishing. While a lot of the fish are school sized reds in the 6 to 8 kg size, there are quite a few +10 kg fish mixed in with the smaller fish to make the fishing interesting.

MAP 33 Price

This little settlement is fringed by dense mangrove forests, which are among the most important fish nursery areas in South Australia. There are two creeks at Price – Shag Creek and Wills Creek – and both teem with juvenile fish life at times. The creeks are tidal, emptying out rapidly during periods of extreme tide variation around the full and new moons. They often carry concentrations of drifting seaweed, which can be a nuisance when launching a boat or trying to fish.

These creeks can be very handy locations for small boat anglers when it's too windy to fish outside on exposed Gulf waters, particularly Wills Creek, which is often good for species like gar, mullet, salmon trout, blue swimmers and the occasional flathead. It can be fished in practically any weather from a car-topper 'tinny' with either an electric or small petrol outboard.

There's a launching ramp on Wills Creek which is fine for conventional tow vehicles around high tide, but a bit tricky once the water drops away. A four wheel drive is definitely the preferred option for safe launching around Price. The fishing outside in upper St Vincent's Gulf is generally good for several species, including snapper, King George whiting, gar, snook, blue swimmers and flathead.

There are plenty of man-made snapper reefs offshore from Price, many of which have been on the bottom for decades, but still produce big reds during the summer spawning run. Some of these are in surprisingly shallow water. Snapper to 30 pounds and above are taken off Price each season, along with occasional nice mulloway.

King George whiting are abundant throughout upper St Vincent's Gulf, but most are small to medium and a lot won't make the minimum legal size of 31 centimetres. The garfish are generally easy to find, too, and this is a popular area for 'dabbing' gar after dark with a spotlight and long-handled net. You'll need a calm night and little or no moon for this exercise.

MAP 33 Port Clinton

This is the last township as you travel up the western shore of St Vincent's Gulf. Its permanent population is around 260, but there are a number of 'weekender' shacks and holiday houses that fill up at vacation times and the place gets quite busy.

Clinton is surrounded by a 1850 hectare conservation park, most of which is dominated by dense mangroves and is home to a diverse range of birdlife. It's also an important nursery area for fish and crustaceans and provides enjoyable light tackle fishing from

King George whiting are the number one target by boaties up Gulf St Vincent.

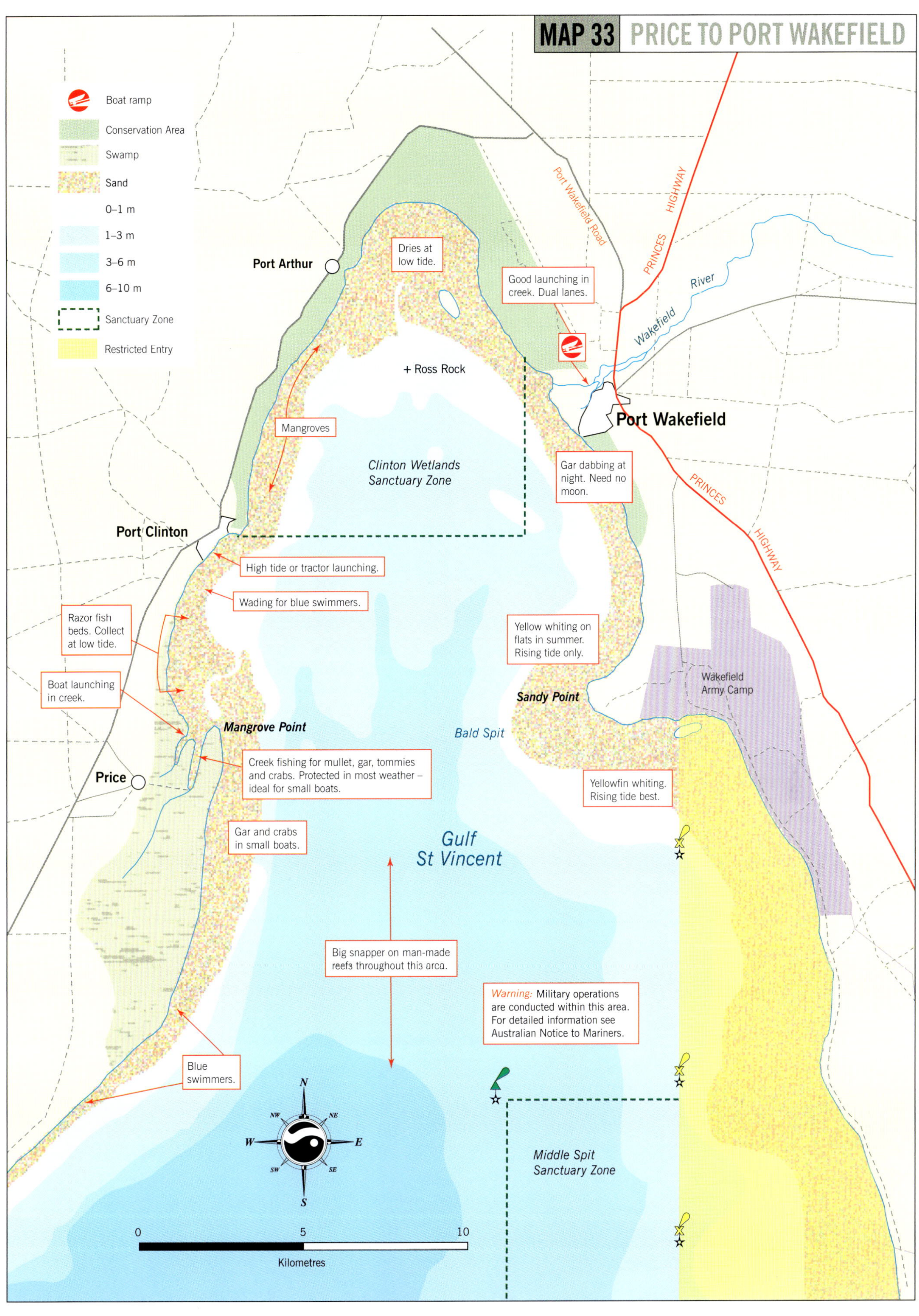
MAP 33 PRICE TO PORT WAKEFIELD
Boat ramp
Conservation Area
Swamp
Sand
0–1 m
1–3 m
3–6 m
6–10 m
Sanctuary Zone
Restricted Entry
Port Arthur
Dries at low tide.
Good launching in creek. Dual lanes.
Port Wakefield Road
PRINCES HIGHWAY
Wakefield River
+ Ross Rock
Port Wakefield
Mangroves
Clinton Wetlands Sanctuary Zone
Gar dabbing at night. Need no moon.
Port Clinton
High tide or tractor launching.
Wading for blue swimmers.
Razor fish beds. Collect at low tide.
Yellow whiting on flats in summer. Rising tide only.
Boat launching in creek.
Wakefield Army Camp
Sandy Point
Mangrove Point
Bald Spit
Price
Creek fishing for mullet, gar, tommies and crabs. Protected in most weather – ideal for small boats.
Yellowfin whiting. Rising tide best.
Gar and crabs in small boats.
Gulf St Vincent
Big snapper on man-made reefs throughout this area.
Warning: Military operations are conducted within this area. For detailed information see Australian Notice to Mariners.
Blue swimmers.
N
NW
NE
W
E
SW
SE
S
Middle Spit Sanctuary Zone
0
5
10
Kilometres

small boats. The available species are much the same as down at Price and many who visit this area will fish both locations over the course of a weekend.

There is small boat launching in the creek, but it's best to launch and retrieve with the tide well up. Expansive tidal flats outside are popular with those wading for blue swimmers. This is a great family activity and something that is traditionally South Australian. The best time to be out on the flats is an hour before low water, then follow the tide back in as it floods. The crabs bury themselves and their presence beneath the sand is usually indicated by a disturbed area and a mound of grey sub-surface grit. You rake over this and, if a crab, is in residence, it can be scooped up and deposited in your floating tub.

Bag limit catches of 40 blue swimmers per person can be taken comfortably when the main crab invasion is in full swing, but size limits and other regulations need to be considered. The minimum size for blue swimmers in SA is 11 centimetres across the carapace and it is illegal to take females carrying external eggs.

PORT WAKEFIELD TO ADELAIDE

Tidal flats, mud and mangroves are the dominant coastal features in the 90 kilometre stretch along the eastern shore of St Vincent's Gulf. There is very little boat launching available and access to the coast is limited to just a handful of locations.

MAP 33 PORT WAKEFIELD

This is one of South Australia's oldest and most historic ports. The township has a population of around 600 and is situated right at the top of St Vincent's Gulf. National Highway One runs adjacent to the town and the service stations and allied businesses thrive due to the huge volume of through traffic. During long weekends and peak holiday times it's an enormously popular place to refuel, buy a take-away meal or simply get out of the car to stretch the legs before resuming the journey north or south.

It's a fact that most people who travel through Port Wakefield don't even realise what lies just off the highway. The town is serviced by a recently refurbished two lane boat ramp with floating boarding pontoons and large car park. The ramp is located on a mangrove-lined creek that leads out into the Gulf and this creek is pretty shallow around low tide, so care needs to be taken, particularly in larger boats.

Those fishing outside Port Wakefield are faced with several attractive options. There are plenty of King George whiting available, especially during the cooler months, but many will need to be measured for length. Upper Gulf waters teem with small KG's all year and it often takes a while to locate a school of legal-size fish. Goolwa cockles or softened squid pieces are the preferred baits and it's best to keep tackle as light as possible.

Squid are a popular target from Gulf St Vincent

Big snapper congregate in several areas and particularly on artificial reefs that have been put down privately over many years. Port Wakefield isn't synonymous with giant snapper, but plenty are caught each season and their captors are more than happy to keep this out of the angling headlines. Tide changes, especially if they occur around dawn or dusk, are prime snapper fishing periods in upper St Vincent's Gulf. Just an hour's fishing either side of a change is generally all that's needed if the big reds are about and hungry. This is especially so after a good blow when the water is still clouded after rough weather.

Snook, squid and gar are pretty easy to find if conditions are right. Gar dabbing is quite popular, both with amateurs and professional fishermen, and there can be no faster way to catch gar in big numbers than with net and spotlight after sunset. Most of the snook are taken by trolling lures and strip baits on lead lines or behind paravanes.

There are plenty of blue swimmers around Port Wakefield, with peak numbers occurring between Christmas and the end of March. The later in this three month period, you try, the bigger the crabs usually are. It's usually a mixture of males and females in December and January and, as the season progresses, the females gradually depart to leave just the big, meaty males that are so delectable to eat.

Snapper, Gulf St Vincent.

MAP 34 PORT PARHAM/WEBB BEACH

Both are very small coastal settlements that are legendary for their blue swimmer catches and attract thousands of crabbers from Adelaide each season. You won't find much in the way of facilities at either location and when the tide goes out, it's often difficult to see the water!

The usual family crabbing day involves a picnic

MAP 34
PORT WAKEFIELD TO ADELAIDE – CRABBING BEACHES
Port Wakefield
Clinton Wetlands Sanctuary Zone
Sandy Point
Wakefield Army Camp
Yellowfin whiting in summer. Live tube worms best bait.
Lorne
Middle Spit Sanctuary Zone
Wild Horse Plains
Windsor
Parham
Mallala
Webb Beach
Dublin
Blue swimmers.
Great Sandy Point
Light River Delta Sanctuary Zone
Port Wakefield Road
Blue swimmers wading with rakes – incoming tide.
Light River
Garfish and whiting offshore.
Salt Creek
Two Wells
Gawler
Middle Beach
Blue swimmers and yellowfin whiting.
Gawler River
Angle Vale
Virginia
Snapper and whiting at Goannas. Look for rocks and low ledges. Berley heavily.
Small boat launching at high tide.
Smithfield
Elizabeth
Sand
0–1 m
1–3 m
3–6 m
6–10 m
Salt lakes
Sanctuary Zone
Restricted Entry
Outer Harbour
breakwaters
Torrens Island
N
NW
NE
W
E
SW
SE
S
0
10
20
Kilometres
Torrens River
Adelaide

LEFT: Yellowfin underwater

BELOW: Collecting seaweed worms to use as yellowfin whiting bait.

or barbecue lunch before low tide, followed by three hours of crab raking as the water begins to flow back in. If the crabs are about in numbers, as they should be during this late summer period, it's not difficult to pick up a good feed and experienced crabbers often get their limit of 40 per person.

Some families enjoy relaxing on the beach after crabbing and will often build a campfire (unless a fire ban applies, of course) or get a gas stove going to cook the catch on site. This is very convenient, as sea water is on hand for cooking and it eliminates the odours and mess that are part and parcel of boiling crabs at home.

Eating fresh blue swimmers with a cold beer or glass of white wine while watching the sunset is a pretty good way to end the day!

Yellowfin whiting are caught from a number of Gulf St Vincent locations.

MAP 34 MIDDLE BEACH

Situated about half an hour's drive north of Adelaide, this is yet another crabbing hot spot. It's also a good location to try for yellowfin whiting in the summer time, with late afternoon and a rising tide generally preferred. By far the most popular baits for the whiting here are marine worms. Live tube worms can be dug from the mud flats and seaweed worms are generally easy to find beneath piles of rotting tape weed. For those without the time or energy to gather their own worms, they can be purchased live from Adelaide tackle stores.

Yellow eye mullet are present at Middle Beach year-round, but the bigger fish seem to be caught from mid March through until May. These are readily hooked on the same baits and rigs as yellowfin whiting, although mullet specialists will often change to a berley spring rig with mincemeat for bait.

Small boat launching is possible at Middle Beach, but only around high tide and with a four wheel drive tow vehicle. There are plenty of good grounds offshore for snapper and whiting, the most famous of which is the Goannas. This is an area of low reef and broken ground with a couple of large rocks and holds reds of mixed sizes, as well as good numbers of whiting year-round. The Goannas is a fair run from Adelaide's northern metro' boat ramps, but it is extremely popular with those in fast, seaworthy craft. It's also a regular stomping ground of great whites, especially when the snapper schools are moving through.

There is a recreation centre with dormitory accommodation at Middle Beach, as well as a kiosk and small caravan park.

MAP 34 THOMPSON BEACH

Again there is excellent crabbing potential on the tidal flats and some opportunities for yellowfin whiting and mullet, but Thompson isn't as popular as the beaches further north. Like all of the mangrove-fringed locations along St Vincent's Gulf's eastern shore, this one is a haven for mosquitos, particularly as the sun starts to set after a calm summer afternoon. Covering up and applying plenty of repellent are mandatory for anyone on the beach at this time of day.

CHAPTER 5
THE ADELAIDE AREA

River Torrens running through Adelaide

The population of Adelaide is around 1.15 million, making it the fifth largest city in Australia. It's less than a third the size of Melbourne and about a quarter the size of Sydney, so pressure on its adjacent fishery is relatively low. This factor, combined with sensible management at Government level, has ensured that the Adelaide area remains very productive for recreational anglers and their families.

It is well serviced in terms of facilities, both for the land-based and offshore angler. There are seven jetties along the metropolitan foreshore that are maintained exclusively for recreational activities, five first class launching ramps and, although shrinking these days, there is still limited access to wharf areas around the Port River.

Due to its location roughly midway along the eastern shore of St Vincent's Gulf, Adelaide's metropolitan coast is largely immune from the influence of ocean swell. Kangaroo Island has a blocking effect and essentially knocks out most extreme weather from the south. This doesn't necessarily mean that Adelaide is immune from heavy wind during winter time, but the coast is nowhere near as exposed as some other capital cities.

Prevailing summer winds are south to south-east and during winter the strong onshore winds blow from the north-west to south-west. Statistically, the calmest months are April, May and June and the highest rainfall period is from June through until September.

Adelaide's metropolitan shoreline is roughly 70 kilometres long, stretching from Outer Harbor in the north to Sellicks Beach in the south. It is a generally flat and shallow coast with a peak tide variation of around 2.7 metres. Heavy shipping uses either Outer Harbor or the Port River and there's a long access channel stretching out into the Gulf in a south-westerly direction from Outer Harbor heads.

MAP 35 Outer Harbor

Established in 1908 to service SA's capital city, Outer Harbor is strategically positioned at the northern end of LeFevre Peninsula. It's a deep water facility with a lengthy wharf that has seen many and varied uses in its hundred year history. Overseas passenger liners still berth there from time to time, it's the site for loading live

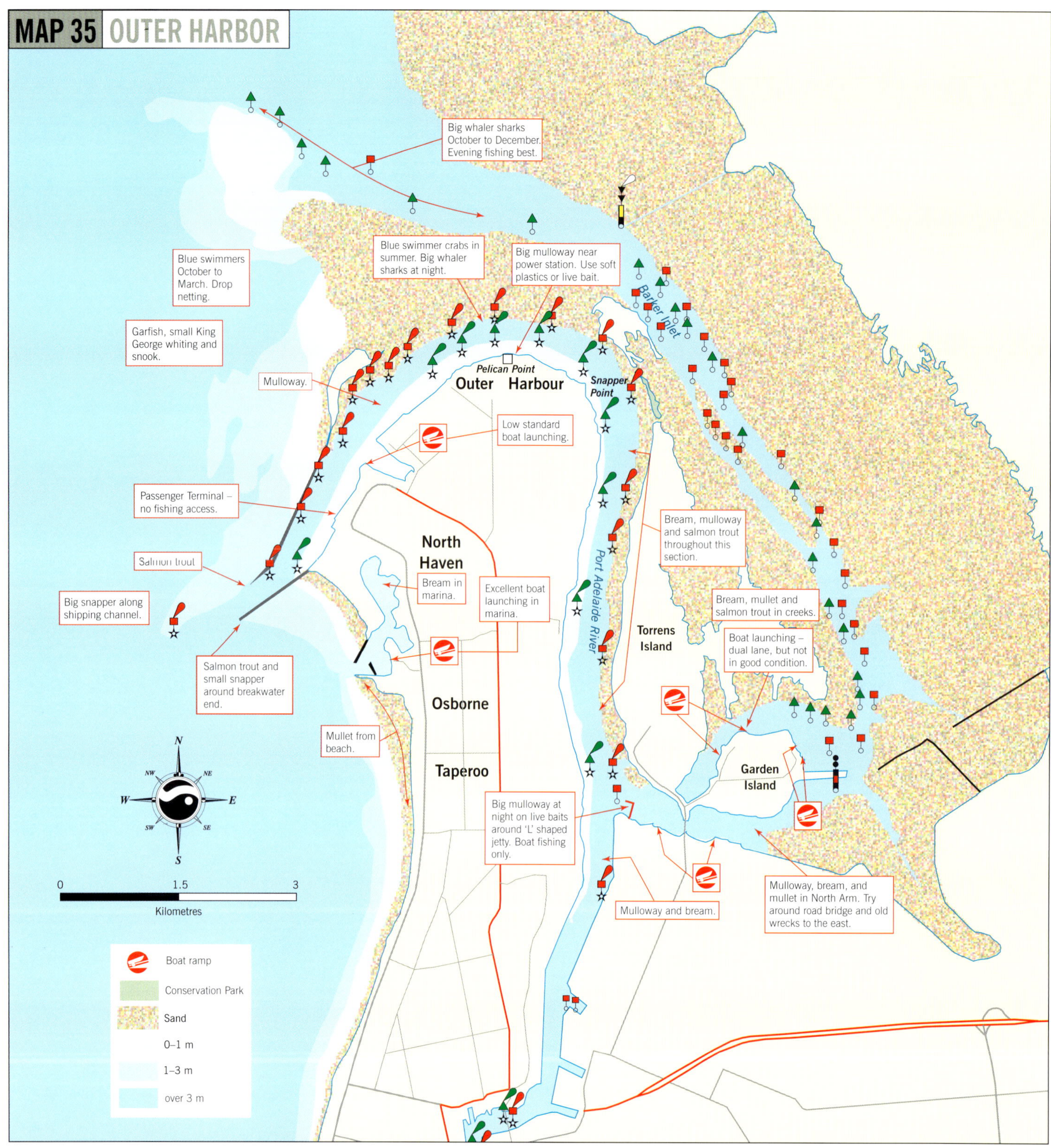

sheep for export to the Middle East.The old and rather dilapidated boat ramp at the northern end of the Outer Harbor complex is still open for use, but its popularity has dwindled in recent years. This single lane ramp has no boarding pontoons, its surface is pot-holed and the adjacent unsealed car park is notorious for vandalism after dark, so it is best avoided if possible.

Unfortunately, the Outer Harbor wharf is now completely off limits to the general public. This is unfortunate, as it was once one of the best land-based locations around Adelaide for truly big fish. Some giant mulloway have been taken from the wharf over the years, usually by those with heavy tackle and using live fish or squid for bait. Jewies to 35 kilograms and more were regular winter captures until the wharf's closure, but are now just happy memories for those fortunate anglers who were there at the right time.

Outer Harbor is protected by a 1.7 kilometre breakwater running parallel to the wharf that knocks out all the winter winds and a second that curves out toward the south-west and blocks summer southerlies. The outer breakwater is a bird sanctuary and is off limits, but the southern wall is open to recreational anglers. Like the main wharf, it has produced some spectacular fish, including big mulloway, jumbo snapper, salmon, snook and even the occasional yellowtail king. There's a neat little platform located at the base of the southern breakwater that was constructed solely for recreational use and this produces some nice fish at times, including mulloway, small snapper and bream.

Small boat fishing is permitted around the seaward end of both breakwaters and good catches of small to medium salmon are common. These are generally hooked on small trolled lures. Big bream, drummer and other rock species are taken around the breakwaters as well, but most who visit concentrate their efforts on salmon.

It is illegal to anchor in the Outer Harbor shipping channel, but big snapper are taken from boats anchored just off the channel edges. These aren't as common now as they once were and there is generally plenty of waiting time between hook ups, but the shipping channel reds are usually giants and worth the time and effort. Specimens of 15 kilograms and more are taken between August and December, usually at dawn or dusk, but occasionally during the day around tide changes.

The Outer Harbor silt grounds, which lie immediately west of the outer breakwater, are enormously popular with small boat anglers who launch at nearby North Haven. This area is generally shallow and attracts large numbers of small to medium King George whiting, garfish, snook, blue swimmer crabs and, in summer time, large whaler sharks. It's just a short boat ride from the North Haven Marina and rarely fails to produce a good mixed bag when tides and weather are favourable.

MAP 36 The Port River

Although it's not a river in strictest terms, this waterway has long been the life blood of Adelaide's commercial shipping. It is essentially a long, deep canal that runs between the eastern shore of LeFevre Peninsula and western side of Torrens Island, joining St Vincent's Gulf at the mouth of Outer Harbor. All up, the Port River is about seven kilometres long and terminates at the southern end at the Bower Road Causeway.

Like most other waterways that carry a heavy traffic load, the Port River has copped its share of pollution over the decades. Until things were tightened up quite recently on the environmental side, much of the industry lining the River used it as a discharge site for waste, resulting in very poor water quality. This situation has now changed, however, and the water is generally much cleaner than it was several decades ago. The fishing seems to have improved in line with water quality, especially on species like bream and mulloway.

The Port River's upper reaches are surrounded by old wharves, although new housing developments have altered the skyline somewhat. High rise apartment complexes on the western bank have sprung up with amazing speed, necessitating the removal of several wharves and jetties that were built close to a hundred years ago. These old structures produced some amazing catches over the decades, particularly big mulloway, and there

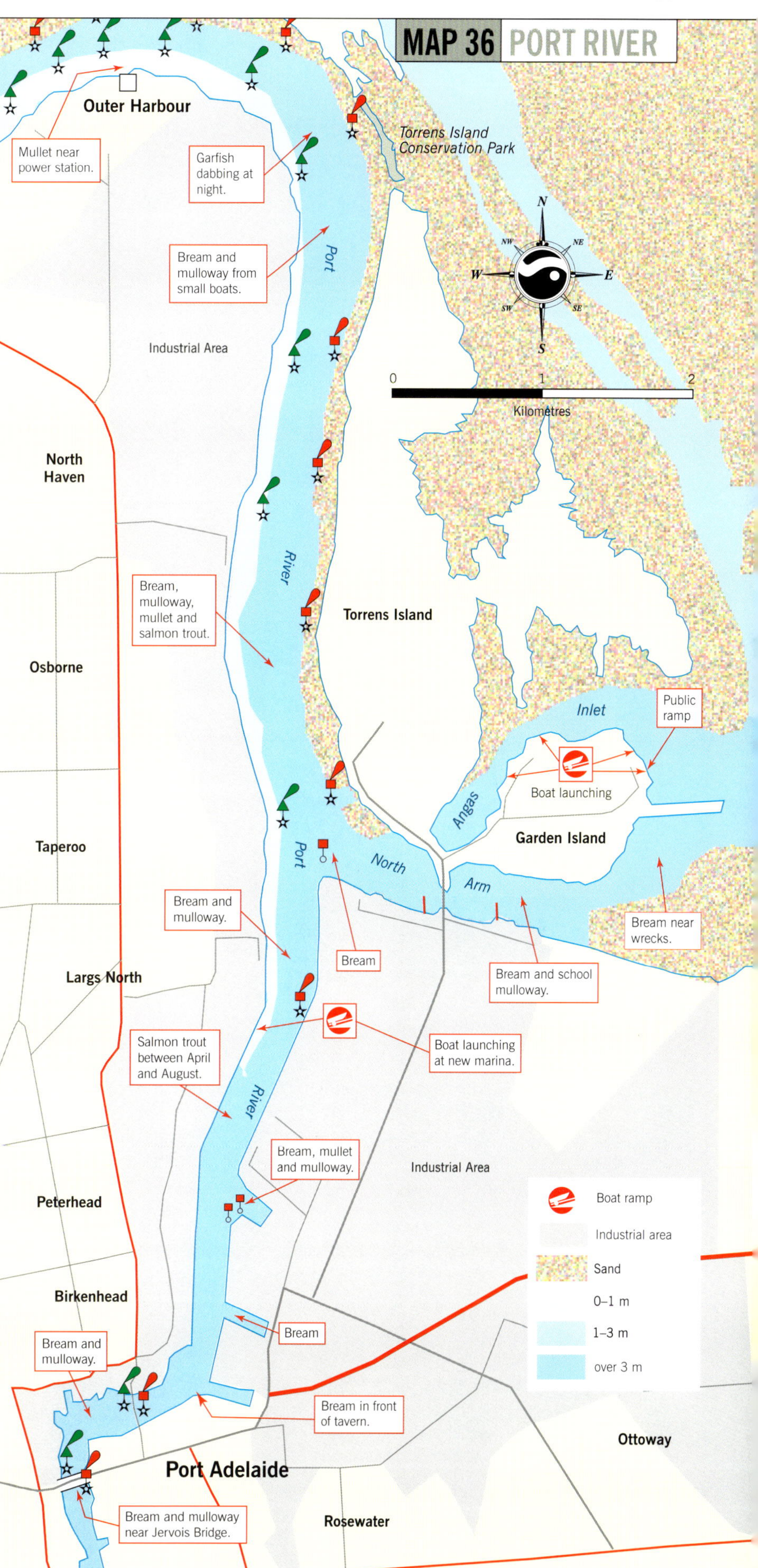

LEFT: Casting lures for bream

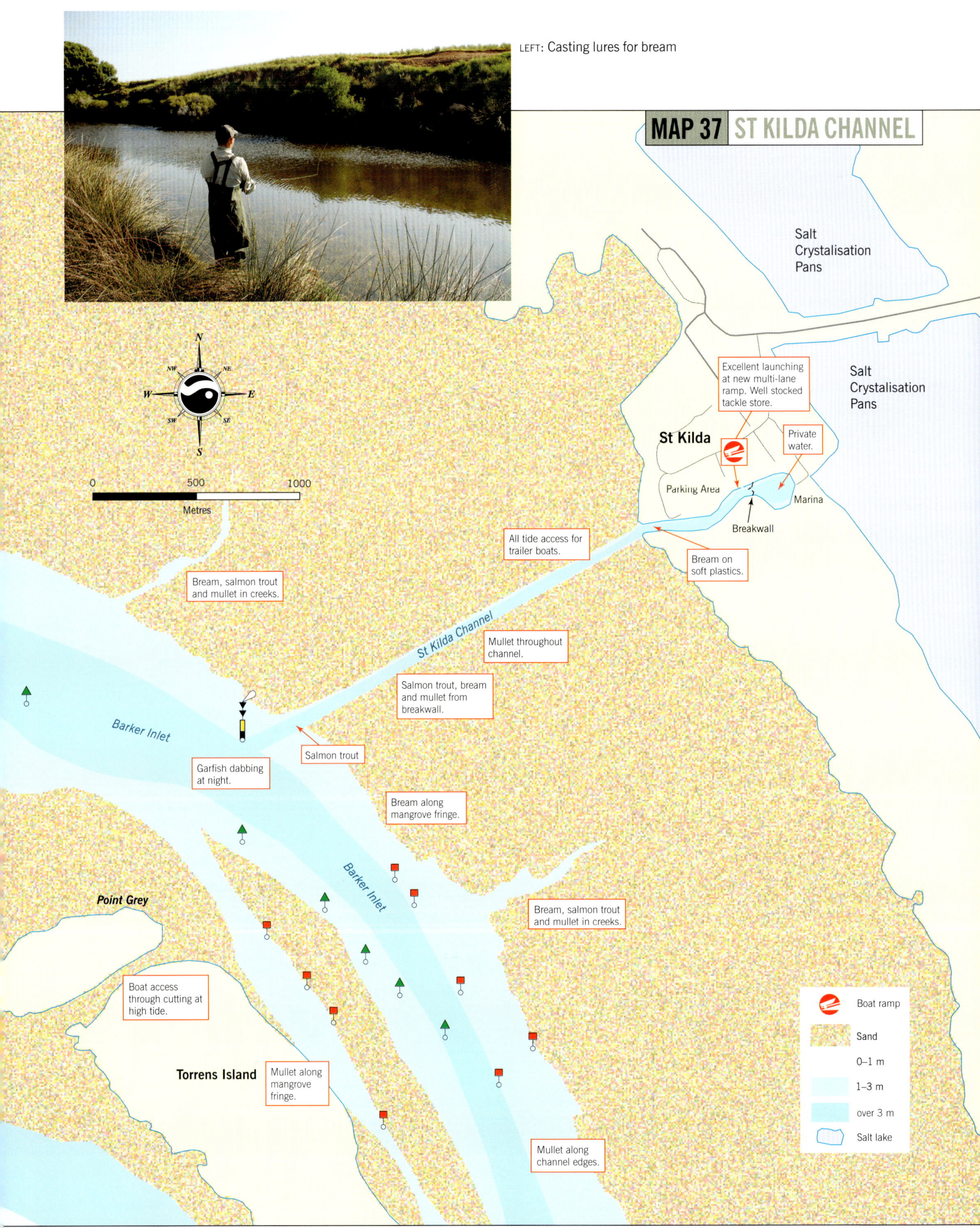

are still quite a few nice jewies taken throughout the system each year.

Unfortunately, access to most of the legendary Port River wharves has evaporated over the past few years, due mainly to the combination of public liability issues and ageing structures. Locations like the wheat silos, Caltex wharf, sugar wharf and Osborne Power Station wharf are now off limits, reducing land-based options considerably. These were all reliable spots to try for bream, mulloway, mullet and salmon trout and were quite handy, as they could be fished in virtually any weather.

The Port River is famous for its winter mulloway, which generally turn up in April and run through until August or September. These vary from 'schoolies' of five or six kilograms all the way up to 35 kilogram giants and are sought consistently by specialist anglers with small boats. Most are hooked on live baits such as salmon trout, mullet and garfish, but there is now a trend toward targeting these magnificent fish on soft plastic lures.

Live baiters seem to do best at night, with most action occurring on or around the turn of low water. Lure tossers, on the other hand, generally achieve more hook ups during daylight hours and once again, low water is prime time. Hooking a 25 kilogram mulloway on a lure and relatively light tackle from a small boat is a true sportfishing experience. These are powerful fish that can strip plenty of line from a reel and it's usually necessary to pull the anchor and give chase after hook up.

Mulloway are caught around all three bridges at the top of the Port River, along the channel edges for most of its length, near the Pelican Point power station and throughout the Outer Harbor area. However, only those who know the fish and know the waterway intimately seem to catch them on a regular basis. Patience and persistence are prerequisites, but the rewards can be great.

Bream fishing in the Port River is now generally a much more active pursuit than was once the case. Up until the last few years, soaking a bait was the generally accepted norm, but these days it's the small boat lure casters who seem to be catching the best bags and biggest fish. Soft plastics, braided line and the right rods and reels to fish them effectively have revolutionised the Port River bream scene, and the River now hosts several well attended tournaments annually.

Bream of varying sizes are present throughout the entire system, including the River's North Arm, which branches off at right angles to the main channel and links up with the St Kilda channel to the north-east. The North Arm forms the southern end of Torrens Island and is crossed by a long road bridge from Port Adelaide. This bridge, although essentially off limits to fishing, has been the scene of hectic school mulloway action over many years. Thousands of schoolies were taken from the bridge during the 1970s, '80s and '90s, but the bite seems to have shut down somewhat now.

Boaties operating at night in the North Arm still catch a few mulloway on lures or live baits and there are plenty of bream to be had around the bridge pylons and the wrecks further to the east. The tide runs strongly through the North Arm in both directions, so it's wise to plan fishing times around periods of slack water. Live trumpeters are probably the most popular school mulloway baits, as they are both easy to catch and quite hardy on the hooks. Mid-sized rubber tail lures are also proven fish catchers in this waterway.

Yellow eye mullet, salmon trout and garfish are generally prolific throughout the Port River's North Arm. All you need to catch a good feed is some light tackle, fresh bait and plenty of berley. Gents (blowfly maggots) are best for gar, but they will also catch mullet, whereas white bait or cockles are preferred for salmon trout. A berley mix of bread, semolina and tuna oil will usually have all three varieties lining up behind the boat.

Live tube worms are without peer for those targeting bream, but not keen on trying lures. It's possible to collect these worms from the Port River's banks at low tide with the aid of a fork or garden spade or they can be bought from local tackle stores at a reasonable price. Practically everything that swims in the Port River will eat tube worms, including school mulloway at times.

There is boat launching at the northern end of Garden Island, although the condition of the dual lane ramp varies somewhat, depending on the current level of maintenance. There's a spacious car park at the Garden Island ramp, but like Outer Harbor, it can be a dicey place to park an expensive tow vehicle and trailer after sundown. Vandalism and theft don't seem to be as much of a problem these days as was once the case, but this is a remote location and one that still sees more than its share of mischief.

There is a lengthy fishing/bird watching jetty that runs parallel with the mangrove canopy adjacent to the Garden Island boat ramp. This attracts a lot of fishing families in fine weather, as it is readily accessible and does produce a few nice bream and mullet. However, it is far from being a fishing 'hot spot'.

The St Kilda Channel, which runs northward from the junction of the North Arm, is a long, meandering stretch of water that leads out into St Vincent's Gulf. It forms the eastern shoreline of Torrens Island and is subject to very strong tidal flow. Big snapper were once a regular catch in certain sections of the channel, but these are now history. Eagle rays are common, as are yellow eye mullet along the mangrove fringe.

There is a series of creeks that run off the eastern side of the St Kilda Channel, most of which are a small boat or kayak proposition only. These fish well for bream, mullet, salmon trout and the occasional school mulloway, but some local knowledge is required to be successful on a regular basis. Casting small soft plastic and hard bodied lures brings the best results from this shallow water environment.

There is excellent boat launching at St Kilda via a recently upgraded multi-lane ramp. A well stocked tackle store is located adjacent to the ramp and the exit channel can be a terrific spot for yellowfin whiting, mullet, bream and salmon trout. Outside the channel there are vast flats that produce blue swimmer crabs in season (November until April), as well as small to medium King George whiting, garfish, snook, salmon trout and tommy ruffs.

In October and November each year members of the Adelaide Game Fishing Club regularly hook large bronze whaler sharks along the edges of the St Kilda channel, especially near the Black Pole. Some of these sharks are three metres long and can weigh upwards of 200 kilograms, providing terrific sport on 24kg tackle. These days most of the sharks are tagged and released, which is far more environmentally sound than was once the case. Big eagle rays are also prolific on the flats, which also make great sport on the appropriate line classes.

Drop netting for blue swimmer crabs is extremely popular in this area as well and when the main summer crab run is on, it's not unusual to see a hundred boats on the water off St Kilda. Most of the crabs are taken in less than five metres of water and bag limit catches of 40 per person are common.

MAP 38 ADELAIDE'S METROPOLITAN JETTIES

The jetties along the Adelaide coast, and particularly those at the northern end, were once important shipping points. These days, however, all seven piers are maintained solely for recreational pursuits and especially fishing. They vary in length and quality of structure, but they have all been subject to storm damage over a long period and are now maintained by the various local councils.

The jetties are enormously popular during good weather, when thousands of people use them. They are seaside drawcards in their own right, which is why the councils value them so highly and pour millions of dollars into their upkeep. It has been estimated that on a warm summer evening as many as 10,000 Adelaide residents walk along the seven jetties and many of these wet a line.

The Largs Bay jetty, situated just south of Outer Harbor on the western side of LeFevre Peninsula, was built way back in 1882. The structure was originally 600 metres long and was commissioned to help establish the suburb of Largs Bay as a seaside resort and to provide an attractive berth for international shipping. At that time Outer Harbor had not been established, so Adelaide had no deep water port.

These days the Largs jetty is only about a third of its original length. Storm damage has shortened it progressively over the decades and although repair work was consistent, the opening of Outer Harbor reduced Largs Bay's value for shipping and a deep water pier was no longer required.

The water around the jetty today is quite shallow; in fact, it is possible to walk around the end of the jetty on really low tides. Despite this, however, it is still a popular fishing and crabbing venue. Nice yellow eye mullet and yellowfin whiting can be caught in the gutters closer to shore, while garfish and blue swimmers are taken nearer the seaward end. Big bream are often seen swimming in and around the jetty piles, but these are notoriously difficult to tempt on the freshest of baits. A roofed shelter at the end of the jetty provides protection from both the rain and intense summer sun.

Semaphore jetty is just a couple of kilometres further south and it, too, has a very interesting history. It is one of the oldest piers and was completed in 1860. Its original length was around 700 metres and it featured a restaurant and dance hall in a two storey complex at the end. In its heyday, Semaphore jetty was the major attraction along Adelaide's foreshore, drawing thousands of visitors annually and adding a lot of colour to the developing coastline.

Today Semaphore is still our longest jetty, but is nearly a hundred metres shorter than it was back in the 1800s. Winter north-westerly gales have taken a heavy toll on this structure, with a significant section breaking off and washing ashore as recently as 1989. Significant on-going repairs have now stabilised the structure, however, and it is a very popular fishing jetty.

Deeper 'gutters' running parallel with the shore and less than a third of the way along the jetty are consistent producers of nice mullet and yellowfin whiting. The mullet are at their best in autumn and early winter, while the whiting peak during the Christmas/New Year period. Live marine worms are the prime bait for both varieties and it's imperative to use the lightest possible tackle.

Night time fishing at Semaphore regularly yields good catches of tommy ruffs and gar. These are surface feeders when the sun goes down and are taken by those using floats and maggot baits. The seaward end of the jetty seems the most productive for both species, which can vary in size and numbers according to season and conditions. The gar are definitely best on warm, calm summer evenings, while the tommies are more of a year-round proposition.

Jetty crabbers do pretty well at Semaphore, with the best catches generally coming after sunset. Both blue swimmers and sand crabs are taken in drop nets, but there are generally quite a few small ones amongst them and these need to be measured and returned if they don't make the grade. Chicken carcasses were once the crab bait of choice, but it's no longer legal to use them in drop nets and both fish heads and squid are now popular substitutes.

Big snapper were once a regular catch from the end of Semaphore jetty, and particularly during strong north-westerly winds in winter. However, the big reds are far less common these days, due mainly to siltation around the seaward end. It's a lot shallower now than it used to be and the snapper seem to stay further offshore. Big sharks are still hooked from the jetty during summer time, most of which are whalers of between 100-200 kilograms. A couple of great whites have also been landed at Semaphore over the years, but these are now protected by law. There are tight regulations governing recreational shark fishing from Adelaide's metropolitan jetties these days, with a ban on shark fishing between 5am and 9pm daily between Outer Harbor and Yankalilla. In addition to the restricted times, recreational fishers are not allowed to use a trace line (wire or monofilament) which exceeds 1mm in diameter and a hook gape greater than 23mm.

Grange jetty is the next pier southward. It was built in 1882 and at 370 metres long it is one of Adelaide's piers that has retained much of its original length. The seaside suburb of Grange is among

BELOW: Fishing for yellowfin whiting in the Shallows at Semaphore.

Largs Bay jetty produces bream, mullet, yellowfin whiting and crabs.

MAP 38 ADELAIDE METROPOLITAN BEACHES
Good jetty fishing for blue swimmer crabs, garfish, squid, tommy ruffs, mullet and yellowfin whiting.
Mullet at river mouth.
Boat launching at Adelaide Shores Marina.
Jetty fishing for squid, tommies and garfish.
King George whiting, garfish and snapper offshore.
Squid drift grounds.
Boat launching in excellent harbour.
Fishing permitted from shore
Jetty fishing for salmon, tommies, squid, gar and mullet.
Boat ramp
Sanctuary Zone
Conservation Park
National Park
Sand
0–1 m
1–3 m
3–5 m
5–10 m
over 10 m
0
2.5
5
Kilometres
N
NE
E
SE
S
SW
W
NW
Tennyson
Grange
Henley Beach
Henley Beach South
West Beach
Glenelg North
Glenelg
Glenelg South
Somerton Park
North Brighton
Brighton
South Brighton
Holdfast Bay
Seacliff
Kingston Park
Marino
Hallet Cove
Port Stanvac
Lonsdale
O'Sullivan Beach
Christies Beach
Port Noarlunga Reef Sanctuary Zone
Port Noarlunga
Port Noarlunga South
Onkaparinga River Sanctuary Zone
Seaford Meadows
Seaton
Findon
Beverley
Croydon
Ridleyton
Fitzroy
Medindie
Royston Park
Payneham
Allenby Gardens
Brompton
Gilberton
Joslin
St Peters
Payneham South
Firle
Trinity Gdns
Kidman Park
Flinders Park
Hindmarsh
Fulham Gardens
Underdale
Thebarton
Beulah Park
Kent Town
Kensington
Lockleys
Torrensville
Fulham
Brooklyn Park
Cowandilla
Mile End
Adelaide
Tusmore
Hilton
West Richmond
Richmond
Keswick
Wayville
Eastwood
Glenside
Frewville
Linden Park
Adelaide Airport
Netley
Marleston
Ashford
Unley
Parkside
Glenunga
Goodwood
Everard Park
North Plympton
Kurralta Park
Hyde Park
Malvern
Millswood
Black Forest
Plympton
Clarence Park
Unley Park
Highgate
Novar Gardens
Camden Park
Glandore
Cumberland Park
Hawthorn
Kingswood
Urrbrae
South Plympton
Westbourne Park
Netherby
Plympton Park
Clarence Gardens
Colonel Light Gardens
Lwr Mitcham
Springfield
Melrose Park
Torrens Park
Glenelg East
Park Holme
Ascot Park
Daw Park
Glengowrie
Clapham
Edwardstown
Panorama
Belair
Morphettville
Mitchell Park
Lynton
Pasadena
Marion
St Marys
Clovelly Park
Warradale
Oaklands Park
Hove
Blackwood
Eden Hills
Sturt
Dover Gardens
Seacombe Gardens
Bedford Park
Bellevue Heights
Darlington
Seacliff Park
Seacombe Heights
Craigburn Farm
Seaview Downs
Coromandel Valley
O'Halloran Hill
Flagstaff Hill
Trott Park
Aberfoyle Park
Sheidow Park
Reynella East
Happy Valley
Old Reynella
Reynella
Woodcroft
Christie Downs
Morphett Vale
Baker Gully
Noarlunga Centre
Hackham West
Onkaparinga Hills
Noarlunga Downs
Huntfield Heights
Hackham

Adelaide's most popular and was the original home of famous inland explorer, Charles Sturt.

The jetty has long been a favourite of gar anglers, who generally do best at night time. Yellowfin whiting and mullet are abundant along the jetty's inshore gutters and anglers are sometimes packed, shoulder to shoulder, when the afternoon bite is in full swing. There are a few nice bream taken from the same gutters and around the jetty pylons, so a mixed bag of quality fish is always on the cards at Grange.

Blue swimmers and sand crabs are regularly available, with the sandies more prevalent after onshore winds have stirred the inshore water. Some of these are quite large and although not as highly regarded as their blue swimmer cousins, they are still fine eating. Night time is best for crabbing at Grange and it is important to be aware of both bag limits and gear restrictions, which are outlined clearly in a recreational fishing guide, produced by PIRSA (Primary Industries and Regions SA).

Young anglers armed with heavy tackle often hook eagle rays, small to medium whaler sharks and the occasional big snapper from Grange jetty. Berleying for larger sharks has been outlawed from all jetties and hefty fines apply for those who ignore regulations.

Henley jetty, a couple of kilometres to the south and almost due west of Adelaide, is probably the busiest along the entire metropolitan coast. This pier is slightly shorter than Grange, but seems to attract more anglers. It is by far the most productive jetty for crabbers and those who know the tides and seasons often come away with a bag limit catch of 40 per person. By far the most reliable time to go crabbing at Henley is during the run-in tide at night time. This often means arriving at midnight and crabbing through until sunrise, which isn't for everyone, but certainly appeals to plenty during summer when the night air is still and warm.

Henley jetty crabbers usually set their nets from about halfway along the pier out to the seaward end. Many use the maximum number of allowable nets (ten single ring nets or three double ring nets) and space them out until the greatest concentration of crabs is discovered. The general rule is to pull the nets at ten minute intervals if the crabs are in moderate numbers or about half that time if they are abundant.

As with the other jetties to the north, Henley is good for yellowfin whiting and gar in the summer months and mullet when the water cools down in autumn and early winter.

ABOVE: Yellowfin whiting can be caught from the Henley jetty and also from the Adelaide Metropolitan beaches during the summer months.

BELOW: Grange jetty is a good one for garfish and tommies after dark.

Henley is by far Adelaide's most reliable crabbing pier.

Glenelg is Adelaide's busiest seaside suburb and its 380 metre jetty was built back in 1859. The original structure had a kiosk, public baths, an aquarium and even a lighthouse at the end to warn incoming ships. It was a significant shipping pier for many years prior to the establishment of Port Adelaide and Outer Harbor, but this has long since changed.

In 1948 the jetty was totally demolished by a hurricane-like storm, which also caused considerable damage to the adjacent foreshore and local housing. The jetty was rebuilt in 1969 and today stands at 215 metres long. Unlike the other piers to the north, Glenelg jetty is all steel and concrete.

It's a popular place for family fishing outings, producing squid, snook, garfish, tommy ruffs, yellowfin whiting and mullet. Crabbing isn't as productive as on the other jetties, but Glenelg offers a greater diversity of available fish species. The gar here are generally larger than those caught further north and it's usual to see a couple of dozen anglers armed with light float fishing tackle chasing them on a warm, calm evening.

Brighton jetty is a few kilometres further south and it's roughly the same length as the pier at Glenelg. Brighton was all but destroyed in a violent storm in the early 1990s, but was rebuilt with funding from one of the larger telecommunications companies. The jetty now carries a tall mobile phone tower at the seaward end.

It's a popular pier with those living in Adelaide's south-western suburbs, but doesn't seem to fish as consistently as most others further north. Squid, tommy ruffs, gar and mullet make up the bulk of the Brighton jetty catch, with a few crabs at times and the odd nice snapper from the end during winter storms. Young anglers also hook eagle rays and occasional whaler sharks in summer time.

Port Noarlunga is the last of Adelaide's metropolitan jetties. It is considerably different from most of the others, in that it stretches from the shoreline and connects with a reef system that runs parallel

Blue crab underwater

with the coast. The original jetty at Port Noarlunga was constructed in 1855, but was destroyed by a gale in the early 1900s and replaced by the current structure in 1921. It's now just under 400 metres long.

The fishing at Port Noarlunga differs markedly from further along the metropolitan coast. The seabed is quite different and so are some of the available fish varieties. The Noarlunga jetty is probably most famous for its invasions of winter salmon, which school up in big numbers and swarm in through the reef when the sea is rough. Most of the salmon are in the 1-2 kilogram range and can really perform on standard jetty tackle.

When news gets around Port Noarlunga and adjacent areas that the salmon are on at the jetty, anglers usually descend en masse. It's often shoulder to shoulder fishing, even when it is pouring with rain and rough enough to have waves crashing over some sections of the jetty. This makes quite a sight, with dozens of fisherfolk clad in brightly coloured wet weather clothing and pulling in big salmon, hand over fist!

Garfish are another of Port Noarlunga's popular jetty drawcards and these are generally large. They are often mixed in with tommy ruffs, which definitely bite best from early evening onward. Mullet, yellowfin whiting and squid are also easy to find from this pier.

The reef system at the jetty's seaward end is an aquatic reserve and is off limits to all fishing activity. This is a very popular location for snorkellers and skin divers, most of whom use the jetty to access the best underwater sites.

MAP 38 Metropolitan beach fishing

Generally speaking, Adelaide's metro' beaches are quiet and lack the surf found on our West Coast and lower Yorke Peninsula. Beach fishing along this stretch of coast isn't particularly popular, but there are some nice fish to be caught on light tackle. Yellowfin whiting are taken from the shore between North Haven and Henley, especially from November through until February. These aren't usually big fish, with most from the legal minimum size of 24 centimetres up to around 30.

Yellow eye mullet are generally abundant and easy to catch when the water cools down a bit and are at their peak between April and June. Garfish are often caught at first light in some of the deeper gutters between Tennyson and Grange, along with a few nice tommy ruffs and salmon trout.

Those with heavier tackle occasionally hook eagle rays, small whaler sharks and the odd elephant fish in springtime.

MAP 39 West Lakes

Created in the early 1970s, the West Lakes system turned a formerly uninhabited and generally uninteresting stretch of coastal marshland into one of Adelaide's true jewels. The project was an enormous one that took seven years to develop and has produced one of the city's elite suburbs. The West Lakes system begins at the southern extremity of the Port River and is connected beneath the road at the Bower Road Causeway. It then meanders southward, concluding about six kilometres away at West Lakes Boulevard.

A major shopping centre and upmarket high rise housing can be found at West Lakes, but it is also one of Adelaide's most popular fishing venues. Tens of thousands of anglers cast a line into the lake system annually and while bag limit catches of any species are the exception rather than the norm, it is still a generally productive place to go fishing.

West Lakes is subject to tidal influence from outside in St Vincent's Gulf. The water flows in via a series of underground pipes and is controlled by gates at the southern end. The water inflow can be quite turbulent at certain times, stirring the lake bed and often stimulating the resident fish into feeding mode. Water movement at the northern end is generally more subtle.

Bream are the dominant fish throughout the West Lakes system and these vary from specimens the size of a fingernail all the way up to kilogram-plus beauties. Most who chase bream do so with natural baits such as live tube worms, prawns, small crabs and mussels, but the use of small lures has gained a lot of popularity in recent times. Both soft plastics and hard body minnows are effective, particularly at dawn and dusk when the fish are most active.

There are plenty of yellow eye mullet scattered throughout the lake and these can often be berleyed up and caught in good numbers. You'll need ultra light tackle for the mullet and hooks as small as size 9. Best baits include worms, cockles and red meat and a berley mix of stale bread, semolina and tuna oil seems to work effectively.

Garfish of varying sizes congregate around the southern end of West Lakes in the warmer months and are often caught on floating rigs using gents (blowfly maggots) for bait. The gar, too, are susceptible to berley and can sometimes be attracted and held in a certain area for lengthy periods. Small tommy ruffs and salmon trout can be a nuisance if targeting garfish and returning undersize bream is a fact of life for those who fish West Lakes regularly.

Although by no means a common capture, mulloway are resident in this system. Most caught are 'schoolies' of legal size (75cm) or just under, but there have been a few in the 15-20 kilogram bracket taken near the southern end. Small live baits are effective on these at night time, but several of the larger jewies have been hooked in daylight on soft plastic lures fished on relatively light threadline tackle. Some of these encounters have gone on for half an hour or longer and there have been several other big mulloway lost after epic struggles.

Blue swimmer crabs and squid are found throughout West Lakes, although neither is targeted heavily. Some of those who live on the water's edge have their own floating pontoons and it's usually possible to pick up a feed of nice crabs by setting a couple of drop nets baited with fish or squid. These pontoons are privately owned and can only be used with the express permission of residents.

There are no power boats permitted on West Lakes, but it's fine to fish from canoes or kayaks, so long as you keep a respectable distance from private pontoons and jetties. A few dedicated young anglers regularly launch kayaks from public reserves and either troll or cast lures for bream and mulloway. There can be quite a bit of paddling involved, but these keen youngsters often catch more fish in West Lakes than their land-based counterparts and thoroughly enjoy the experience.

MAP 40 The Patawalonga

Situated at Glenelg, one of Adelaide's more affluent western suburbs, the Patawalonga is quite a complex system with a long history. In essence, it's an estuary that serves as an outlet for Sturt Creek and a couple of other minor drainage waterways, flowing into St Vincent's Gulf through a relatively narrow access channel. It is affectionately known as the "Pat" by most who live near or around it and its history dates back to the time of Adelaide's first settlement in 1836. It was at the mouth of the Patawalonga that Colonel William Light, Adelaide's founder, anchored and came ashore to proclaim the city.

The Patawalonga was once a vibrant recreational fishery, but diminished water quality has seen the catch fall away somewhat over the years. Back in the 1960s and '70s it was a great spot to catch yellow eye mullet and bream, but the water quality is unpredictable these days and most who fish there now do so for catch and release only. The "Pat" is the outlet point for a lot of Adelaide's storm water run-off and although sophisticated equipment has been installed to control and monitor water flow, it's still a major concern.

At the southern end of the Patawalonga system a series of lock gates regulate water levels inside, enabling the lake to maintain consistent depth. There is an entry and exit point here for boats, which are kept inside on private moorings or berthed in the public marina. Millions of dollars worth of recreational fishing craft are

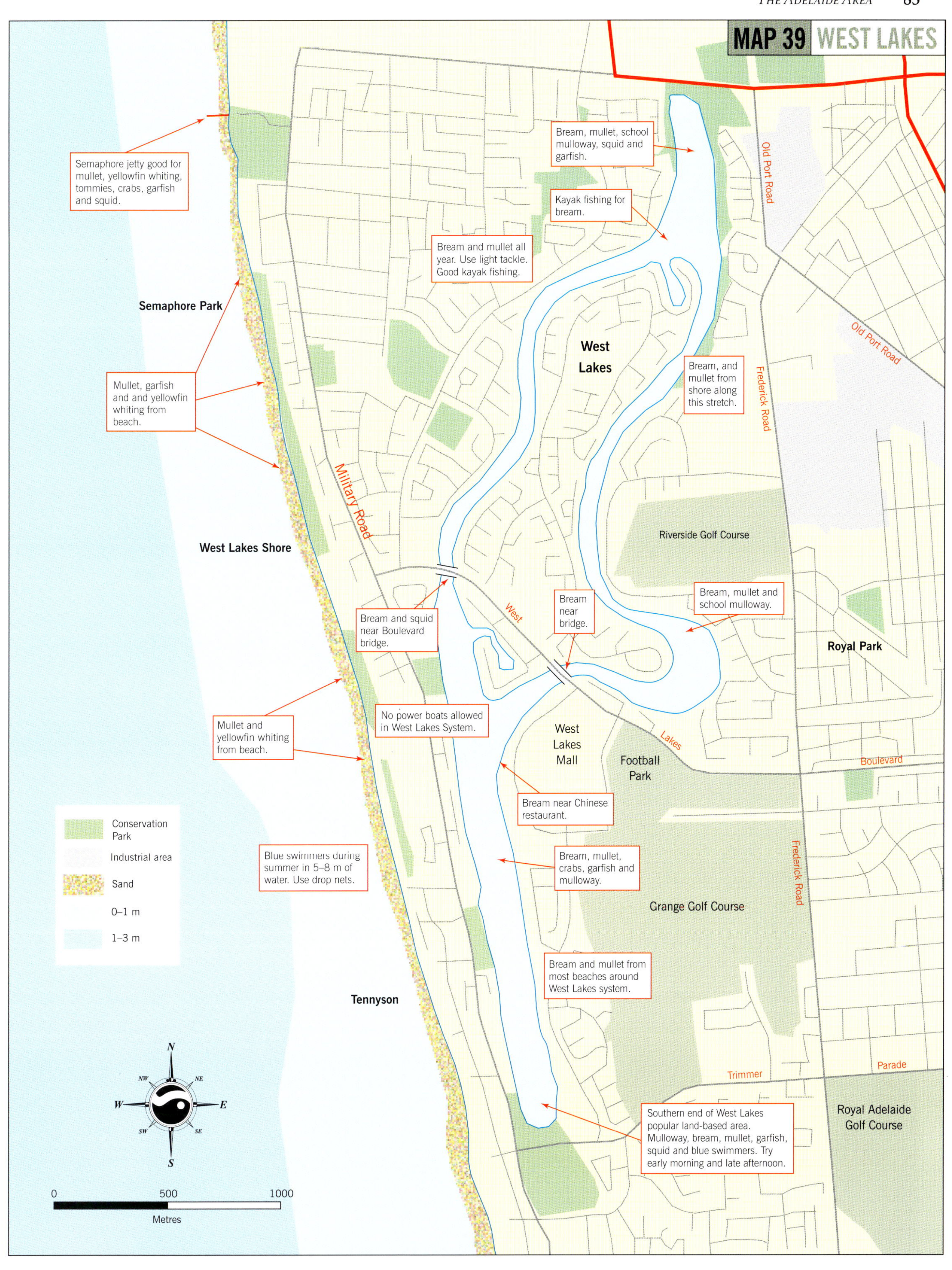
MAP 39 WEST LAKES
Semaphore jetty good for mullet, yellowfin whiting, tommies, crabs, garfish and squid.
Semaphore Park
Mullet, garfish and and yellowfin whiting from beach.
West Lakes Shore
Mullet and yellowfin whiting from beach.
Blue swimmers during summer in 5–8 m of water. Use drop nets.
Tennyson
Bream, mullet, school mulloway, squid and garfish.
Kayak fishing for bream.
Bream and mullet all year. Use light tackle. Good kayak fishing.
West Lakes
Bream, and mullet from shore along this stretch.
Military Road
Old Port Road
Frederick Road
Riverside Golf Course
Bream and squid near Boulevard bridge.
Bream near bridge.
Bream, mullet and school mulloway.
Royal Park
No power boats allowed in West Lakes System.
West Lakes Boulevard
West Lakes Mall
Football Park
Bream near Chinese restaurant.
Bream, mullet, crabs, garfish and mulloway.
Grange Golf Course
Bream and mullet from most beaches around West Lakes system.
Trimmer Parade
Southern end of West Lakes popular land-based area. Mulloway, bream, mullet, garfish, squid and blue swimmers. Try early morning and late afternoon.
Royal Adelaide Golf Course
Conservation Park
Industrial area
Sand
0–1 m
1–3 m
N
NE
E
SE
S
SW
W
NW
0
500
1000
Metres

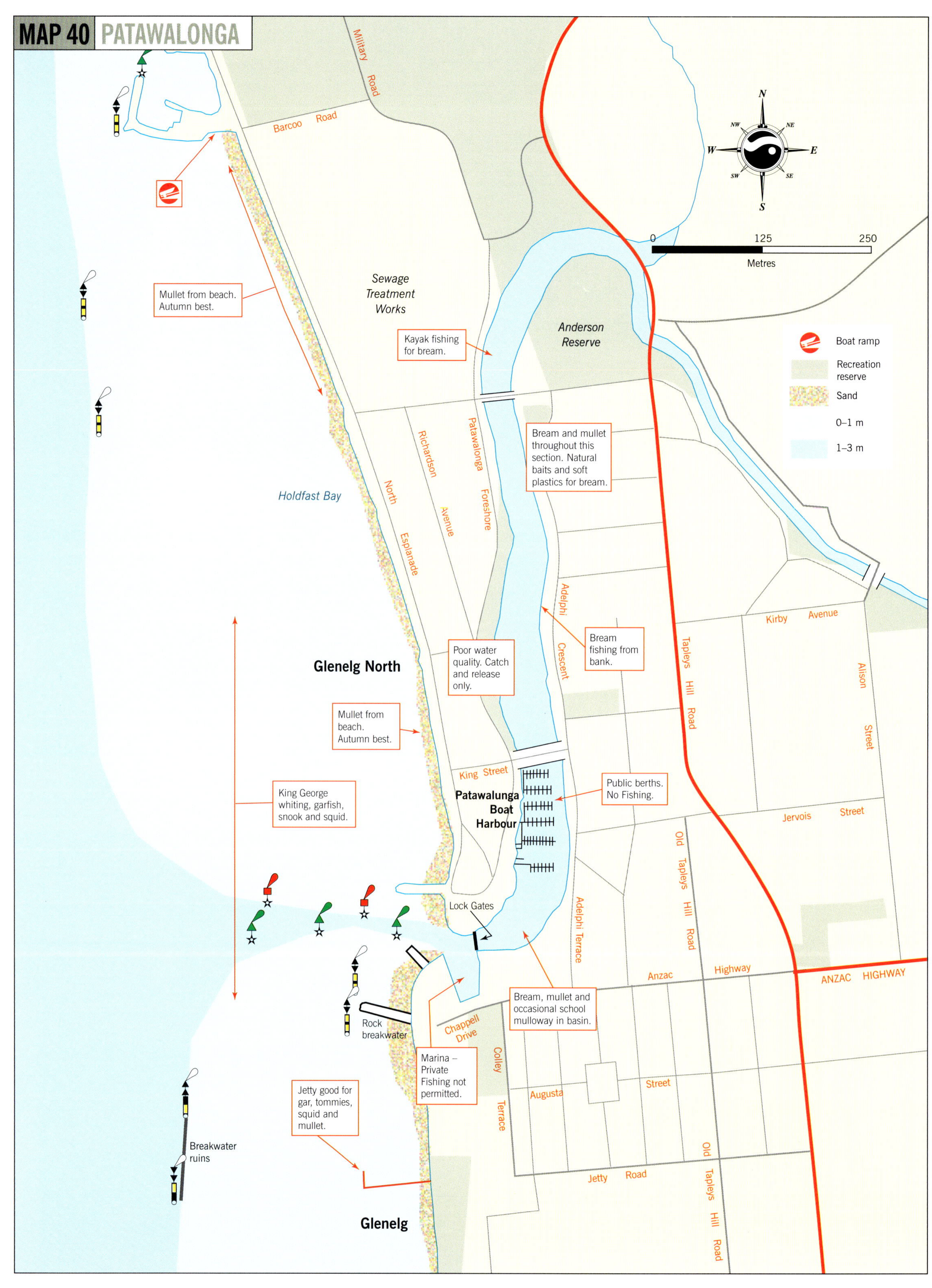
MAP 40 PATAWALONGA
Military Road
Barcoo Road
Sewage Treatment Works
Anderson Reserve
Mullet from beach. Autumn best.
Kayak fishing for bream.
Bream and mullet throughout this section. Natural baits and soft plastics for bream.
Holdfast Bay
Richardson Avenue
Patawalonga Foreshore
North Esplanade
Adelphi Crescent
Bream fishing from bank.
Poor water quality. Catch and release only.
Glenelg North
Mullet from beach. Autumn best.
King Street
Patawalunga Boat Harbour
Public berths. No Fishing.
King George whiting, garfish, snook and squid.
Lock Gates
Adelphi Terrace
Tapleys Hill Road
Kirby Avenue
Alison Street
Jervois Street
Old Tapleys Hill Road
Anzac Highway
ANZAC HIGHWAY
Bream, mullet and occasional school mulloway in basin.
Rock breakwater
Chappell Drive
Colley Terrace
Marina – Private Fishing not permitted.
Augusta Street
Jetty good for gar, tommies, squid and mullet.
Breakwater ruins
Jetty Road
Glenelg
N
NE
E
SE
S
SW
W
NW
0
125
250
Metres
Boat ramp
Recreation reserve
Sand
0–1 m
1–3 m

tied up inside the "Pat", some of which belong to members of the SA Game Fishing Club.

Unfortunately, the Patawalonga entrance is constantly subject to siltation and requires regular dredging to remain safely navigable. There's a relatively new marina complex located just outside the lock gates and the big boats berthed here are generally more upmarket than those inside. The old Glenelg boat ramp, which used to be located directly opposite the new Holdfast Shores Marina, has been demolished and replaced by expensive high rise housing.

MAP 41 The Onkaparinga River

South Aussies are renowned for shortening the names of popular locations and the Onkparinga River is more commonly referred to these days as simply the "Onk". It's quite a long river, originating near Mount Torrens in the Mount Lofty Ranges and flowing some 95 kilometres to the sea at Port Noarlunga. It traverses many of Adelaide's south-eastern and southern suburbs and is broken near the township of Clarendon by the Mount Bold Reservoir. The only other significant river near Adelaide is the Torrens, which flows through the city centre into St Vincent's Gulf at West Beach.

While there are redfin perch and a few trout available in the Onkaparinga's fresh water section, it is the estuary and first few kilometres upstream from the sea that hold most interest for recreational anglers. From the mouth, just south of Port Noarlunga jetty, to the township of old Noarlunga, the River turns from salt to brackish and provides the ideal habitat for fish varieties like bream, mulloway, salmon trout, yellowfin whiting, flathead and yellow eye mullet. This is a bountiful estuary system that attracts thousands of anglers annually and provides some first class fishing.

Bream are easily the most sought after species and these are targeted with both fresh bait and lures. There are thousands of undersize bream in the lower Onkaparinga and getting through them to find the better ones can sometimes be a problem. However, there are kilogram-plus specimens in residence as well and persistent local anglers use several strategies to hook them. Larger, robust baits like rock crabs are quite resilient and can withstand the onslaught of 'pickers' until a larger bream comes along. The same applies to substantial strips of fish, which big bream take with relish.

Light tackle lure tossing has become extremely popular in the lower "Onk" and the usual outfit consists of a 2500 size threadline, two metre light-tipped rod and 2-3 kilogram braid. A rod like this will throw ultra light soft plastics or tiny hard bodies far enough to catch a bream and if you are lucky enough to hook a big one, the ensuing battle can be very exciting.

School mulloway are caught regularly between the Onkparinga mouth and Old Noarlunga and these days most fall to lures. It's unusual to hook a mulloway of more than six or seven kilograms in this waterway and indeed most caught are below the legal minimum size of 75 centimetres and have to be thrown back. However, even these undersize 'soapies' are good fun on light line and attract a lot of sportfishers to the River in the warmer months.

Perry's Bend, not far upstream from Port Noarlunga township, is probably the best known fishing location in the Onkaparinga. It can be a busy place when the bream are biting and is probably best avoided if you're serious about catching bigger fish. Prime time to be on this river is from late afternoon through until the first hour of darkness, particularly if mulloway is the target species.

Because of its significance as a bream nursery and spawning site, a closed season on bream is in place upstream of the Main South Road bridge at Noarlunga between September 1 and November 30 inclusive.

The mouth of the "Onk", situated at Port Noarlunga, often teems with salmon trout, which can be caught on small, lures or natural baits like anchovies, cockles and fish pieces. Most of these

The Onkaparinga River still produces some good black bream in the deeper sections of the river.

MAP 41 ONKAPARINGA RIVER
Port Noarlunga
Port Noarlunga Reef Sanctuary Zone
Fishing permitted from shoreline within the Port Noarlunga Sanctuary Zone.
Bream mullet and school mulloway.
Noarlunga Downs
Onkaparinga River
Kayaking good in these stretches for bream and school mulloway.
Salmon trout, mullet and bream throughout lower estuary.
Onkarparinga River Sanctuary Zone
Commercial Road
Onkaparinga River
Salmon trout, mullet, and yellowfin whiting at river mouth.
Onkaparinga River Recreation Park
Onkaparinga Head
Bream, mullet and school mulloway.
Seaford Meadows
Port Noarlunga South
Esplanade
Closed season on bream between September 1– November 30 upstream of Main South Road bridge.
Seaford
Seaford Road
Main South Road
Robinson Point

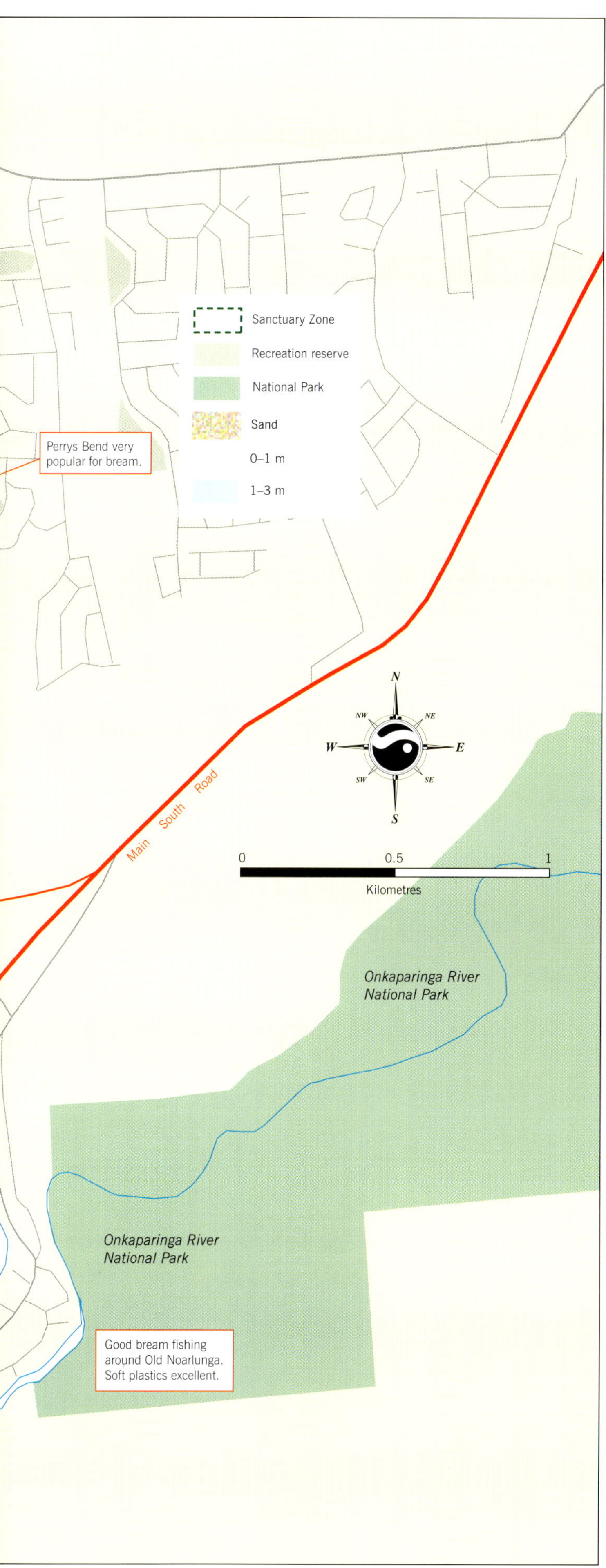

fish weigh less than a kilogram, but they are great sport on ultra light gear and quite good on the plate if put on ice immediately after capture and eaten fresh.

MAP 42 & 43 Adelaide's offshore fishing

Although it sees plenty of boating traffic in good weather, Adelaide's metro coast and adjacent offshore waters continue to offer good fishing. The most popular species is King George whiting and although capital city stocks aren't as healthy as those in Spencer Gulf, Kangaroo Island or the West Coast, local whiting specialists still do pretty well.

Whiting can be caught from Outer Harbor in the north all the way down to Sellicks Beach and beyond. They vary in both size and quantity according to location and each section of coast has its own 'gun' spots. Competing for a bag of whiting, particularly on fine weekends, can be interesting at times and it's not unusual to see 20 boats anchored in an area the size of an average house block when the fish are really on!

Some of the better known King George whiting locations along Adelaide's metropolitan coast include the 'Buckets', the 'North-West', the 'Norma', the 'John Robb' and the 'Goannas', all off Outer Harbor. Moving southward, Semaphore Reef, Wonga Shoal, Grange tyre reef and Glenelg tyre reef are all well patronised for much of the year, with the most consistent catches coming in winter and springtime.

Southern school whiting (also known as transparent whiting) are readily caught along Adelaide's metro coastline. This variety of whiting is quite tasty, but does not grow to the same sizes as King George or yellowfin, with a 25cm school whiting being a good sized fish. These whiting can be caught on the same grounds as King George, but are seen in better numbers in the shallower grounds from Hallett Cove through to Maslin Beach.

There are snapper grounds along this stretch as well. The John Robb wreck, Fairway beacon, Port Stanvac barges and Fred's ground off Glenelg all produce snapper of varying sizes in summer. Again, there is plenty of competition when the big reds show up, but those who know the tides and seasonal fish movements well generally pull enough to make the effort worthwhile. There are also several man-made 'drops' well offshore from Adelaide towards the middle of St Vincent's Gulf, most of which are kept secret by their creators. These produce snapper to 30 pounds from early summer through until March. Some inshore snapper can be caught around natural reef along Adelaide's southern metro coastline, from Christies Beach and Seaford through to Red Ochre at Maslin Beach. Most of these inshore fish are in the 40 to 60cm size range, and respond well after a decent blow.

Drop netting for blue swimmers off Adelaide is very popular with boat owners of all persuasions. Most of the best crabbing takes place within five kilometres of the coast and in water less than ten metres deep, so you don't need a large craft to grab a good feed when the crabs are running. Wonga Shoal, just off Semaphore, is a very reliable crabbing venue, as are the Outer Harbor silt grounds and the area of broken ground directly offshore from the Football Stadium.

There is also good snook fishing to be had in the same areas. Snook are easy fish to catch from a small boat and although those close to Adelaide aren't generally huge, they are big enough to take home. Trolling small lures behind the boat at walking pace is the most popular fishing method and this is often done with the aid of a paravane or lead line to keep the lures well down. Prime snook time is spring through until Easter, when the fish tend to thin out and move further offshore. Schools of salmon are sometimes found by boaties from O'Sullivan Beach through to Port Willunga. When these fish are seen feeding on the surface they respond well to trolled hard body lures and metal slugs cast into the foray, but when the fish push deep, floating down a half pilchard often brings good results.

MAP 42 & 43 ADELAIDE'S METROPOLITAN BOAT RAMPS

There are five major launching sites between St Kilda and O'Sullivan Beach and all offer first class facilities. They are all pretty busy on fine, calm weekends, but nowhere near as hectic as the ramps around Melbourne's Port Phillip Bay.

The newest of these facilities is located at Snowdens Beach on the banks of the Port River. It is well equipped, with dual lane launching and a large sealed car park. This is the first decent launching ramp ever built on the Port River's western side and is a welcome boost for those who fish this waterway regularly.

The St Kilda launching site is a dual lane complex with floating boarding pontoons and spacious car park. A well stocked tackle store/café is located just west of the ramp and this is open quite early each morning to supply anglers with fresh bait, ice and food. Launching at St Kilda provides ready access to St Vincent's Gulf, as well as the Port River and Outer Harbor.

St Kilda is a very convenient site for Adelaide's northern suburbs boaties. It's within easy reach of heavily populated suburbs like Salisbury and Elizabeth and reduces driving time to the coast. At the time of writing (mid 2016), a launch fee of $7.50 applied to St Kilda.

North Haven Marina, located about 17 kilometres north-west of Adelaide, is the largest launching site in South Australia. The complex is owned and maintained by the Cruising Yacht Club of SA and it sees the bulk of our local boating traffic annually. The North Haven ramp has undergone quite a deal of change recently, with the main basin now home to a lot of large permanent berths, but the ramp is still the best in town.

It boasts a massive secure car park, a wash down area, multi-lane launching and plenty of protection in windy weather. North Haven is quite close to most of the better northern metro fishing grounds and is just a short ride from Outer Harbor. A launch fee of $13 applied to North Haven at the time of writing.

Adelaide Shores Marina, situated between West Beach and Glenelg, is a much smaller facility, but one that still sees plenty of traffic. The ramp here was built to replace the defunct launching site at the Patawalonga entrance. Its construction in the mid 1990s heralded quite a deal of controversy, as it was predicted that any marina built in this location would disrupt natural sand movement along the Adelaide coast. There was a lot of public outcry as the bulldozers moved in to begin excavation in 1995, but the facility was completed in '96 and continues to attract plenty of trailer boat traffic. An $11 fee applied for single use launch and retrieve at the Adelaide Shores Marina at the time of writing.

The multi-lane ramp is nestled within a small harbor with strategically positioned breakwaters. It's a bit of a walk back to get the tow vehicle and trailer prior to retrieving, as a causeway links the ramp apron and parking area, but aside from this, Adelaide Shores is first class. Like the other marinas, its entrance silts up from time to time and requires dredging, but this is a fact of life along most shallow coasts in South Australian gulf waters.

The fifth launching facility is well located for southern suburbs boaties at O'Sullivan Beach. The coastal geography here is significantly different from further along the eastern shore of St Vincent's Gulf, as it is quite rocky and the water is generally deeper. The O'Sullivan Beach Harbor is larger than that of Adelaide Shores and the multi-lane ramp does cop a bit of surge occasionally when the wind is in the north-west.

The facility was built in 1983 and received its first major upgrade in 2000, when the ramps were widened, new boarding pontoons were installed and new concrete approaches were laid. A well stocked tackle store is located on site and there is ample car parking to cope with heavy weekend usage. At the time of writing a $10 launch fee applied for O'Sullivan Beach.

O'Sullivan Beach provides convenient access to many of Adelaide's best southern offshore fishing grounds, such as the barges off Port Stanvac, Marleys and Fred's. Many big snapper are brought into the ramp and, in fact, the O'Sullivan Beach Harbor Kiosk holds an annual competition for the heaviest red weighed in. This is also a good stretch of coast for squid and King George whiting, which are often larger than those caught further north.

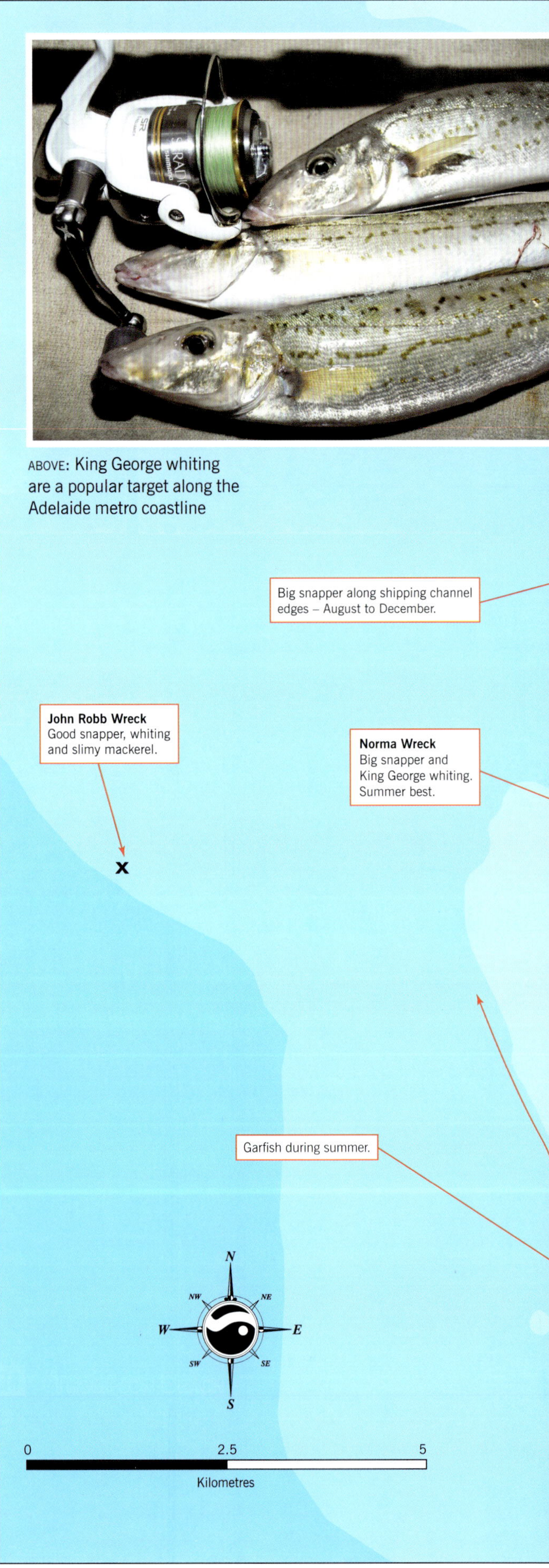

ABOVE: King George whiting are a popular target along the Adelaide metro coastline

MAP 42 ADELAIDE OFFSHORE FISHING – NORTH
Crabs
Spoil
Ground
Silt grounds.
King George whiting,
snook and crabs.
Outer Harbour
Blue swimmers on
shoal in summer.
Largs Bay
Wonga
Shoal
Semaphore Anchorage
Semaphore Reef
King George whiting
Outfall
Blue swimmers
in drop nets.
St Kilda
Salt
Crystalisation
Pans
Point Grey
Barker
Inlet
Pelican
Point
Outer
Harbour
Snapper
Point
Lefevre Peninsula
North
Haven
Gulf Point
Marina
Osbourne
Taperoo Beach
Taperoo
Port Adelaide River
Angas
Inlet
North Arm Creek
North Arm Creek
Salt
Crystalisation
Pans
Largs North
Largs Bay
Peterhead
Semaphore
Exeter
Birkenhead
Gillman
Glanville
Semaphore
South
Ethelton
Port Adelaide
Ottoway
Wingfield
Rosewater
Pennington
Angle
Park
Semaphore Park
Queenstown
Alberton
Athol
Park
Mansfield
Park
West Lakes
Woodville
North
Ferryden
Park
Cheltenham
West Lakes Shores
Woodville
Gardens
Royal Park
Hendon
Woodville
Kilkenny
Albert Park
Woodville
Park
Croydon
Park
Recreation
Park
Sand
0–1 m
1–3 m
3–5 m
5–10 m
over 10 m

MAP 43 ADELAIDE OFFSHORE FISHING – SOUTH

CHAPTER 6
FLEURIEU PENINSULA

Bluefin tuna are readily caught from Victor Harbor during the late summer and into autumn

Situated at the point where St Vincent's Gulf and the Southern Ocean meet, this small peninsula was once joined to Kangaroo Island; in fact, millions of years ago Kangaroo Island was an extension of the Fleurieu that broke away and is now separated by Backstairs Passage.

French explorer, Nicolas Baudin, charted and named the peninsula in 1802 after hydrographer and fellow explorer, Charles Pierre Claret de Fleurieu. It stretches approximately from Aldinga Bay on the western side around to Goolwa in the east and encompasses some 140 kilometres of coastline. Due to its relative proximity to Adelaide's southern suburbs, the Fleurieu Peninsula is extremely popular as a weekend fishing/camping/surfing venue and sees tens of thousands of visitors annually.

There is a wide range of accommodation options on the Peninsula, varying from well appointed caravan parks and camping grounds to upmarket holiday houses, motels and apartments. Tourism is one of the Fleurieu's major money spinners and visiting fisherfolk make a significant injection into the local economy.

The angling opportunities around Fleurieu Peninsula are many and varied. There are several productive surf beaches, plenty of rock ledges and headlands, top class jetties, a handful of rivers and access to some great offshore fishing from several well maintained marinas and boat ramps.

ALDINGA TO CAPE JERVIS

This stretch of coastline, situated at the southern extremity of eastern St Vincent's Gulf, is now quite heavily populated. Urban sprawl has seen housing estates spring up consistently over the past decade, linking previously isolated townships and creating a population band that now stretches from Adelaide's southern suburbs all the way to the northern Fleurieu.

MAP 44 ALDINGA BEACH

Aldinga Beach itself is probably best known as the place where Rodney Fox was mauled and nearly killed by a great white shark back in the 1960s. There is plenty of reef fishing not far offshore for species like snapper, drummer, trevally and Australian salmon and there are yellow eye mullet, salmon trout and yellowfin whiting from the beach when conditions are right. The mullet are best from Easter through until early winter, while the yellowfin prefer warmer water over the Christmas/New Year period.

Aldinga isn't a surf beach as such and has few natural gutters, so it is wise to select a likely location and berley heavily to bring the fish to you. A mixture of soaked stale bread, pilchard scraps and a few drops of tuna oil makes a great berley for mullet, while crushed cockles, prawn shells or razor fish is best for yellowfin whiting.

A few nice flathead are taken from Aldinga Beach in the autumn and early winter and occasionally a school of medium Australian salmon will move in to feed on the afternoon rising tide.

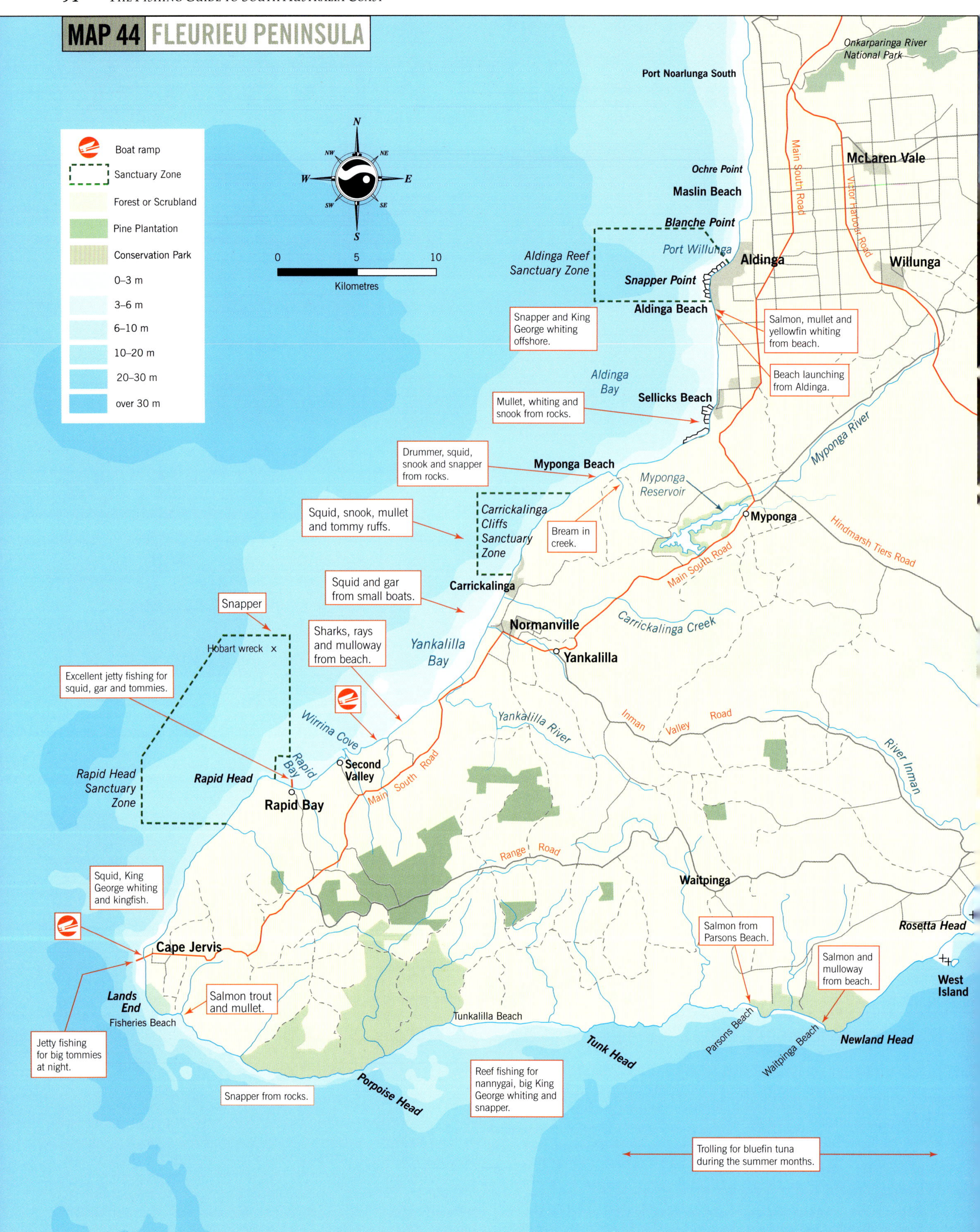
MAP 44 FLEURIEU PENINSULA
Boat ramp
Sanctuary Zone
Forest or Scrubland
Pine Plantation
Conservation Park
0–3 m
3–6 m
6–10 m
10–20 m
20–30 m
over 30 m
N
NE
E
SE
S
SW
W
NW
0 5 10
Kilometres
Onkarparinga River National Park
Port Noarlunga South
Ochre Point
Maslin Beach
McLaren Vale
Main South Road
Victor Harbour Road
Blanche Point
Port Willunga
Aldinga
Willunga
Aldinga Reef Sanctuary Zone
Snapper Point
Aldinga Beach
Snapper and King George whiting offshore.
Salmon, mullet and yellowfin whiting from beach.
Beach launching from Aldinga.
Aldinga Bay
Sellicks Beach
Mullet, whiting and snook from rocks.
Myponga River
Drummer, squid, snook and snapper from rocks.
Myponga Beach
Myponga Reservoir
Myponga
Squid, snook, mullet and tommy ruffs.
Carrickalinga Cliffs Sanctuary Zone
Bream in creek.
Hindmarsh Tiers Road
Main South Road
Squid and gar from small boats.
Carrickalinga
Snapper
Normanville
Carrickalinga Creek
Hobart wreck
Sharks, rays and mulloway from beach.
Yankalilla Bay
Yankalilla
Excellent jetty fishing for squid, gar and tommies.
Wirrina Cove
Yankalilla River
Inman Valley Road
River Inman
Rapid Bay
Second Valley
Main South Road
Rapid Head Sanctuary Zone
Rapid Head
Rapid Bay
Range Road
Waitpinga
Squid, King George whiting and kingfish.
Rosetta Head
West Island
Cape Jervis
Salmon from Parsons Beach.
Salmon and mulloway from beach.
Lands End
Salmon trout and mullet.
Fisheries Beach
Tunkalilla Beach
Parsons Beach
Waitpinga Beach
Newland Head
Jetty fishing for big tommies at night.
Tunk Head
Reef fishing for nannygai, big King George whiting and snapper.
Snapper from rocks.
Porpoise Head
Trolling for bluefin tuna during the summer months.

MAP 44 Myponga Beach

This rocky beach isn't generally regarded as a top fishing venue, although a few yellowfin whiting, mullet and tommy ruffs turn up from time to time. It's the rocky ledges at the southern end of Myponga that attract the interest of visiting anglers and particularly those chasing snook, salmon, drummer and the occasional nice snapper. There are large bronze whaler sharks hooked here from time to time as well, but you've got to have the right equipment and a sense of adventure to land them. There are also plenty of squid caught from these rocky platforms when the water is clear. Casting and retrieving squid jigs is a popular method off the rocks, but some people set a fresh teaser bait under a float, which often brings good results.

The Myponga Creek has occasional runs of bream and some are nice fish indeed. You'll need light tackle and either fresh live bait or soft plastic lures to hook a bream and best times are dawn, dusk and the first couple of hours of darkness. Yellow eye mullet and salmon trout enter the creek when it breaks out after winter rain and these are often easy to catch.

MAP 44 Normanville

There is some reasonable beach fishing to be had around this delightful little resort, mainly for mullet, yellowfin whiting and flathead. School mulloway are hooked from time to time, along with rays and small sharks, but you've got to be prepared to put in long hours on the beach after sunset.

The Normanville jetty is extremely short and sees very little fishing action, but there are a few small beaches and rock ledges between Normanville and nearby Carickalinga that are worth fishing with light tackle. Mullet, garfish and snook are hooked from the shore and there are plenty of squid over the inshore weed beds for those with small boats.

King George whiting are taken offshore and there are several snapper grounds within easy reach. There's a beach launching ramp to the south of the Normanville jetty, but it's suitable only for smaller craft and those with four wheel drive vehicles.

MAP 44 Wirrina

Situated in a natural cove just eight kilometres south of Normanville, Wirrina is the site of an upmarket resort and also a well protected marina and launching ramp. This is the best boat launching facility between O'Sullivan Beach and Cape Jervis and it sees plenty of traffic during periods of fine weather. There is excellent King George whiting fishing on the grounds south of Wirrina and some top class snapper action further offshore.

Snook and squid are also found in good numbers, particularly during the warmer months, along with plenty of big slimy mackerel. The wreck of the Ulonga, a 119 tonne ketch that sunk off Wirrina in 1976, has been a magnet for big snapper since its exact location was discovered. Reds to 30 pounds are hooked around the wreck in the summer months, along with the occasional mulloway and yellowtail kingfish. It's a fair run from the Wirrina ramp, however, and should only be fished from larger boats in good weather.

There is also some good shallow water snapper fishing through Wirrina's inshore waters. There are plenty of natural inshore reefs which produce snapper – mainly pan sized fish – but some better fish to around 8kg are caught, The use of berley and fishing around sun up or sun down are prime times to be on the water for snapper in this area. A few gummy sharks are also caught.

Those with smaller boats can expect to score good numbers of calamari in the summer and autumn, with bag limit hauls quite

Some nice mulloway are caught from the surf from southern Fluerieu Peninsula beaches.

common when the water is clear. Drifting over the inshore weed beds is the most productive technique, normally with a teaser line deployed to attract squid to the boat.

Redfin perch are caught in several of the rivers near the Wirrina facility and also in the lake within the resort. Most are small, but they are easy to catch on tiny lures and make great family fishing.

MAP 44 Second Valley

Located within a comfortable hour's drive of Adelaide, this quaint little township is very popular with weekenders and day-tripping fisherfolk. The short jetty produces consistent fishing for tommy ruffs, squid, garfish and the occasional snook and it's often difficult to get a spot on the pier when the weather is fine and the fish are on the bite.

A well appointed caravan park provides plenty of accommodation at Second Valley and there is also the more upmarket option of holiday units and a motel. There is no boat ramp, but Wirrina is just a few kilometres to the north and provides ready access.

MAP 44 Rapid Bay

The long, deep water loading jetty at Rapid Bay was for decades a major angling drawcard and has attracted thousands of anglers to Fleurieu Peninsula. However, when the ageing pier was declared unsafe and subsequently closed in the late 1990s, a lot of fisherfolk were extremely disappointed. There was much discussion over the jetty's future and when a massive repair/restoration estimate was handed down, it looked like Rapid Bay's fate as a recreational fishing venue was sealed.

Fortunately, the SA State Government recognised the value of this jetty to the Fleurieu Peninsula economy and the decision to build a new structure close to the old one was widely applauded. Although the new Rapid Bay jetty is only about half as long as the original pier, it has quickly proven popular with the angling masses and especially with those chasing calamari.

Bag limit catches of squid are easy to achieve almost year round and especially when it is calm and the water is clear. Garfish, tommy ruffs, silver trevally and snook are hooked from the new jetty as well, but it's probably not long enough to attract the likes of yellowtail kingfish, sharks and other heavyweights for which the original pier was renowned.

Small boat fishing around nearby Rapid Head often yields big snook, squid, kingfish, slimy mackerel and trevally, but launching off the beach here is definitely a four wheel drive proposition only. It's just a short boat ride from Wirrina Marina to Rapid Bay for those with larger craft and it's certainly worth the trip when the King George whiting are biting in springtime. These are generally good sized fish and can be caught in reasonable numbers. Most of the better grounds lie between Second Valley and Rapid Bay and within a couple of kilometres of shore. There are often plenty of snook in this area as well.

MAP 44 Cape Jervis

Located at the foot of Fleurieu Peninsula, this small, but busy fishing village provides access to Backstairs Passage and Kangaroo Island. It is the site of the Sealink Ferries, which operates a regular car and passenger ferry service across Backstairs Passage to Penneshaw on Kangaroo Island.

There is a small boat harbor at Cape Jervis with multi-lane launching ramp, which sees plenty of traffic in good weather. The basin here has been dredged to handle large ferries and it's the ideal place to launch bigger trailer boats. There are several fishing charter operations based at Cape Jervis, most of which fish Backstairs Passage, Kangaroo Island's eastern end and the nearby Pages Islands.

Backstairs Passage is a very productive stretch of water, but it's not easy to fish and isn't for small boats. It is subject to a heavy tide run and regularly chops up badly, especially when the wind pushed against the tide, so it is best left to experienced boaties with plenty of local knowledge. Generally speaking, a boat of 20 feet and over is required and it is mandatory to have an accurate and up to date weather forecast before venturing out.

This is big snapper territory and although the reds aren't as prolific or predictable as they once were, Cape Jervis still sees plenty of good ones brought in. Snapper are the mainstay of the local charter fishing industry and are also sought by commercial fishermen during the summer months. Because of the substantial tide run through Backstairs Passage, it is usually necessary to fish with big sinkers and tackle far heavier than that used further north in St Vincent's Gulf. However, 20 pound snapper are still caught in good numbers, so the effort is generally worthwhile.

Some big gummy and school sharks are caught from the deeper waters of backstairs passage. Fishing around the tide change or during periods of slower tides is preferred in this area due to the flow. You will still need fair lumps of lead to hit the bottom, even during periods of slower tidal movement. Squid heads are popular baits, so too are fillets of fresh fish such as mackerel and herring.

The Pages Islands, situated about 15 miles to the east of Cape Jervis, are prolific producers of big snook and Australian salmon in the spring and summer months. Southern Bluefin Tuna have had a resurgence around the Pages and surrounding waters in recent years after a long absence. These fish are typical school size SBTs of 10 – 20kg, and offer fantastic sport on the right tackle. Trolling 4" to 5" skirted lures has been bringing good results, with the months of January to April being the most consistent period.

There are snapper grounds in this area as well, but once again this is big boat/fine weather territory only. Great white sharks are regular visitors to the Pages, so it pays to be vigilant, particularly when gaffing large fish at boatside.

There is some excellent shore-based fishing east of Cape Jervis, with salmon, snook, mullet, tommy ruffs, squid and a few snapper available. Locations like Fisheries Beach and Porpoise Head attract visiting anglers from time to time, but care should be taken when accessing these areas, particularly if it has been raining.

CAPE JERVIS TO GOOLWA

Access to the coastline east of Cape Jervis is quite limited. There are a few small coves and beaches that can be reached, but a four wheel drive vehicle is a wise option. The further east you travel from the Cape, the more difficult the coastal terrain becomes and safe fishing venues are few and far between. This coast fronts Backstairs Passage, which is a notoriously rough and swell-affected waterway, and extreme care should be taken while rock fishing anywhere along its length.

From the Cape Jervis launching ramp it's a relatively short trip out to the deep water grounds, but you really need to know where to go and when to be there. This is where the local charter operators come into their own. These guys run big, fast boats and know precisely where to go and at what state of the tide you need to be fishing. Most have been fishing their home waters for many years and regularly produce good catches.

MAP 44 Fisheries Beach

Easily accessible from the main road into Cape Jervis, this is a delightful little location that is popular with weekend visitors. It's often very productive for the light tackle brigade, particularly for salmon trout, mullet and good sized tommy ruffs. All you need is a good supply of berley and either pilchards or cockles for bait. A selection of small metal lures is handy in case a school of salmon trout ventures within casting distance.

MAP 44 PORPOISE HEAD

This is a rock fishing area that's not for the inexperienced, but does produce some lovely snapper at times. It should only be visited in good weather and low swell and under no circumstances should anyone consider fishing there solo. You'll need a long handled gaff and relatively heavy tackle to fish Porpoise Head and plan your visit around tide changes.

MAP 44 PARSONS AND WAITPINGA BEACHES

Situated off the Cape Jervis-Victor Harbor Road, both Parsons and Waitpinga were once fantastic beaches for the surf salmon fisherman. However, heavy professional purse-seine netting over many years has changed this situation somewhat and it is now no longer a formality to turn up and catch as many eight and ten pounders as you like. In fact, salmon of this size are now the exception rather than the rule.

Having said that, however, Waitpinga Beach is still a worthwhile surf fishing venue. Most of the salmon are between one and two kilograms these days, but they are still a lot of fun on light tackle and definitely better to eat than the bigger models. Half pilchards, blue bait or squid are the preferred baits, but the salmon will also grab small metal lures or soft plastics.

The headland which separates Parsons and Waitpinga Beaches is a consistent producer of mixed-size salmon and this is where float fishing can be quite effective. Styrene floats on either threadline or sidecast tackle work well and the fish are most reliable either early or late in the day. Whole pilchards, strips of garfish or squid will catch salmon from the rocks, as will metal lures on occasion.

Big mulloway have been taken at Waitpinga, especially during the spring and summer months, and these are always worth a try. The key is to pick a substantial surf gutter and be on the beach about an hour before sunset. Fish through into the night and use either fresh squid, live salmon trout or fish fillets for bait. Naturally, tackle for mulloway needs to be heavier than that used for salmon.

Mullet and salmon trout can be caught on lighter gear for much of the year from both beaches. Autumn and early winter is prime time for mullet, which definitely bite best on a rising tide. A few bream can be caught in the adjoining Waitpinga Creek, especially once the mouth has been opened to the sea at the end of winter. Some big sea run bream are occasionally caught from the surf around the ocean side of the mouth, and offer great eating should you be lucky enough to land one.

MAP 45 VICTOR HARBOR

Victor is the unofficial 'capital' of Fleurieu Peninsula. It has a population of around 11,500, which may swell to over 30,000 during high season vacation periods. It's very much a holiday town and, as such, offers a wealth of services and accommodation options. The town is situated on the shores of Encounter Bay, which was so named by Matthew Flinders in 1802 to mark the historical meeting between his ship, *Investigator*, and *Le Geographe*, captained by French explorer, Nicolas Baudin. Victor is picturesque southern location, with rolling hills surrounding the town and a couple of islands dotted within the bay. These islands buffer the southern swell, which is fairly consistent along this coastline.

Due to its close proximity to and easy access from Adelaide, Victor Harbor is enormously popular as a weekend fishing destination. It offers both land-based and offshore options, varying from light tackle bream through to medium tackle blue water. There's pretty much something for every angler, regardless of experience or aspirations.

Both the Hindmarsh and Inman rivers flow into Encounter Bay and although not as productive as they once were, they still yield nice bream and both brown and rainbow trout in the higher reaches. The Hindmarsh is worth a try anywhere from the mouth to several miles upstream and definitely fishes best for bream when it has had a decent flush of fresh water and is open to the sea. There are a lot of undersize bream in both rivers, so it's wise to use large, resilient baits like rock crabs and unpeeled green prawns.

Victor Harbor has two main fishing jetties – one at the Bluff and the other on Granite Island – and both are worth a shot at the right time of year. Reaching the screwpile jetty involves a lengthy walk across the Granite Island Causeway, which isn't a lot of fun if you're carrying a heap of heavy fishing gear and bait. Some regular anglers load their equipment onto purpose-built trolleys for the trip.

Salmon trout are the staple catch around Granite Island, but the screwpile jetty also produces barracouta, snapper, small sharks, tommy ruffs, mullet and the occasional large mulloway. It seems to fish best during the cooler months, particularly for salmon trout and barracouta, which can be in plague proportions at times.

The small jetty at the Bluff (Rosetta Head) is nearly always busy. You can drive cars right up to the pier, which is a good one for big squid in winter time, as well as tommy ruffs, gar and a few nice snapper after a decent blow. The Bluff jetty sees regular overnight anglers, who often do battle with huge stingrays, seven gill sharks and the odd bonus mulloway.

The shallow waters of Encounter Bay are ideal for small boat anglers when the weather is favourable. It's possible to catch a feed of King George whiting, gar, squid and mullet from a 'tinny', particularly when the outside ocean swell is down and the water is clear. Mullet can also be taken from the beaches to the east, with Chiton Rocks usually reliable in autumn and winter time. School sized mulloway can be caught from Bashams Beach and Chiton Rocks in the deeper holes adjacent to the reef. These are generally smaller mulloway in the 4 to 8kg size, but still offer a good reward for those who put in the time.

Victor Harbor's main boat ramp, located just east of Rosetta Head, was upgraded early in 2009 and is now a first class facility. It features dual lanes, floating boarding pontoons, a spacious car park and short protective breakwater on the southern side. The entrance channel hasn't changed and is still a little shallow at dead low tide, but this rarely presents a problem.

The blue water fishing outside of Encounter Bay can be really good, but it is influenced by the weather and ocean conditions. The Southern Ocean swell often makes life difficult for trailer boaters for days at a time and it's wise to keep an eye on predicted swell height before planning a trip out wide. The stretch of water immediately south of the boat ramp outside Rosetta Head can become quite nasty when the swell is up and there's some breeze about and this is best avoided in a small boat.

Victor Harbor has been a popular location in recent years during Bluefin season, and when the fish are on, it can be hard to secure a park at the local ramp. Long line-ups are the norm on weekends when the weather is fine, and for good reason with plenty of school sized tuna caught a short distance from the Harbor. Tuna have been regular visitors to the reef systems from Waitpinga Head in the west, through to the Murray Mouth in the east, usually in water deeper than 20m. It's been a real boon for the local area. The fish have been falling to skirted lures and hard body lures in the 120mm to 160mm size. January to April have been the most consistent months for schools of Bluefin in this area.

There are two substantial reef systems south of Victor Harbor that fish well in the summer and autumn months and these are extremely popular during the Christmas holiday period. The first of these is about seven miles from the boat ramp. It's good for silver trevally, snook, snapper and slimy mackerel in the summer and also offers the bonus of sea bream (warehou) when the water cools down. Small mako sharks are regular visitors to this reef system and many are hooked on baits intended for snapper or trevally.

MAP 45 VICTOR HARBOR

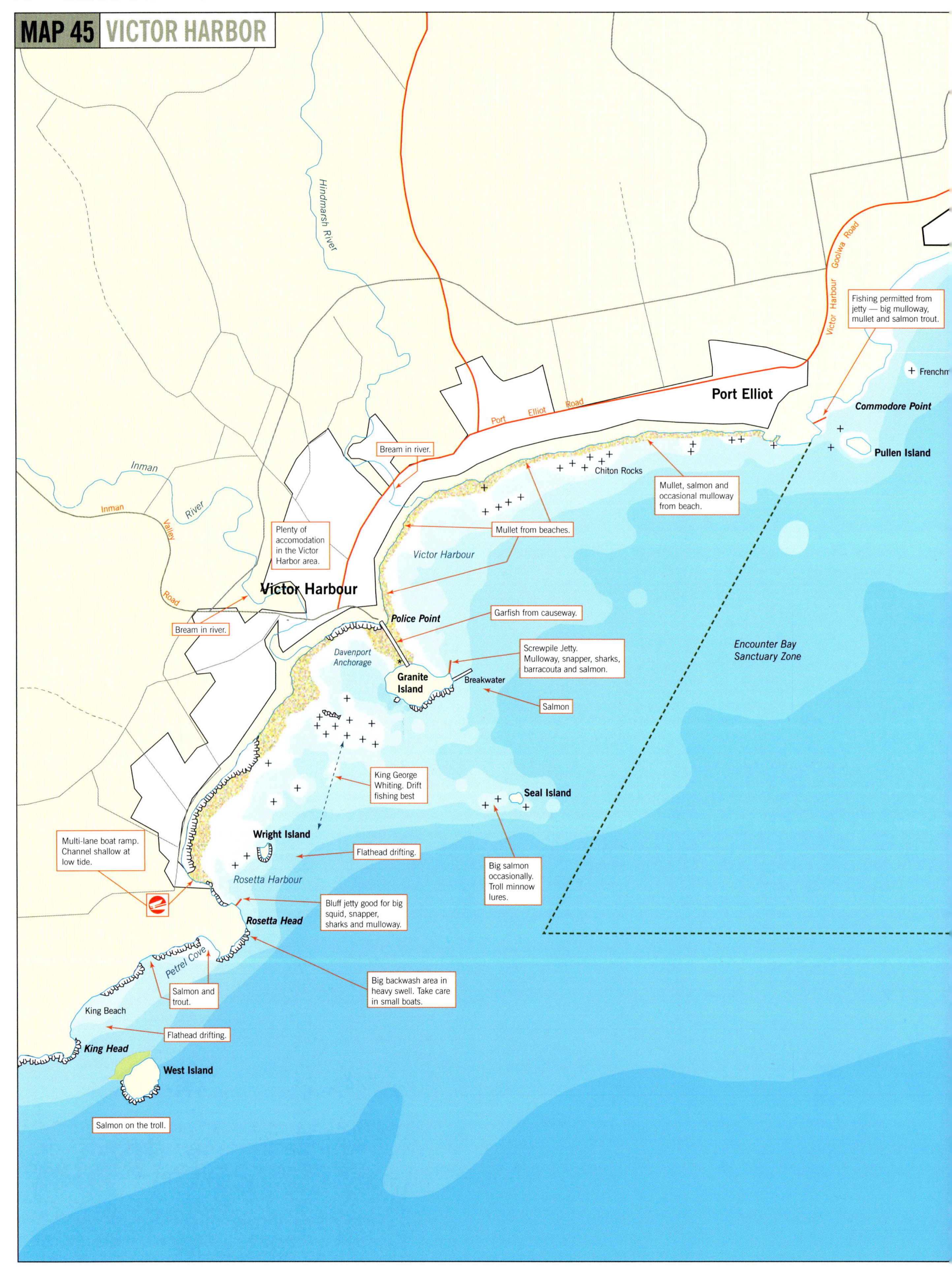

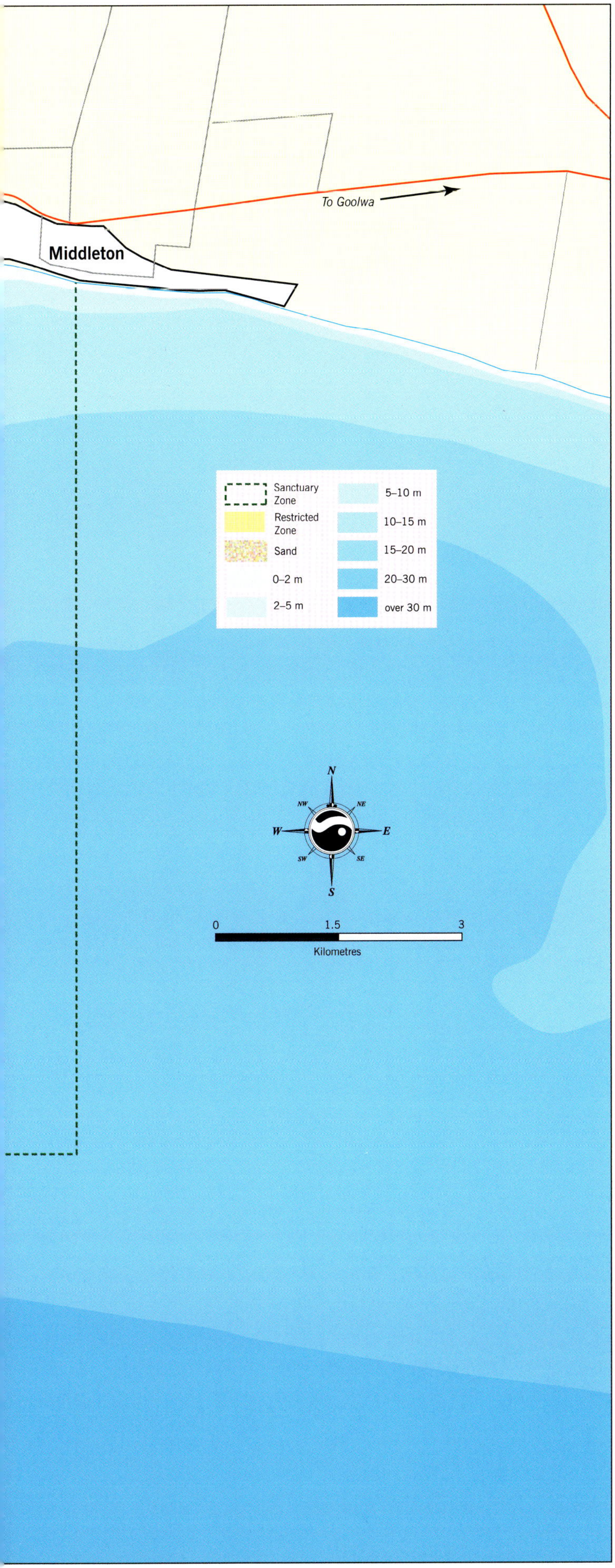

Middleton

To Goolwa

Sanctuary Zone		5–10 m	
Restricted Zone		10–15 m	
Sand		15–20 m	
0–2 m		20–30 m	
2–5 m		over 30 m	

N NE E SE S SW W NW

0 1.5 3

Kilometres

MAP 45 PORT ELLIOT

Located just a short drive to the east of Victor Harbor, Port Elliot is another very popular tourist destination and offers some handy land-based fishing. There is no boat launching, but a few offshore reefs make the trip from Victor Harbor well worthwhile. The short jetty inside Horseshoe Bay often produces mullet and salmon trout, particularly at first light, along with some surprisingly large mulloway and giant black stingrays.

Only dedicated anglers who are prepared to fish all night catch mulloway on a regular basis, however. Live mullet are the bait of choice, but jewies to better than 30 kilograms have been caught on fresh squid heads, salmon fillets and whole dead mullet.

MAP 46 GOOLWA

Fleurieu Peninsula officially terminates at the mouth of the River Murray, which spills into the Southern Ocean about 15 kilometres east of Goolwa. The township of Goolwa is one of SA's most historic ports and was once a busy hub for commercial paddle steamers and cargo vessels. These days, however, it's primarily a tourist town. Goolwa has been affected by drought conditions and fluctuating water levels in years gone by, but these low levels have largely returned to normal, bringing stability back in to this historic township.

One of southern Australia's most popular baits, the Goolwa cockle, is available from the surf beach adjacent to the town. Commercial cockle harvesters work the stretch to the east of the Murray mouth, while the beach to the west is very popular with amateurs keen to stock up on bait for King George whiting. All you need to gather cockles is a four wheel drive vehicle, a bucket and a reasonable day when the swell is down. The cockle season is open from the 1st November through until the 31st May.

The Goolwa surf beach is relatively flat, producing mullet, salmon trout, small sharks and school mulloway, but it's certainly not one of the best beaches along Fleurieu Peninsula for visiting anglers. The Murray mouth, however, is a different story. This has been the scene of some fabulous mulloway catches over the years, with fish to 40 kilograms taken on both lures and baits.

Fishing in this area is heavily dependent on water flow, but is generally best in November and April/May. Heavy metal lures and big rubber tails are proven mulloway takers, both of which are most effective when worked quite slowly. Live and dead baits drifted out into the surf also account for a lot of big mulloway, but this can be a

Goolwa is a well known beach for collecting cockles.

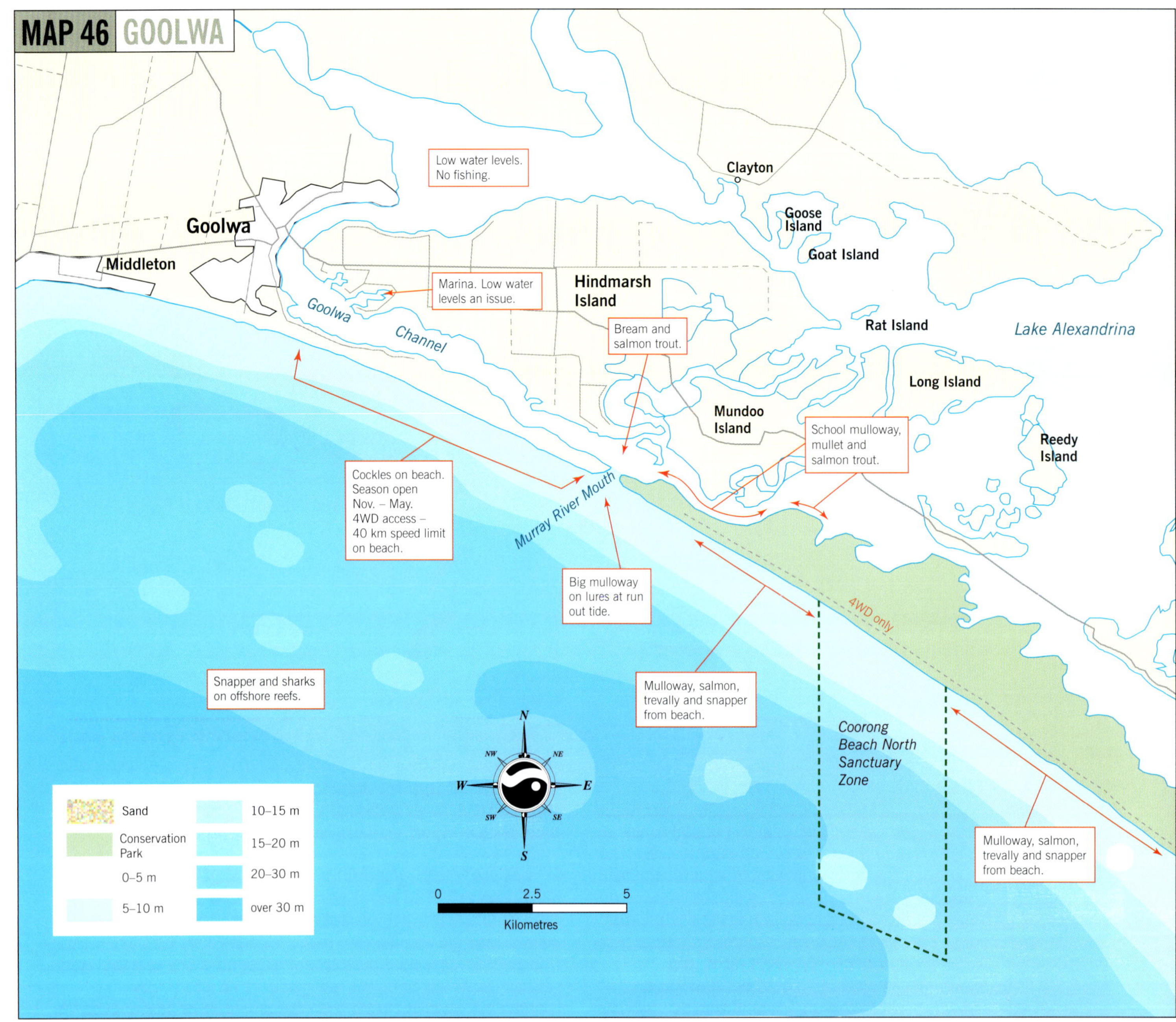

dangerous area when the water is flowing out at full volume. There have been tragedies at the Murray mouth, so taking extreme care is vital. No fish, however big, is worth risking your life over and this should always be foremost in the thinking of any surf fisherman.

MAP 46 Coorong

The Coorong is a large saltwater tidal lagoon, separated from the fresh water of Goolwa and Lake Alexandrina by a series of weirs which regulates the flow into the Coorong. The lagoon waters extend for approximately 130 km in a south east direction, and are separated from the Southern Ocean by Younghusband Peninsula. The Coorong is well known for its bird life, wetlands and natural beauty, but it's also a popular location for fishing for smaller recreational vessels.

There are three main launch sites for accessing the Coorong, No 19 Beacon is a concrete ramp located downstream of Goolwa Barrage, plus Mundoo Channel and Sugars Beach on Hindmarsh Island. Sugars Beach offers the closest access point to the Murray Mouth, but is a sand ramp best suited for smaller boats with a shallow draft.

Mullet and salmon trout are the two mainstay species within the Coorong, offering consistent fishing through the deeper sections of the waterway. Provided the barrages aren't flushing too much water down the Coorong and the flow isn't too strong, setting up a berley pot will soon have fish around the back of the boat.

School mulloway up to around 90 cm are caught within the Coorong, especially by those using live baits in the deeper sections around the Mouth and down towards the Tauwitchere barrage. The size limit for mulloway within the Coorong is smaller than in other waters of South Australia, at 46 cm, with a bag limit of 10 per person. Overcast conditions and a bit of freshwater released from the barrages create good conditions for school mulloway within the Coorong. Some big black bream can be caught in the Coorong too, especially in the Mundoo Channel.

Sand bars and water depth within the Coorong and around the Murray Mouth change regularly depending on the level of freshwater released from the adjoining barrages. As well as affecting the fishing, it also affects navigation, so care must be taken. Camping within the Cooring is a popular pastime, but you must book and pay for your camping permit on-line before you go. Visit *www.parks.sa.gov.au/coorong* to secure your camping permit.

CHAPTER 7
KANGAROO ISLAND

A couple of Kangaroos in the Flinders Chase national park.

If you count Tasmania as a state rather than an island, SA's Kangaroo Island is the second largest piece of offshore real estate in the country. Only the Northern Territory's Melville Island is bigger. Discovered and named by Matthew Flinders in 1802, Kangaroo Island is roughly 155 kilometres long by 57 kilometres at its widest point. It boasts some 540 kilometres of coastline, covers 4,400 square kilometres and has a permanent population of just under 4,500.

Kingscote, Penneshaw and Parndana are KI's three major population centres, with Kingscote being credited as South Australia's first European settlement. It was established in 1836 and is now home to around three quarters of KI's total population.

Agriculture is and has always been very significant to Kangaroo Island's economic well being, but tourism has also become a huge money spinner and the place is now well geared to handle tens of thousands of visitors annually. A lot of those are fisherfolk, who regularly spend a week or longer exploring the coastline or venturing offshore in their boats. Kangaroo Island offers a wide range of angling options, including surf, river, estuary, pier, rock and offshore, so the possibilities are endless.

The Island is accessible from Adelaide by air or by ferry from Cape Jervis on Fleurieu Peninsula. It's just a half hour flight or 45 minute ferry crossing, with the latter option enabling visitors to take trailer boats, cars, caravans and motor homes. The road surfaces on KI vary from very good to poor and it's a fact that a few visitors get into trouble on unsealed roads and tracks each year. Consequently, care needs to be taken while travelling around, particularly in some areas after heavy rain.

The fishing on and around Kangaroo Island is pretty much a twelve month proposition, but there are certain seasons that suit some styles and some locations best. Autumn is definitely the preferred option of those intending to head offshore, as the weather is generally at its most stable and most predictable. This is the time when southern bluefin tuna are available off the Island's western end and it's also a great time for big King George whiting throughout Investigator Strait.

Salmon fishing from several surf beaches is usually at its peak in winter, while summer is best for snapper, snook, squid and garfish. Summer can be a windy time, however, with incessant south-easterly winds making life difficult for small boat anglers.

THE NORTH COAST

Stretching from Point Marsden in the east to Cape Borda at the western tip, KI's northern shore is extremely popular with both land-based and offshore fishers. There is roughly 100 kilometres of coastline, which consists of tall cliffs, small sheltered coves, rocky headlands and a handful of pristine beaches and bays. Settlements are few and far between and fishing pressure is generally light.

MAP 47 Boxing Bay

Once you round Point Marsden and head west, Boxing Bay is the first inlet and provides great shelter from strong summer south-easterlies. It's not generally recognised as a hotspot for any fish variety in particular, but does produce occasional catches of nice King George whiting, snook, garfish, salmon and even the odd mulloway. Boxing Bay is readily accessible from the Emu Bay launching ramp, which is just a five minute boat ride away in good weather.

MAP 47 EMU BAY

Situated just a short drive from Kingscote, Emu Bay is a truly delightful part of KI's north coast. It is very popular over the holiday season, offering both beach and offshore fishing for a variety of species. It has the only established launching facility on the north coast, as well as a short pier and a superb beach that stretches for three kilometres. There's a caravan park (no showers due to a lack of mains water) and several upmarket holiday rental options, most of which are in high demand over the Christmas/New Year period.

Emu Bay's boat ramp features a main central lane and two smaller offshoots to the side. The central ramp is quite steep and can be severely affected by strong winds from the northerly quarter, so it's not for the inexperienced unless conditions are perfect. However, the ramp provides access to some great offshore fishing in Investigator Strait and it's consequently busy on fine weekends and particularly during vacation time.

The Emu Bay jetty isn't a reliable producer of quality fish, but

does yield a few squid, King George whiting, tommy ruffs and garfish when the water is clear. It's a safe pier for family fishing and is within walking distance of the caravan park.

The Emu Bay beach consists of pure white sand and is open to those with four wheel drive vehicles. Each summer a few mulloway are hooked from the beach, along with eagle rays, small sharks and salmon. However, it's the autumn mullet run that attracts most interest from visiting anglers. Plump yellow eye mullet begin to arrive in March and are usually at their peak in April and early May. These are best taken on light tackle, with seaweed worms, pieces of cockle (pippi), mince meat or even bread dough effective baits.

A berley mix of soaked stale bread, semolina and a dash of tuna oil will have the Emu Bay mullet lining up and waiting to pounce on your baits. Most of the fish are good ones of between 25-35 centimetres and, due to the very clean environment, make great table fare.

For those with small boats, squid, garfish, tommies and King George whiting are the staple fare in Emu Bay. Big squid are often prolific and the most productive method of catching a good feed seems to be drifting through the boat moorings with a couple of artificial jigs and a teaser line baited with a whole tommy ruff. Bag limit catches of 15 per person are common when the squid are on.

From a four metre 'tinny' it's possible to catch King George whiting within a few hundred metres of shore. Emu Bay is well protected from strong summer south-easterlies and is ideal for those with 'car topper' aluminiums, kayaks and similar lightweight craft. The reef at Cape D'Estaing, at the western end of Emu Bay, is always worth a shot for salmon and snook, which can be targeted effectively on small trolled lures.

MAP 47 Smith Bay

Heading westward, Smith Bay is just a short boat ride from the Emu Bay ramp and it's a great spot for snapper of varying sizes, silver trevally, snook and some thumper King George whiting. The water in the bay is quite deep and there are several reef systems scattered offshore. Some of these reefs are easy to pick up on the average echo sounder and the usual procedure is to move around until a good showing of fish is recorded. It's then a matter of deploying a berley cage and waiting for the fish to start biting.

Some of the KG whiting in Smith Bay are well over a kilogram each, which makes this a very attractive location for visiting boaties. It's open to winds from north-west around to north-east and can chop up quickly when the breeze gets up, but its proximity to the Emu Bay ramp makes Smith a good small boat option. Trolling for snook is generally productive and the snapper can vary from just legal size (38cm) up to ten kilograms, so it's always worth setting a large bait on the bottom.

MAP 47 Dashwood Bay

The next inlet westward is a favourite with whiting and squid fishers. Dashwood again is accessible from Emu Bay and although there's not much natural reef throughout the bay, there are several low ledges that regularly hold nice King George. Whiting to over 50 centimetres are taken here, with the majority between 38-45. Snapper of varying sizes turn up at times and there are gummy sharks, small bronze whalers and eagle rays for those after some light tackle sport.

Drifting through the shallower parts of the bay often yields good bags of squid when the water is clear and calm and there are garfish, tommy ruffs and salmon according to season.

MAP 47 Cape Cassini

This is the most northerly point of Kangaroo Island. It was discovered and named by Captain Nicolas Baudin in 1802 and again is within reach of trailer boats launching at Emu Bay. Cassini is a substantial rocky headland that is totally exposed to any wind from the northerly quarter, but can produce excellent fishing when conditions are right.

A few snapper are taken on the bottom, as there are plenty of ledges and low reef adjacent to the cape. The best fishing method in this area, however, is trolling parallel to the shore. Big salmon, snook and the occasional yellowtail kingfish are caught by boaties within a few hundred metres of the rocks, usually on bibbed minnow lures. It is also possible to reach Cape Cassini by conventional car and casting metal lures from the rock ledges often yields nice salmon.

MAP 47 & 48 Stokes Bay

There is a small group of holiday homes clustered along the shoreline at Stokes Bay, but not a lot else. The bay is accessible from KI's North Coast Road and it is also within trailer boat range of Emu Bay in good weather. There is a boat ramp at Stokes, but launching here involves navigating through a narrow opening in a fringing reef and isn't for the inexperienced.

The fishing offshore from Stokes is excellent, particularly for big King George whiting and small to medium snapper. There are plenty of offshore reef systems to explore in water depths varying between 15-28 metres, but this area is subject to heavy tidal influence, particularly around the full and new moons.

Gummy and school sharks are quite common out in Investigator Strait and it is well worth keeping a large bait on the bottom for these. Silver trevally of various sizes, blue morwong, swallowtail and nannygai are also available, so a good mixed bag is always possible out of Stokes Bay.

For land-based anglers there is some good rock fishing to the west of the Stokes holiday homes. Salmon, sweep, tommies, King George whiting, snook and squid are all taken from the shore. To the east of the houses lies a beach that can be accessed through a rock chasm and this is often good for a feed of mullet, tommies, salmon trout and a few King George whiting.

MAP 48 King George Beach

This is one of the better rock fishing areas along KI's north coast. Big silver trevally are hooked here consistently, along with the odd snapper and nice whiting. Calm weather is mandatory to try from the rocks and you'll need a good supply of berley to attract the fish. Pilchards and cockles (pippis) are the most productive baits and it's a good idea to use two rods – one set on the bottom and a second with a floating rig. Quite often big salmon will venture in close here and these will scoff a pilchard rigged under a float.

The offshore whiting action here is pretty consistent and there are also trevally, snapper, morwong, nannygai, snook and squid for the boaties. Beach anglers can grab a bag of mullet, salmon, flathead and whiting to the east of the King George holiday houses.

LEFT: A typical catch from KI's north coast.

Admirals Arch in the Flinders Chase national park is a popular tourist location.

MAP 48 Snellings Beach

This is one of the north coast's most scenic beaches and can be very productive for several fish species. School mulloway have been caught here, as well as big salmon, mullet, tommy ruffs, flathead and a sprinkling of King George whiting. The beach definitely fishes best when the wind and swell are down and it can become quite difficult when dead seaweed piles up after strong north-westerlies. There is some good rock fishing adjacent to the beach, especially for salmon, trevally and the occasional snapper.

It's possible to launch small boats from the beach at Snellings when conditions are calm, but you'll need a four wheel drive to do it. Trolling along the rocks to the east of the beach often produces salmon and big snook and there have been small kingfish hooked here as well.

Middle River flows into Investigator Strait at Snellings Beach and this is always worth a try for bream. There are a lot of small fish to contend with, but larger specimens are available for those who know how to catch them. Tough baits like rock crabs are often the answer, but both soft plastic and hard bodied lures will often attract the bigger bream.

MAP 48 Western River Cove

The offshore grounds in this area are legendary producers of quality fish, such as big King George whiting, snapper, silver trevally, school and gummy sharks, blue morwong, nannygai and samson fish. Most of the grounds lie within five miles of shore, but there is no launching for bigger boats within comfortable range, so fishing pressure is generally light. The Emu Bay ramp is a long way to the east and you'll need good weather and plenty of fuel to make the trip.

An alternative for those wishing to sample the offshore action here is a charter service, which is based just west of the cove in a private marina. Kangaroo Island Fishing Adventures takes clients out into Investigator Strait in a large boat and rarely disappoints. This unique operation also offers onshore cottage accommodation.

The beach adjacent to the Western River mouth is often good for nice mullet, salmon, tommy ruffs and a few King George whiting. The river itself is a good one for bream, especially in springtime, and there are yellow eye mullet between the foot bridge and the mouth. Western River Cove has a great camping area with toilets, barbecue and under cover picnic area.

MAP 48 Snug Cove

This small, picturesque inlet is a popular overnight venue for commercial crayfishermen, as well as those with larger offshore cruisers. It is well outside the range of trailer boats launched at Emu Bay, so the waters are lightly fished. Snug Cove is famous for its whiting fishing, with kilogram-plus specimens caught just a couple of miles from the entrance. There are also plenty of grounds that hold snapper, silver trevally, sharks, nannygai and samson fish.

Snug Cove is a terrific overnight anchorage in most weather, as it is protected by towering cliffs, but it can become dangerous in winds from the north around to north-west. Wreckage of a commercial fishing boat was strewn on the beach for several years, providing a timely warning for those who ignore weather warnings.

MAP 48 Cape Torrens/Cape Forbin

This is big boat territory only that provides access to big King George whiting quite close to shore. Whiting to 60 centimetres are taken here, generally by drifting when the sea is calm. Big salmon often move along the cliffs and these are caught on trolled lures.

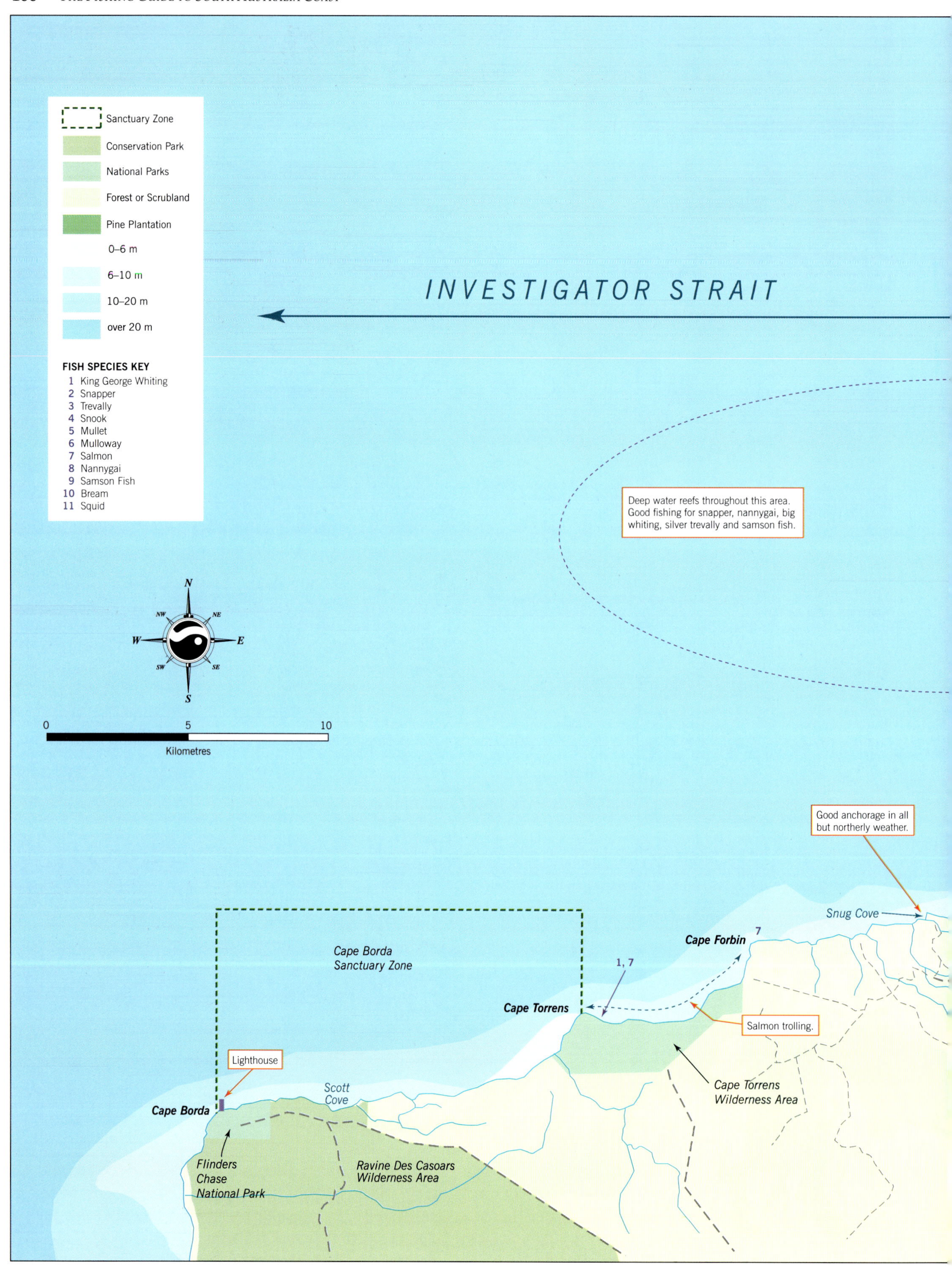

Sanctuary Zone
Conservation Park
National Parks
Forest or Scrubland
Pine Plantation
0–6 m
6–10 m
10–20 m
over 20 m
FISH SPECIES KEY
1 King George Whiting
2 Snapper
3 Trevally
4 Snook
5 Mullet
6 Mulloway
7 Salmon
8 Nannygai
9 Samson Fish
10 Bream
11 Squid
N
NW
NE
W
E
SW
SE
S
0
5
10
Kilometres
INVESTIGATOR STRAIT
Deep water reefs throughout this area. Good fishing for snapper, nannygai, big whiting, silver trevally and samson fish.
Good anchorage in all but northerly weather.
Snug Cove
Cape Forbin
7
1, 7
Cape Borda Sanctuary Zone
Cape Torrens
Salmon trolling.
Lighthouse
Scott Cove
Cape Borda
Cape Torrens Wilderness Area
Flinders Chase National Park
Ravine Des Casoars Wilderness Area

MAP 48 STOKES BAY TO CAPE BORDA
INVESTIGATOR STRAIT
Big tide area.
Good offshore whiting fishing.
1, 2, 3, 4, 7
Stokes Bay
Ledges for whiting and snapper.
1, 2, 3, 4, 7, 11
Cape Dutton
King Georges Beach
Snellings Beach Salmon, flathead and mullet.
Bream in river. Springtime best.
1, 2, 3, 5
Western River Cove
Waterfall Creek Sanctuary Zone
1, 5, 7, 11
10
7
Bream in river.
Western River Wilderness Area
Good bream fishing.
Western River
Middle River
Middle River Dam
Middle River
Cygnet River

THE WESTERN END

The stretch of rocky headlands, tall cliffs and small beaches between Cape Borda and Cape Du Couedic is undoubtedly the lightest fished section of Kangaroo Island's 540 kilometre coastline. It's rugged, exposed to the Southern Ocean and quite remote, so it can only be fished safely in perfect weather. There is absolutely no small boat access.

MAP 49 Sandy Beach

Located at the mouth of Sandy River, this small beach is a very reliable spot for salmon, which can vary from 1-4 kilograms, but generally average 1.5-2kg. They will take lures, but are best on whole pilchards. Also available from the beach are big mullet, tommies, trevally and gummy sharks at night.

Rock fishermen can expect bigger trevally, salmon and snook, but only when the Southern Ocean swell is right down.

MAP 49 West Bay

It is possible to camp in a designated area just above the beach at West Bay, but as this is National Park, permits are required. There is good rock and beach fishing around West Bay, with salmon, trevally, snook, whiting, mullet and sharks all available when conditions are right.

MAP 49 Offshore

Due to its remoteness and distance from the nearest launching ramp, the waters of KI's western end are close to untouched. A couple of charter operators visit this area from time to time and their catches are often spectacular. Southern bluefin tuna travel past in summer and autumn and there are some massive samson fish, yellowtail kings, blue groper, sharks and enormous King George whiting.

Those with large offshore cruisers can expect to do well along this stretch of coast, with West Bay and Weirs Cove reasonable overnight anchorages in good weather.

Remarkable Rocks, Flinders Chase National Park

Weirs Cove

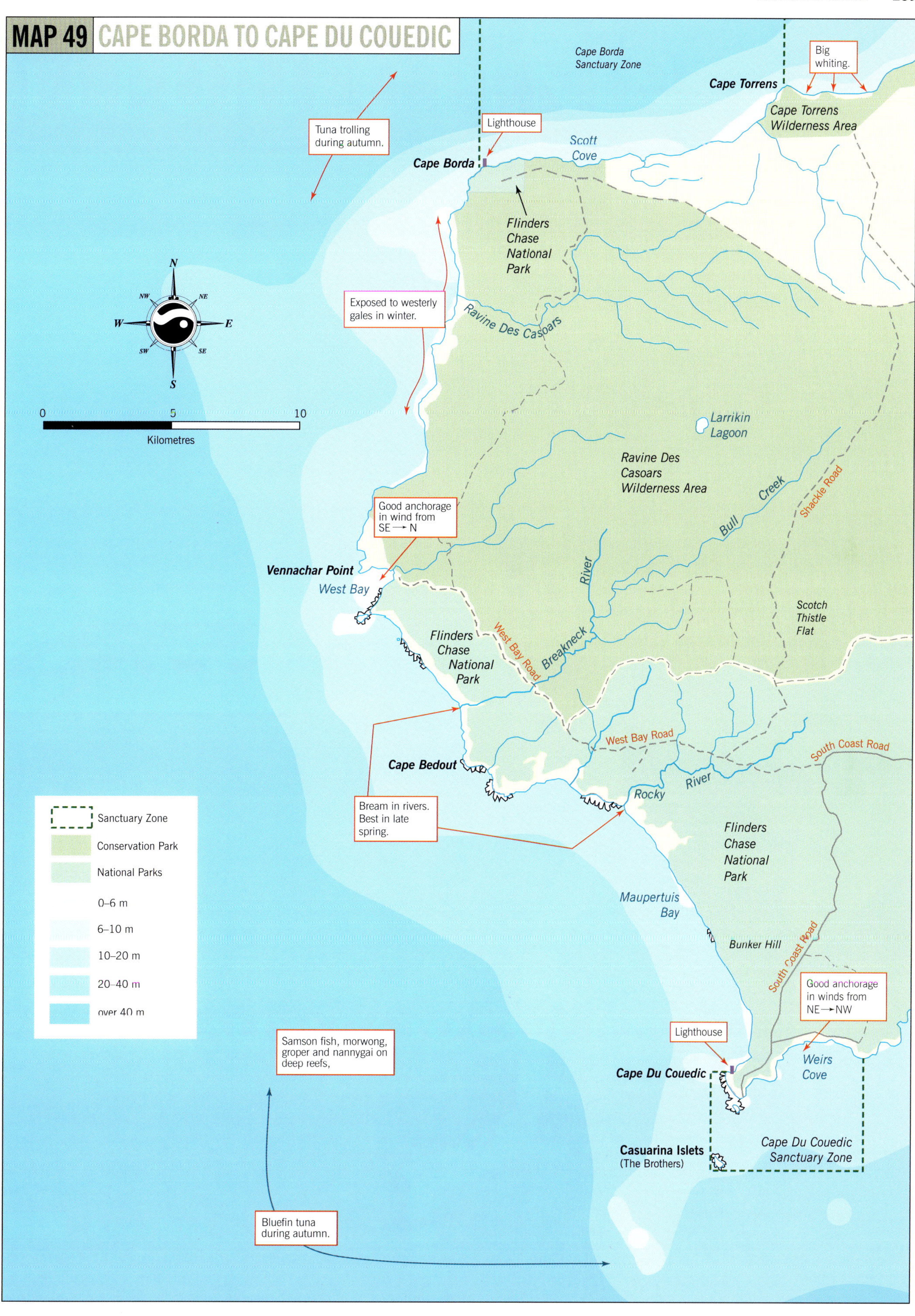
MAP 49 CAPE BORDA TO CAPE DU COUEDIC
Cape Borda Sanctuary Zone
Big whiting.
Cape Torrens
Cape Torrens Wilderness Area
Lighthouse
Tuna trolling during autumn.
Scott Cove
Cape Borda
Flinders Chase National Park
Exposed to westerly gales in winter.
Ravine Des Casoars
N
NW
NE
W
E
SW
SE
S
0
5
10
Kilometres
Larrikin Lagoon
Ravine Des Casoars Wilderness Area
Bull Creek
Shackle Road
Good anchorage in wind from SE → N
Vennachar Point
West Bay
River
Breakneck
Scotch Thistle Flat
Flinders Chase National Park
West Bay Road
West Bay Road
South Coast Road
Cape Bedout
Rocky
River
Bream in rivers. Best in late spring.
Flinders Chase National Park
Sanctuary Zone
Conservation Park
National Parks
0–6 m
6–10 m
10–20 m
20–40 m
over 40 m
Maupertuis Bay
Bunker Hill
South Coast Road
Good anchorage in winds from NE → NW
Lighthouse
Weirs Cove
Cape Du Couedic
Samson fish, morwong, groper and nannygai on deep reefs,
Casuarina Islets (The Brothers)
Cape Du Couedic Sanctuary Zone
Bluefin tuna during autumn.

THE SOUTH COAST

Kicked consistently by the Southern Ocean, this long and totally exposed section of coastline offers much for the adventurous angler. There is great rock fishing in some sections, a handful of productive surf beaches, several rivers and although restricted by weather and access, plenty of top notch blue water fishing.

MAP50 HANSON BAY

There are two beaches at Hanson Bay, both of which can be worth fishing in good conditions. The first beach is just a short stroll from the car park at the entrance to South-West River and it's often good for a feed of mullet and salmon trout. South-West River is one of

KI's better bream waterways and fishes best when the mouth is open and flowing to the sea. Big yellow eye mullet also push up into the river on good tides, providing a bonus for light tackle anglers.

A bit further eastward, a long and often turbulent surf beach regularly produces big salmon, school sharks and a few nice flathead. Dedicated anglers often try their luck here after dark, which is when most of the sharks are hooked. A light wire trace is needed if targeting school sharks, as they are equipped with needle-sharp teeth.

When the swell is down and the wind is in the north, some exceptional rock fishing is available west of the river mouth at Hanson. Accessing the better rock platforms involves a bit of a walk, but the possibility of hooking big sweep, drummer, salmon and even blue groper regularly entices keen rock hoppers.

The Southern Ocean Lodge, Kangaroo Island's premier upmarket resort, is situated at Hanson Bay. This superb facility isn't cheap to stay at, but it is nicely located within a wilderness area and very handy to some great land-based fishing.

River
Eleanor
Big squid, trevally, and tommy ruffs from jetty. Night time is best.
8
8
5 8
Vivonne Bay
Vivonne Bay
1, 2, 3, 4, 6, 9, 12
Nobby Island
Seal Bay Sanctuary Zone
North West Snare
ape Kersaint
Rock fishing for sweep salmon and drummer.
South East Snare (breaks at times)

Sanctuary Zone

FISH SPECIES KEY
1 King George Whiting
2 Snapper
3 Trevally
4 Snook
5 Mullet
6 Salmon
7 Nannygai
8 Bream
9 Squid
10 Bream
11 Sweep
12 Tommy Ruffs
13 Bluefin Tuna

Conservation Parks
National Parks
0–3 m
3–6 m
6–10 m
10–20 m
20–30 m
over 30 m

MAP 50 VIVONNE BAY

This is one of the most picturesque bays on Kangaroo Island's south coast and is home to the only jetty open to recreational angling. Vivonne offers a fair variety of fishing options, including rock, beach and river, and attracts visiting anglers over the course of a year. There is no boat launching facility, but a well stocked general store provides basic grocery needs and fuel and there is some privately owned holiday accommodation within easy reach of the jetty.

Southern Ocean swell rolls into Vivonne Bay when the seas are up outside, which is why commercial lobster fishermen hoist their tender dinghies up onto the jetty. Many large commercial boats have permanent moorings in the bay, which are used regularly during the lobster season.

The Vivonne Bay jetty produces huge tommy ruffs in winter time, with the best fishing available from late afternoon through into the evening. Some of these fish are better than 30 centimetres long and are great fun to catch on light tackle. Silver trevally, snook, garfish and squid are taken from the jetty during the daytime, with a few school sharks taken at nightBoth Harriet and Eleanor Rivers are reliable streams for bream specialists and generally fish best in springtime. Small bream can be a real nuisance when you're targeting the bigger specimens and you'll need tough baits and plenty of patience. However, fish to well over a kilogram are taken by those who know the rivers well. The bankside vegetation is quite thick for the most part, so access is limited. A kayak opens up the options, giving access to overhanging trees and sunken snags that are hard to fish from the shore. Small hard body and soft

Vivonne Bay jetty

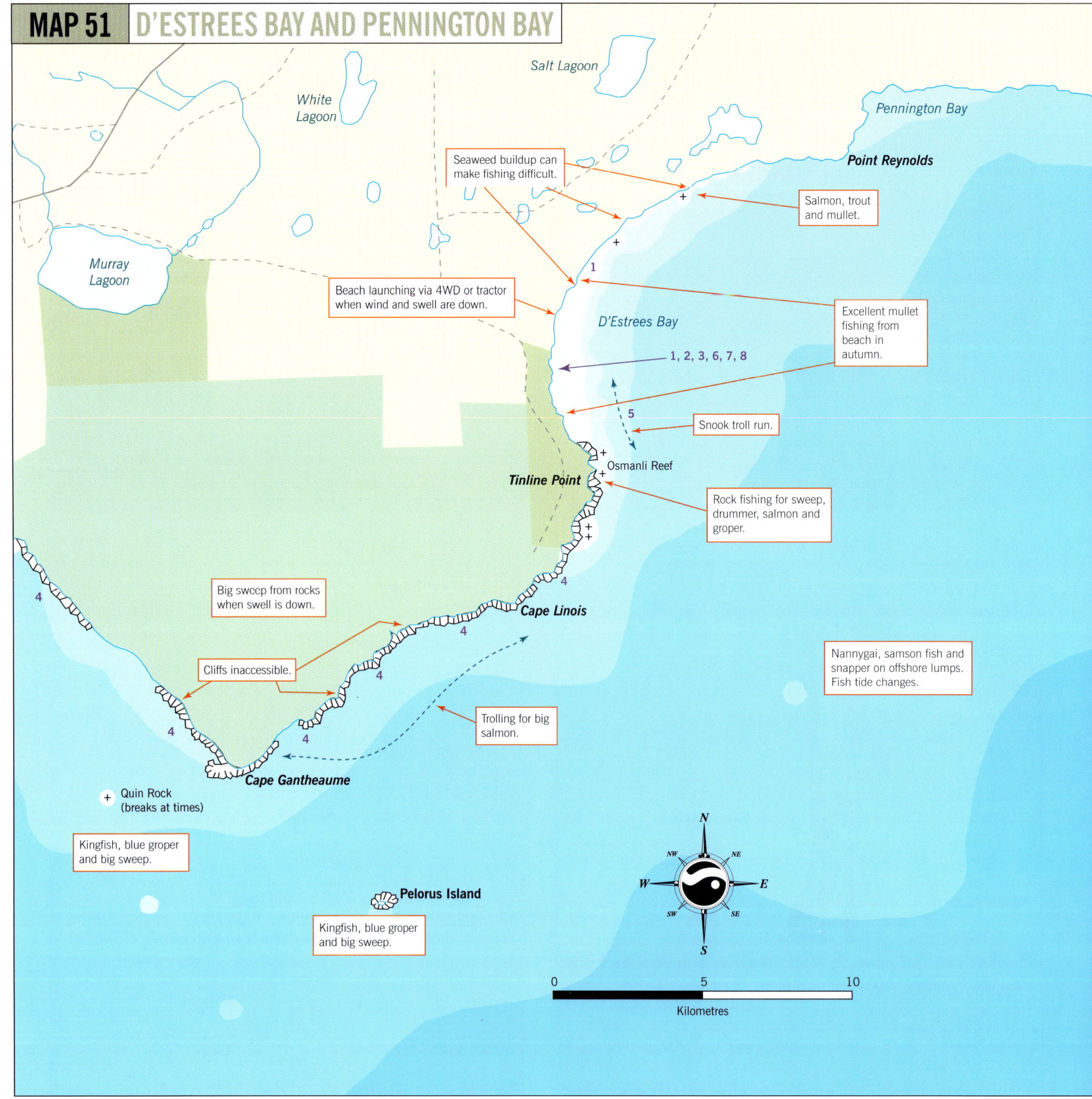

plastic lures in the 45 to 60mm size are preferred, along with baits including green prawns, nippers and whitebait. Using larger baits will help to wean through hoards of smaller fish.

Beach fishing around Vivonne Bay can be quite productive, particularly for salmon and mullet. Surprisingly, a few big bream are taken from the beach as well, providing a definite bonus on light gear. Nearby Point Ellen is a handy location for rock fishermen, with sweep, salmon, trevally and drummer available when ocean swell is minimal. Care needs to be taken when fishing anywhere along this coast and you should always avoid fishing alone.

The offshore action south of Vivonne Bay can be sensational at times and particularly during the autumn months when the weather is stable and the bluefin tuna are running. Young Rocks, which lies more than 20 miles offshore, is a regular tuna haunt and also holds yellowtail kingfish, but only those with big, seaworthy boats should contemplate a visit. Snapper, nannygai, harlequin fish and blue morwong are regularly caught from the deeper reefs wide of Vivonne.

MAP 51 D'Estrees Bay

Named by Nicolas Baudin, D'Estrees is a large, sweeping inlet that provides some good light tackle beach fishing, particularly for big yellow eye mullet and a few King George whiting. Because it's open to ocean swell, the beach at D'Estrees often clogs up with dead seaweed, which can make fishing difficult. Autumn and early winter is prime time for mullet, which often top 30 centimetres and bite strongly on a rising tide. Seaweed worms, which are readily available, are definitely the top bait.

There is a beach launching ramp at D'estrees Bay, but seaweed

ABOVE: Pennington Bay on the south coast is a regular salmon haunt. Check out the school in the centre of the beach.

BELOW: Red snapper are available from the deeper reefs along KI's coastline.

build up dictates that a tractor or robust four wheel drive vehicle is mandatory. The offshore fishing can be terrific, with big KG whiting, snook and salmon trout for light tackle anglers and a host of bigger fish on the deep reefs. Nannygai, snapper, big trevally, small sharks and blue groper are hooked out wide, but you'll need a decent boat and the right tackle for these.

Wreckers Beach, just west of D'estrees Bay, is another location for surf fishers to try. It can be a be a bit hit and miss, but generally produces mullet, flathead, King George whiting, salmon and trevally, and a good spot to try for school and gummy sharks at night..

MAP 51 PENNINGTON BAY

This beautiful inlet from the Southern Ocean is something of an enigma. It looks as though it should be the most productive surf beaches on the island, but in reality it runs hot and cold. Big schools of salmon move in occasionally, providing great sport for those on the beach at the right time. Some of these fish top four kilograms and can be caught on both bait and lures.

Mullet move into Pennington Bay in the autumn, along with some thumper flathead, which can be tempted with soft plastic lures. There are also school sharks to be caught at night and tailor have been reported occasionally.

Rock fishermen can hook nice sweep, trevally, salmon, drummer and leatherjackets from the headlands either end of the beach, but only when conditions are kind.

THE DUDLEY PENINSULA

This substantial promontory is Kangaroo Island's most easterly point and offers ready access to good all-round fishing. Backstairs Passage separates Dudley Peninsula from the mainland and it's in these often turbulent waters that some terrific deep water catches are made. There is also river, beach, rock and jetty fishing available, with the township of Penneshaw a great location in which to base an extended angling vacation.

MAP 52 PENNESHAW

This is KI's second largest settlement and also the closest point to Fleurieu Peninsula. It's from here that the regular Sea Link Ferry Service across Backstairs Passage operates – a trip of some 18 kilometres that takes around 45 minutes. Penneshaw has a jetty that attracts thousands of anglers annually and it's nearly always good for a feed of tommy ruffs and squid. Big salmon enter the bay at Penneshaw at times, providing hectic action for those on the jetty.

Hog Bay can be a very rewarding small boat venue, often yielding King George whiting, flathead, salmon, garfish and squid. This bay is usually protected from most winds except north-easterlies and is ideal for visiting anglers with aluminium dinghies and kayaks.

Just around the corner from Hog Bay lies Christmas Cove, which is now equipped with a terrific little marina and multi-lane launching ramp. This facility provides ready access to both

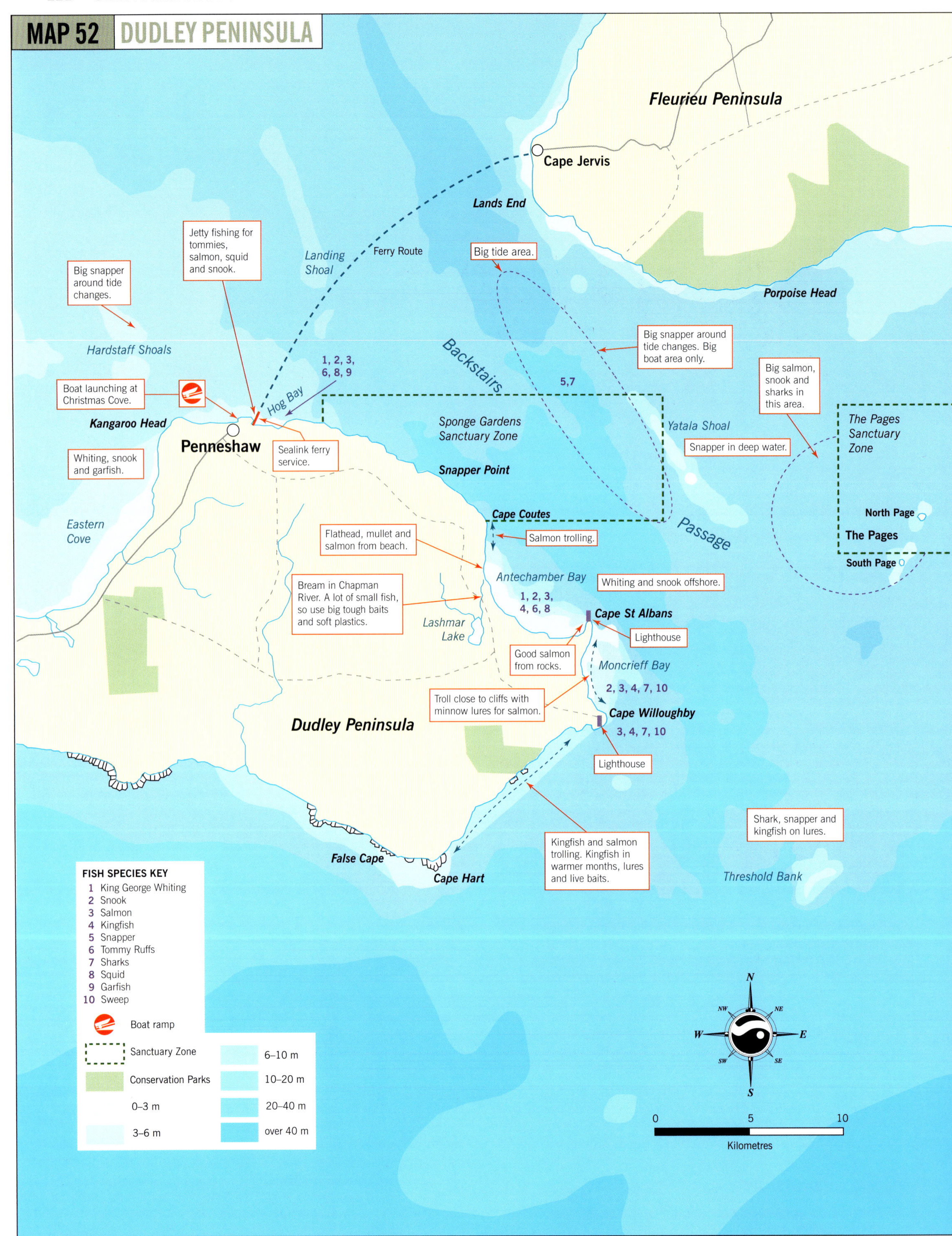
MAP 52 DUDLEY PENINSULA
Fleurieu Peninsula
Cape Jervis
Lands End
Porpoise Head
Landing Shoal
Ferry Route
Big tide area.
Jetty fishing for tommies, salmon, squid and snook.
Big snapper around tide changes.
Hardstaff Shoals
Big snapper around tide changes. Big boat area only.
Backstairs
5,7
Big salmon, snook and sharks in this area.
1, 2, 3, 6, 8, 9
Hog Bay
Boat launching at Christmas Cove.
Kangaroo Head
Penneshaw
Sealink ferry service.
Sponge Gardens Sanctuary Zone
Yatala Shoal
Snapper in deep water.
The Pages Sanctuary Zone
Whiting, snook and garfish.
Snapper Point
Eastern Cove
Cape Coutes
Salmon trolling.
Passage
North Page
The Pages
South Page
Flathead, mullet and salmon from beach.
Antechamber Bay
Whiting and snook offshore.
Bream in Chapman River. A lot of small fish, so use big tough baits and soft plastics.
1, 2, 3, 4, 6, 8
Cape St Albans
Lighthouse
Lashmar Lake
Good salmon from rocks.
Moncrieff Bay
2, 3, 4, 7, 10
Troll close to cliffs with minnow lures for salmon.
Cape Willoughby
3, 4, 7, 10
Dudley Peninsula
Lighthouse
Shark, snapper and kingfish on lures.
Kingfish and salmon trolling. Kingfish in warmer months, lures and live baits.
False Cape
Cape Hart
Threshold Bank
FISH SPECIES KEY
1 King George Whiting
2 Snook
3 Salmon
4 Kingfish
5 Snapper
6 Tommy Ruffs
7 Sharks
8 Squid
9 Garfish
10 Sweep
Boat ramp
Sanctuary Zone
Conservation Parks
0–3 m
3–6 m
6–10 m
10–20 m
20–40 m
over 40 m
N
NE
E
SE
S
SW
W
NW
0
5
10
Kilometres

RIGHT: The Sealink ferries operate between Cape Jervis and Penneshaw.

Backstairs Passage and Eastern Cove, which are both great producers of quality fish.

The rock fishing to the east of Penneshaw is generally good, with drummer, sweep, leatherjackets and salmon of varying sizes all available in good weather. Trolling in close to these rocky ledges often produces plenty of salmon, along with small yellowtail kingfish and big snook.

MAP52 ANTECHAMBER BAY

This is one of Dudley Peninsula's most popular and most productive areas for King George whiting and, because of its relative proximity to the mainland, often draws anglers who launched at Cape Jervis. The whiting are generally big and easy to locate, particularly from April through until September.

Huge snook – some topping three kilograms – are taken in Antechamber Bay during the warmer months. These are generally caught on slowly trolled lures, but will also respond to whole pilchards fished unweighted in a steady berley trail at anchor. Salmon of varying proportions can be expected on the same baits and rigs, but these are generally far less predictable.

Antechamber can be reached by car and makes a pleasant day trip from Penneshaw for beach casters. The western end of the bay is most productive for salmon, mullet, big flathead, tommies and the occasional school mulloway. The Chapman River is one of KI's legendary bream streams, but due to its accessibility and proximity to Penneshaw, it cops plenty of fishing pressure. Bream to over a kilogram are caught among hordes of smaller ones, but you'll have to be patient. Dusk, dawn and early evening are prime times in the Chapman.

MAP 52 CAPE WILLOUGHBY

Marked by a prominent lighthouse, Willoughby is the easternmost point of Kangaroo Island. The surrounding area consists of high cliffs, rocky headlands and a few stony beaches, but much of the adjacent coastline is inaccessible. Salmon are the most popular fish from the rocks around Cape Willoughby and there are a few locations between Willoughby and nearby Cape St. Albans that can be fished safely in good weather.

The salmon vary a bit in size, but generally average 1.5-2 kilograms and will usually pounce on metal lures retrieved at speed. Quite often some bigger salmon will stray into this area and then the fun really begins! They can also be trolled from boats motoring just off the shoreline.

During the summer months yellowtail kingfish patrol the coast between Cape Willoughby and Cape Hart to the south-west, but this is big boat territory. It's accessible from Christmas Cove on a nice day and when the kings are on, the fishing can be quite spectacular. They are often hooked on big, deep-diving minnow lures or live baits such as salmon and garfish. Whichever method you choose, however, the tackle has to be up to the job. Kings are dirty fighters and this is difficult terrain, so don't mess with substandard equipment or tie mediocre knots!

Windmill Bay, which lies just around the corner from Cape Willoughby, holds both big kingfish and salmon to five kilograms at times. You can hook in around the corner of the bay to escape south-easterly winds and this is also a reasonable overnight anchorage.

THE KINGSCOTE REGION

With three quarters of Kangaroo Island's permanent population living in or around Kingscote, it's an area that cops plenty of fishing pressure, but still produces the goods. Treble this figure over the high season holiday period and you can understand that things can get a little crowded.

There's some top notch jetty fishing available here, particularly during the warmer months, and plenty of grounds within Nepean Bay and the Bay of Shoals for the visiting small boat enthusiast.

MAP 53 KINGSCOTE

On a warm, still summer evening Kingscote jetty is a great place to be. The long pier is within easy walking distance of the main street and caravan park and it's generally very productive for those who know when and where to fish. Countless ink stains along the inshore half of the jetty indicate that this is the place to try for calamari and indeed there are thousands caught each summer. Artificial prawn-style jigs are quite effective, although wire jags with a whole fish for bait can sometimes prove superior.

Apart from squid, the jetty is also a beauty for big snook, which patrol the areas around overhead lighting in search of baitfish. Small minnow lures cast out into the dark and retrieved through the light will generally score strikes from snook, some of which weigh two kilograms or better. Salmon can be taken using the same tackle and technique, but these are the exception rather than the rule and shouldn't be relied upon.

Other jetty targets include silver trevally, tommy ruffs, yellowtail kingfish and the occasional bronze whaler shark. King George whiting are also a viable proposition, with the majority caught after dark. These aren't the monster whiting boated out in Investigator Strait or Antechamber Bay, but they are usually well over legal size and often in numbers that make a bag limit catch possible. Cockles (pippis) are the standard jetty whiting bait, but they will also take prawns, worms and pieces of pilchard.

MAP 53 NEPEAN BAY

This is easily KI's most popular whiting fishing area and with good reason. Both commercial and recreational whiting fishermen

MAP 53 THE KINGSCOTE AREA

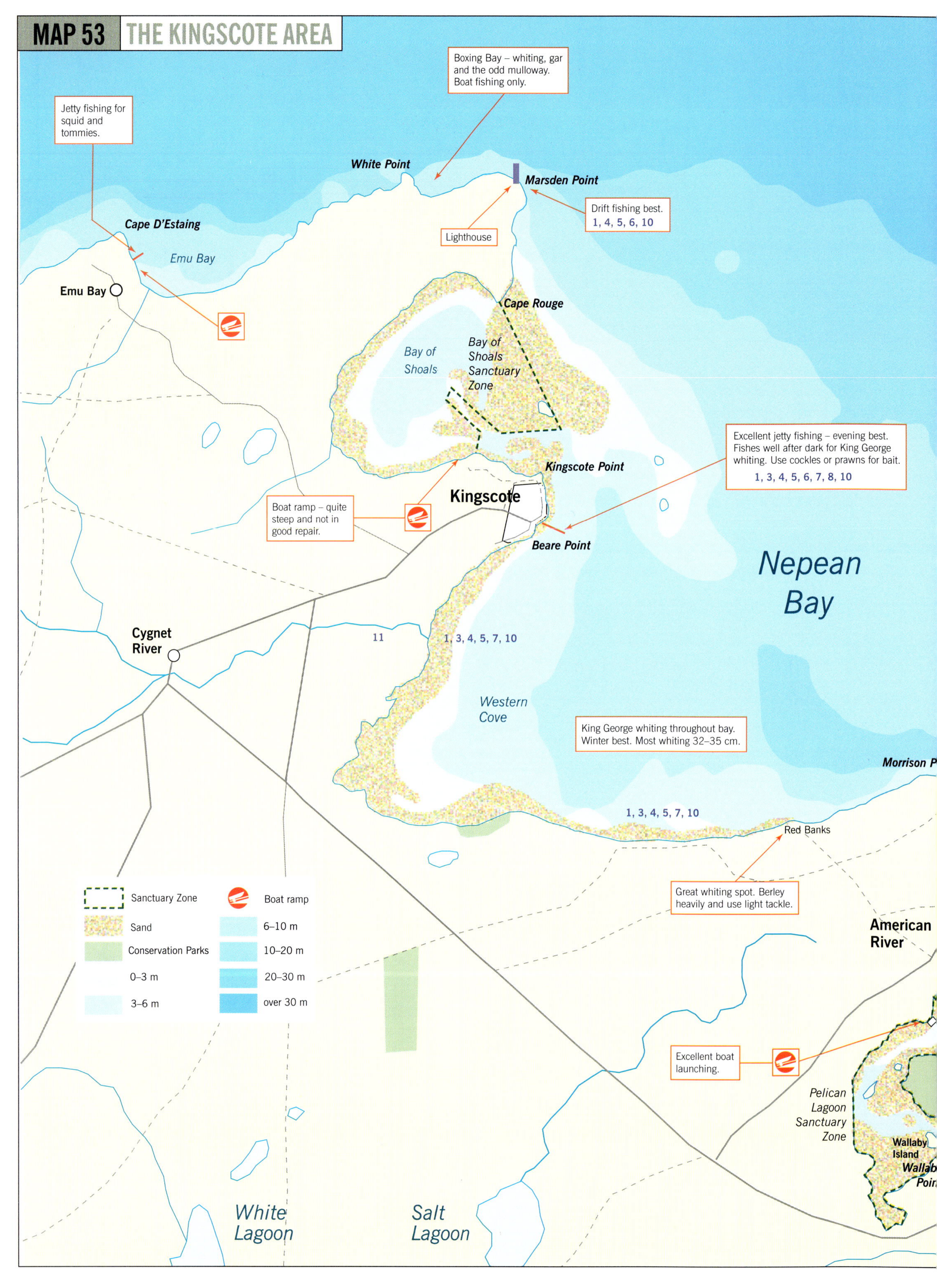

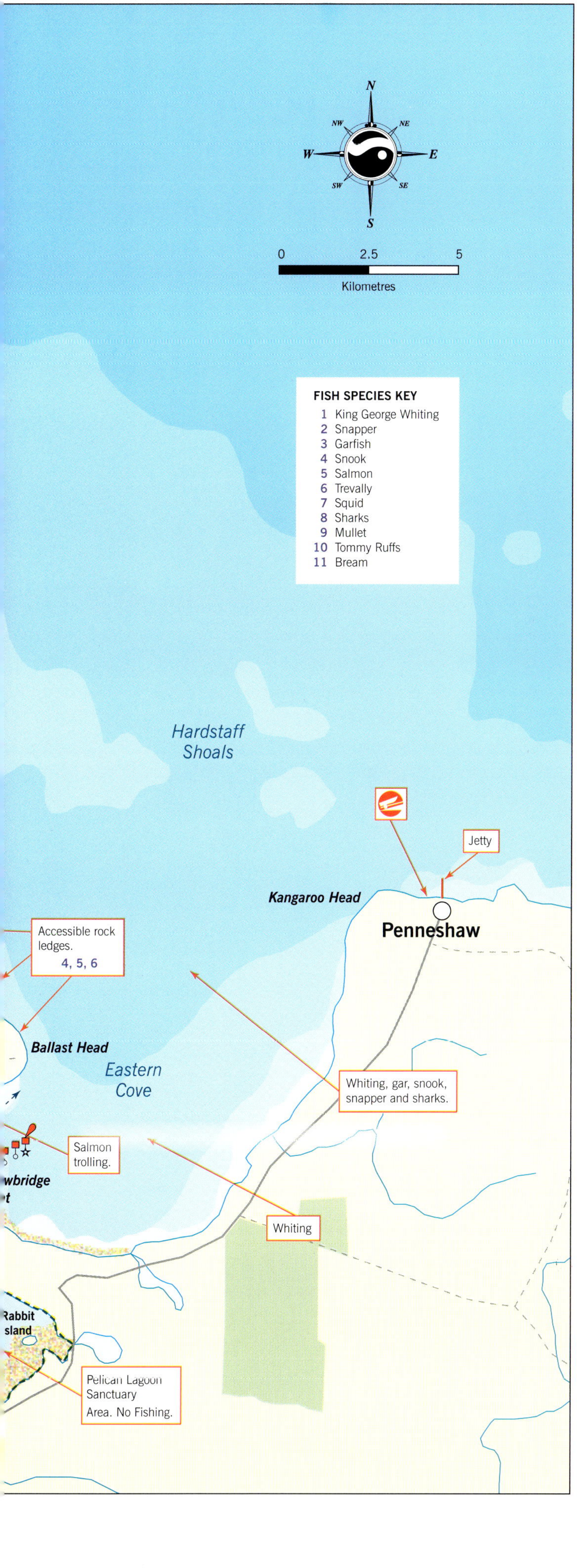

N
NW
NE
W
E
SW
SE
S

0 2.5 5
Kilometres

FISH SPECIES KEY

1 King George Whiting
2 Snapper
3 Garfish
4 Snook
5 Salmon
6 Trevally
7 Squid
8 Sharks
9 Mullet
10 Tommy Ruffs
11 Bream

Hardstaff Shoals
Jetty
Kangaroo Head
Penneshaw
Accessible rock ledges. 4, 5, 6
Ballast Head
Eastern Cove
Whiting, gar, snook, snapper and sharks.
Salmon trolling.
wbridge
t
Whiting
Rabbit
sland
Pelican Lagoon Sanctuary Area. No Fishing.

operate throughout the bay year-round and it's not often they return to the boat ramp empty handed. As is the case in the Bay of Shoals, the whiting generally aren't huge, but they are abundant in certain areas at certain stages and easy to catch.

Red Banks, on the southern side of the bay, is one of the more consistent areas. The water averages around 5-8 metres deep and there's not a great deal of tide flow through this section, so light tackle is a viable option. Hooking King George whiting on three or four kilogram line is a heap of fun and you'll also catch nice tommy ruffs, salmon trout, gar, smallish trevally, snook, squid and a few flathead. Dabbing gar after dark is popular here as well.

MAP 53 AMERICAN RIVER

Originally settled by American sealers in the early 1800s, this delightful little township is situated on the shores of a peaceful waterway that attracts thousands of visitors annually. There is plenty of holiday accommodation available, ranging from a caravan park and camp ground to upmarket resorts and practically everything in between. American River is just a 20 minute drive from Kingscote and a similar distance from Penneshaw, so it is very conveniently located.

The boat ramp is a modern facility featuring floating boarding pontoons and multi-lanes, suitable for trailer boats of all sizes at any stage of the tide. The only catch with launching here is the strong tidal rip across the ramps, but this isn't as much of an issue now as it was before the ramp upgrade.

There are plenty of good fish to be caught in American River and in the adjacent Eastern Cove. Salmon are abundant throughout the narrow channel to the north-east of the boat ramp and these are caught on small trolled lures. The salmon rarely exceed a kilogram or so, but are good fun nonetheless. Snook are hooked in the same location, but most are small.

Out in Eastern Cove there is plenty of good bottom for King George whiting. These fish are generally small to medium, but every so often some bigger KG's show up. Garfish, tommy ruffs, rugger snapper, gummy sharks and silver trevally are among the every day catch and it's not unusual to return to the boat ramp with a very good bag of quality table fish.

The American River wharf is quite popular with visiting anglers and can often turn up reasonable catches. Salmon, tommy ruffs, mullet and a few whiting can be expected, but the wharf area is subject to strong tidal flow and cops more than its share of drifting weed. Whitebait, pilchard pieces and cockles (pippis) are the preferred baits and these will catch practically anything.

Pelican Lagoon, just to the south-west of American River, is one of Kangaroo Island's most important fish nursery areas. It's off limits to angling, but is worth seeing by boat because of its abundant bird life. Tammar wallabies and western grey kangaroos are common around the fringes of the lagoon, particularly late in the day, and round out a truly wonderful wildlife experience.

Some good sized bream are available in the rivers on KI in between the smaller models.

CHAPTER 8
THE SOUTH EAST

Robe Jetty

The stretch of coastline between the Coorong National Park and the Victorian border is known simply as the South-East or the Limestone Coast. The latter name has become quite popular and, given the geographical nature of the region, it really is quite appropriate.

As far as coastal terrain and geography go, the South-East is a little different from much of SA. The entire coast is open to the Southern Ocean, with many kilometres of turbulent surf beach, several large, sweeping bays and just a handful of significant population centres. It's a ruggedly beautiful part of South Australia and one that doesn't receive as much angling publicity as it deserves.

The surf fishing possibilities are many and varied; Australian salmon, giant mulloway, sharks, silver trevally and even the odd snapper are hooked along the expansive Coorong beaches and there are plenty of mullet, salmon trout and garfish in quieter waters. Offshore there are big King George whiting, snapper, gummy and school sharks, as well as barrel-sized southern bluefin tuna, big albacore and mako sharks for those with the right boats and tackle.

There are piers at Beachport, Port MacDonnell, Cape Jaffa and Kingston that produce good bags of mullet and tommy ruffs on a regular basis and some top shelf estuary fishing in the Glenelg River for bream and school mulloway. Facilities for visiting anglers are generally excellent, with well appointed caravan parks, motels and private rental accommodation abundant in most towns. Mount Gambier is SA's largest regional town, and makes a great base for fishing such locations as Port MacDonnell and the Glenelg River.

So, despite its relatively low profile in the overall scheme of South Australian fishing, the South-East has a great deal to offer and is growing in popularity as an angling holiday destination.

COORONG BEACHES TO KINGSTON

It is generally accepted that the South-East starts on the eastern side of the Murray mouth, about 20 kilometres from the township of Goolwa. Younghusband Peninsula separates the protected waters of the Coorong from the Southern Ocean and it's from the beaches fronting this section that some of the best surf fishing in the state is available. Access to the beach can be had in a handful of locations, but some of the Coorong crossings close at different times of the year, depending largely on seasonal condition of the tracks.

MAP 54 The 42 Mile Crossing

The most popular area along the Coorong Beach would be the stretch between the 42 Mile Crossing and the Tea Tree Crossing at Salt Creek. The channels run very deep in close to shore, which means anglers are not required to wade out into the water to cast. The beach north of the Tea Tree Crossing is blocked off to vehicles from October 24 to December 24. This is to protect the eggs and young of the hooded plover that nest above the high tide mark.

MAP 54 COORONG TO SALT CREEK
Lake Alexandrina
Narrung
Albert Passage
Ashville
PRINCES HIGHWAY
Lake Albert
Coorong National Park
The Coorong
Meningie
McIntosh Road
Narrung Road
4WD only
National Park
Conservation Park
0–5 m
5–10 m
10–15 m
15–20 m
20–30 m
over 30 m
Drive along beach until a decent gutter is found. Fish rising tide. Evening is best.
Coorong National Park
Needles Island
Snake Island
Rabbit Island
Magrath Flat
4WD access along entire beach, but sand conditions change constantly. Best with 2 vehicles and recovery equipment.
Beach very exposed to ocean swell.
Coorong National Park
Woods Well
4WD only
Policemans Point
Salt Creek
Beach fishing at Salt Creek for mulloway, salmon and sharks. 4WD access via marked crossings. Beach can be swell affected and can clog with weeds.
N
NE
E
SE
S
SW
W
NW
0
10
20
Kilometres

LEFT: The surf beach crossing at Salt Creek offers mulloway.

Anglers heading towards the Murray mouth should exercise extreme care, as this area is only lightly fished, so all vehicles should be well equipped and in good mechanical condition. Deflating your tyres down to around 18psi certainly makes this sand driving easier, with less strain on the vehicle and less chance of 'chewing' the track for other users. Notify someone of your intended return so a retrieval team can be called if necessary and travel in the company of another vehicle if possible.

Although mulloway are the main prize, they are not the only fish caught along the beach. Flathead averaging a kilo, but occasionally larger are a common catch. Gummy sharks, school sharks and small to medium bronze whalers also frequent the surf and prefer fish flesh baits. The best shark action is generally had at night, with October to December the peak months for gummy sharks along this stretch of coast. Salmon to over four kilograms can be caught all year round, however the bigger catches occur during winter. Even a few snapper are caught from the deeper areas, particularly during autumn.

When camping along the beach for a few days, bait supply can become a problem. If you run out of bait for smaller fish, you do have the option of a readily available supply of cockles when in season. They can be found in many areas along the beach and can sometimes be spotted as the waves recede. Another method is to wriggle your toes and feet in the receding waves to bring the cockles to the surface, where they are then easily picked up. Mullet and small salmon suitable for bait can then be caught in the shallows on pieces of cockle flesh.

Camping on the beach is allowed, but camping behind the beach is permitted only in the areas marked for such. Remember to take any rubbish out with you and if someone else has done the wrong thing, take a few minutes to make it right again.

MAP 55 The Granites

The Granites, situated about 18 km north of Kingston, mark the start of mulloway territory for most anglers, although those with four wheel vehicles will often prefer the deeper water further along the beach. Experienced anglers look for a hole or gutter running close to the beach and preferably with a channel leading out to the sea. These gutters regularly hold baitfish such as mullet, salmon trout and whiting, which in turn attract the larger predators.

The turn-off to the Granites, north along the Adelaide Road, is clearly marked. A three kilometre drive along the unsealed road will take you through to the beach. While mulloway can be caught between the Granites and Kingston, the better water starts north of the Granites. Some of the favoured spots to fish are recognised by the number of miles from Kingston. This is how the '32 Mile' and '42 Mile' names originated.

MAP 55 The Wreck

The Wreck, or '32 Mile' as it is known, is a hot spot. The wreck of an old ship a short distance offshore creates an ideal holding area for fish. It's here that snapper are taken, some of which are well in excess of ten pounds. It's also the scene of some good mulloway catches and the odd big silver trevally.

MAP 55 Kingston

Kingston is described in the tourist brochures as the "northern gate to the southern ports" and is a town that provides strong commercial support for a large number of cray boats and also the agricultural enterprises in the area. It is popular with anglers due to the relatively calm waters of Lacepede Bay and the close proximity of great beaches to the north.

The inshore waters adjacent to Kingston produce catches of King George whiting, garfish, salmon and mullet. A simple paternoster is the best rig for fishing this area, especially if casting into the ribbon weed beds. A flat spoon style sinker will assist in retrieving your rig and tying the hooks above will keep your bait out of the weed.

Releasing a school shark

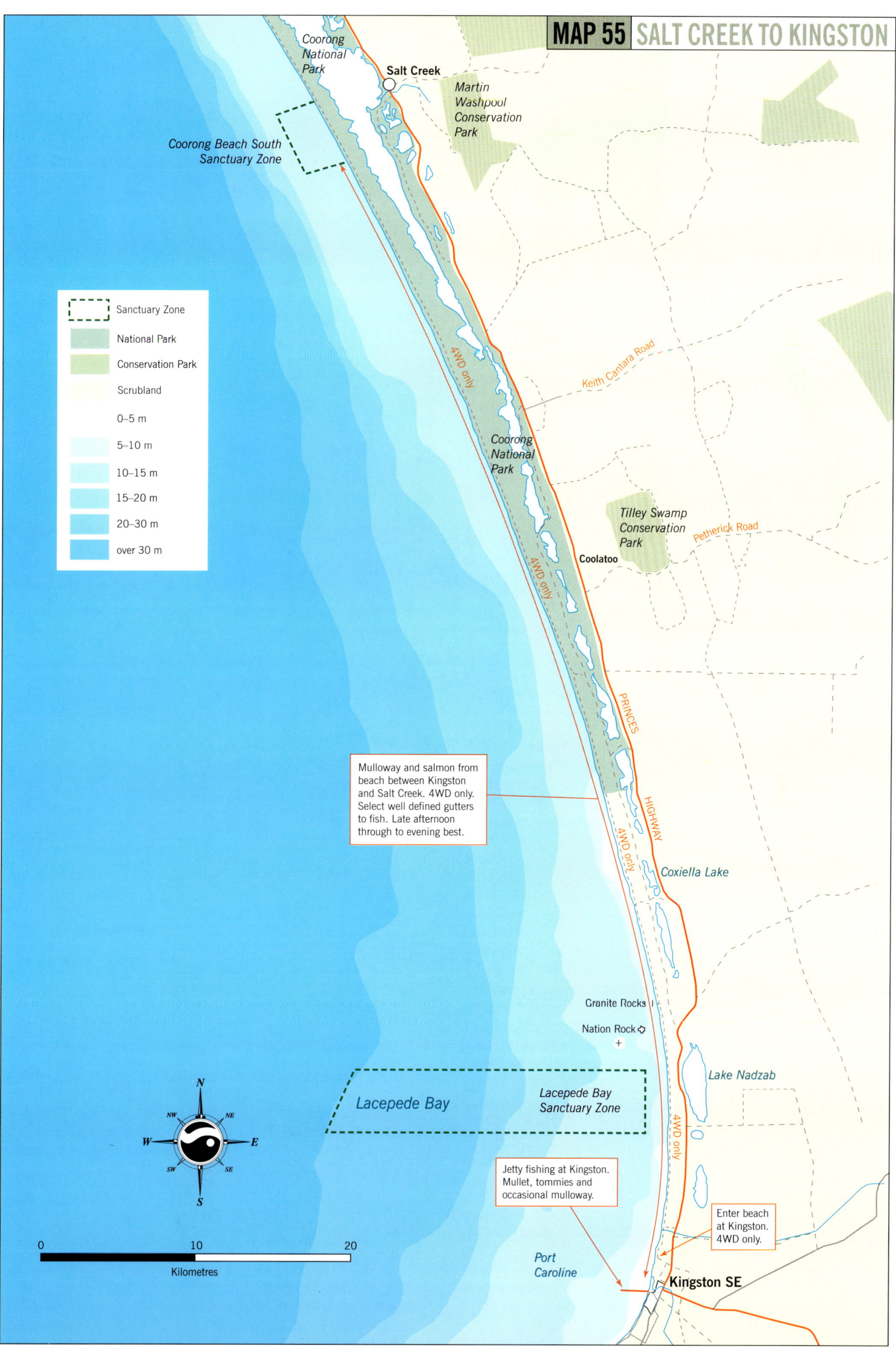
MAP 55 SALT CREEK TO KINGSTON
Coorong National Park
Salt Creek
Martin Washpool Conservation Park
Coorong Beach South Sanctuary Zone
Sanctuary Zone
National Park
Conservation Park
Scrubland
0–5 m
5–10 m
10–15 m
15–20 m
20–30 m
over 30 m
4WD only
Keith Cantara Road
Coorong National Park
Tilley Swamp Conservation Park
Petherick Road
Coolatoo
4WD only
PRINCES
HIGHWAY
Mulloway and salmon from beach between Kingston and Salt Creek. 4WD only. Select well defined gutters to fish. Late afternoon through to evening best.
4WD only
Coxiella Lake
Granite Rocks
Nation Rock
Lake Nadzab
Lacepede Bay
Lacepede Bay Sanctuary Zone
N
NE
E
SE
S
SW
W
NW
4WD only
Jetty fishing at Kingston. Mullet, tommies and occasional mulloway.
Enter beach at Kingston. 4WD only.
0
10
20
Kilometres
Port Caroline
Kingston SE

The drain between Cape Jaffa and Wyomi Beach is recognised as a good area for light surf fishing for flathead and whiting. Using a running sinker rig, cast out towards the edge of the weed line and slowly retrieve for best results. An ideal spot for children to catch both mullet and tommy ruffs is adjacent to the boat ramp and entrance to open water. Another alternative on calm evenings along Pinks Beach and Wyomi Beach is spearing flounder and dab netting garfish. An underwater light will make it easier to spot and net both varieties.

The long pier at Kingston is probably the pick of the South-East jetties. At night, berleying will bring large numbers of nice tommy ruffs in under the lights and excellent catches are common. A good feed of squid can also be caught by casting prawn style jigs over the weed patches and retrieving slowly.

Mulloway of all sizes are regular visitors, attracted to the jetty lights and the baitfish that aggregate in the immediate area. The larger specimens are usually caught on live baits such as mullet, tommies or squid. During the day a few whiting can be taken over the sandy patches towards the end of the jetty and mullet are often plentiful in close to the beach. Worms are an ideal bait for the mullet and these can be dug from the masses of rotting ribbon weed that collects on the beach. Most of the locals choose to fish the right side of the jetty, as for some reason this side produces most of the fish.

For boaties, Kingston's Lacepede Bay would probably be the safest area along the South-East coast. Boat launching is possible anywhere along the beach between Cape Jaffa right through to the Granites, situated about 18 kilometres to the north. A boat ramp through the man-made channel about 500 metres north of the Kingston jetty is a good alternative for those not keen on beach launching.

Off the Kingston coast the bottom terrain is mainly flat and featureless. The broken bottom, consisting of ribbon weed interspersed with sand patches, is ideal for garfish and whiting. Trolling for snook is also very productive using either garfish strips or deep diving lures. The area about a hundred metres offshore from the main drain entering the bay between Kingston and Cape Jaffa is a top spot for snook.

About a kilometre south-west of the Granites is Nations Rock, which has a reputation as a salmon hot spot and is also a good area for sweep, snapper and small sharks. This area can be dangerous, however, and can usually be spotted by the waves breaking over the top of the reef, even in a good sea, so approach carefully and do not anchor too close.

KINGSTON TO ROBE

There is plenty of coastal access along this stretch and also some terrific boat fishing, but it's weather dependent. As is evident from the Giant Lobster, which is something of a landmark in Kingston, this is crayfish territory. A substantial commercial lobster fleet works this section of coast and many of the locals also set recreational pots on the various inshore reefs.

Targeting rock lobsters is very popular, with lobsters being taken diving, setting hoop and drop nets, and dropping baited pots. If dropping pots, you will need to have the pot registered with PIRSA before being used. Note there are tight regulations surrounding the recreational lobster fishery, including a closed season which extends from the 31st May through until the 1st October for the Southern Zone.

MAP 56 CAPE JAFFA

This delightful little resort is recognised as one of the prime boating locations of the South-East. Professional crayboats use Cape Jaffa as a base and in recent years, as the fishing reputation spreads, the increasing numbers of visiting anglers and holiday makers have made this part of the South-East a popular destination.

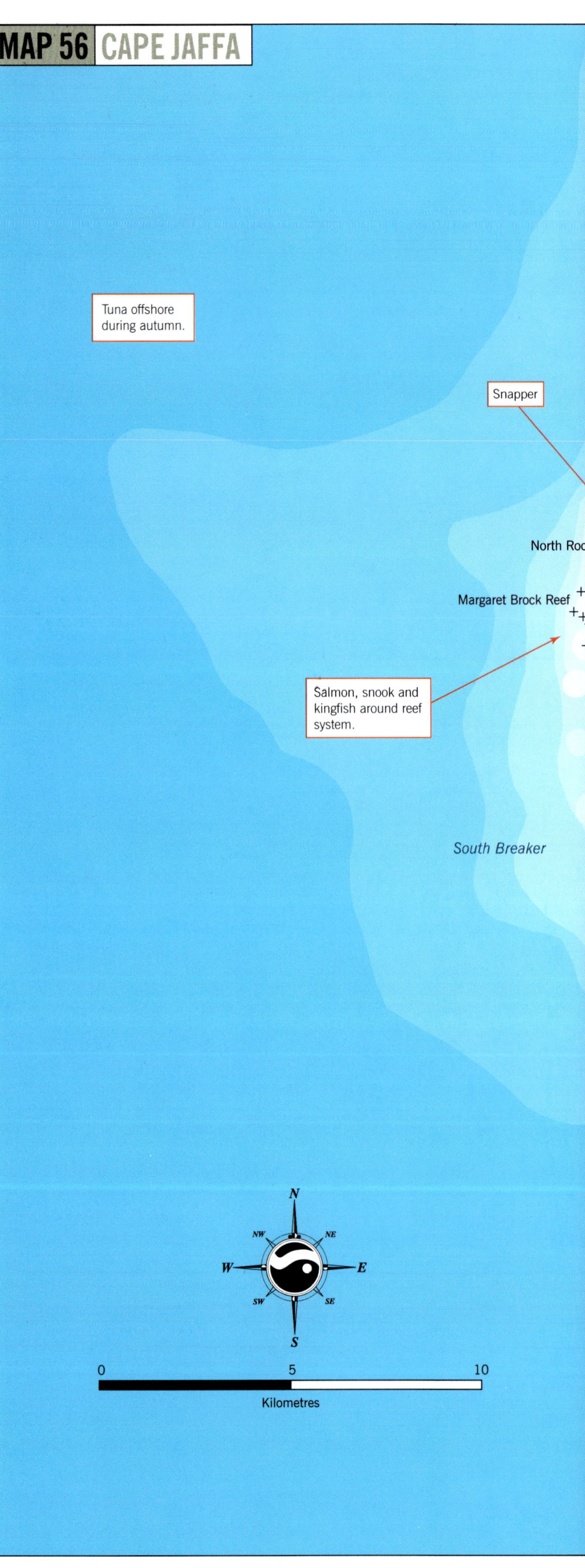

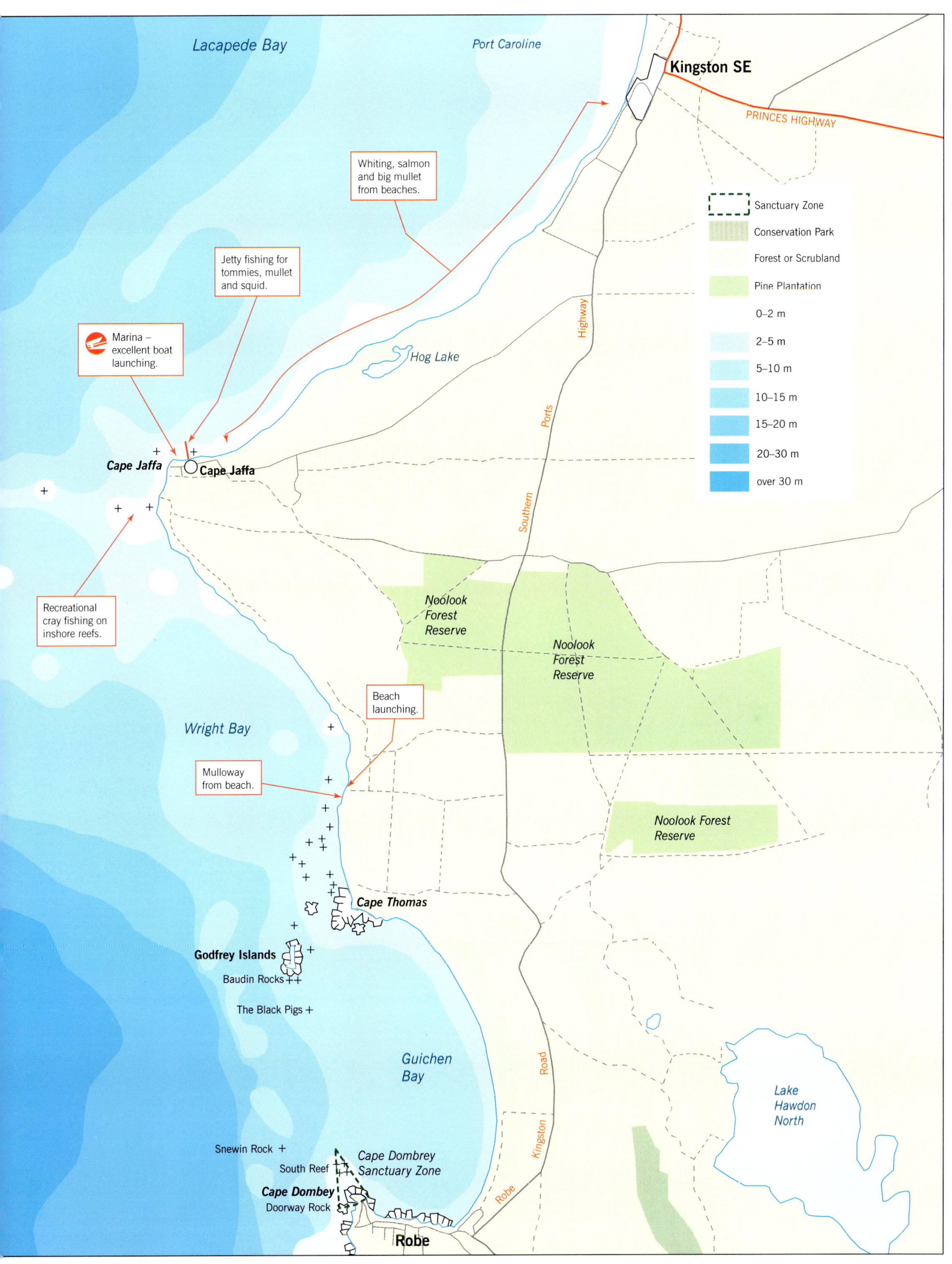
Lacapede Bay
Port Caroline
Kingston SE
PRINCES HIGHWAY
Whiting, salmon and big mullet from beaches.
Jetty fishing for tommies, mullet and squid.
Marina – excellent boat launching.
Hog Lake
Highway
Ports
Southern
Cape Jaffa
Cape Jaffa
Recreational cray fishing on inshore reefs.
Sanctuary Zone
Conservation Park
Forest or Scrubland
Pine Plantation
0–2 m
2–5 m
5–10 m
10–15 m
15–20 m
20–30 m
over 30 m
Noolook Forest Reserve
Noolook Forest Reserve
Beach launching.
Wright Bay
Mulloway from beach.
Noolook Forest Reserve
Cape Thomas
Godfrey Islands
Baudin Rocks
The Black Pigs
Guichen Bay
Road
Kingston
Robe
Lake Hawdon North
Snewin Rock
South Reef
Cape Dombrey Sanctuary Zone
Cape Dombey
Doorway Rock
Robe

LEFT: Giant Lobster at Kingston

100 metres off King Rock and in an area 1–2 kilometres further south. Another popular mark for the same species is the 'Pinnacles', a reef area located about two kilometres from the lighthouse on Margaret Brock Reef. This area is also very popular with divers.

Margaret Brock Reef, about eight kilometres offshore from the Cape, marks a prime location for a wide variety of fish. When weather forecasts are favourable and sea conditions are good, monster King George whiting to well over a kilogram, snapper to eight kilos, big Australian salmon, trevally and snook frequent this area, making it well worth the boat ride from Cape Jaffa.

Good catches of whiting and flathead are taken within a kilometre of the reef and on days with light winds and low swell, some boats are known to travel through the small gap in Margaret Brock Reef. The sheltered area inside the reef is frequented by good numbers of salmon, trevally, whiting, flathead and snook, but some care is needed fishing here. If the wind or swell picks up, it's time to be somewhere else.

Snapper and school sharks are also caught in good numbers in the deeper waters west of Margaret Brock and along the two kilometre stretch to North Rock. Further north from this point North Reef runs for about 15 kilometres. Good catches of snapper and sharks are made in this area, with drifting a very effective technique in favourable weather. Although the fishing can be excellent, these outer reef areas do present hazards and visitors to the area are best advised to team up with other experienced anglers who know the waters well.

The Cape Jaffa jetty is a popular spot for visiting anglers and produces tommy ruffs, garfish, whiting and mullet. Snook are also a chance in the early mornings and evenings, preferring lightly weighted fish fillets, blue bait or pilchards. Fishing at night with prawn style squid jigs often yields a good feed of squid. As with all fishing, berleying from the jetty will definitely improve results.

The recent establishment of a brand new marina is predicted to see Cape Jaffa's population escalate from under 50 to over 2,000 in coming years. Known as The Anchorage Marina, this terrific new facility has been welcomed by most as a true forward step and potential economic boost for the region, but not by some locals, who are afraid of the effect the marina will have on local fish stocks and the environment in general.

Boat fishing from Cape Jaffa right through to Kingston is considered relatively safe due to the Cape and outer reefs blocking nearly all the ocean swell, so the main consideration is usually wind strength. Before The Anchorage Marina was established, most boats were launched from the beach, making a four wheel drive vehicle a definite advantage. Some still choose to launch their boats from the beach about a kilometre east of the town jetty. The concrete slabs will get you through the soft sand down to firmer ground, where two wheel drive vehicles can launch tinnies and small fibreglass boats. The other launching area is off the point at the lighthouse cottage ruins to the left of the township. Access is over a sandy track and is suitable for four wheel drive vehicles only.

A small dinghy and a set of oars are all that are required to put anglers in suitable territory to bag a few whiting, garfish and squid between Cape Jaffa and Kingston. Bottom terrain consists of extensive ribbon weed beds interspersed with sand holes and rock bottom. The edges of these sand holes are the prime areas to target whiting and flathead. If garfish or squid are your target, fish over the ribbon weed beds. Drifting is a popular method of fishing here for flathead, snook and squid. The same species can also be caught on the anchor, together with snapper, whiting, trevally and salmon.

For anglers keen to explore the fishing grounds a little further out, there are good numbers of snapper, school sharks, whiting and flathead caught in waters as close as 50-

RIGHT: Dropping baited pots is a popular way of securing a feed of lobster in the south east.

Salmon are caught from the beaches of the south east.

MAP 57 LONG BEACH

This is one of the few beaches that allows relatively safe access for two wheel drive vehicles. Between December and April the beach is usually quite firm, but care still should be taken to ensure you are not caught by the incoming tide. This pristine beach offers excellent swimming, surfing and fishing. Mulloway are the main target, along with flathead and even a few snapper in the deeper water.

MAP 57 GUICHEN BAY

Boat fishing in Guichen Bay is relatively safe in good conditions. In the waters directly out from the entrance of the boat haven and towards Long Beach, good catches of garfish and the occasional flathead make the effort worthwhile. If sweep and snapper are sought, the reef areas account for the most consistent catches. Quite a number of anglers target the snapper in the deeper water around South Reef, but take care, as waves will break on the inside of the reef.

Baudin Rocks (also known as Godfrey Islands), towards the far end of Guichen Bay and about three kilometres off Boatswain Point, also fish well for sweep, snapper, garfish and trevally. Small reef and weed patches hold flathead and schools of whiting. During summer the area is popular with boaties launching at Robe and travelling the eight kilometres across the bay. However, take extreme care around the reefs known as 'The Black Pigs', as they have claimed a number of lives over the years.

The Baudin Rocks area has large stands of reef and hazardous rocky outcrops and visitors should, where possible, seek local advice or team up with local boats if planning a trip across the bay.

When calm seas prevail and the weather forecast is good, quite a number of boats also head around past Goat Island and fish for

The Obelisk, erected in 1852, is an aid to navigating vessels into Guichen Bay.

Mulloway are caught off the beaches around Cape Jaffa, with the beach along from the lighthouse cottage ruins towards Wright Bay often worth a try. Whiting, salmon and mullet are also caught in good numbers from the beaches around Cape Jaffa and indeed, all the way to Kingston. Flounder spearing and dab netting garfish at night using an underwater light is also a popular activity. October to May is the best time to fish this area, not only because the fishing is at its most reliable, but the prevailing south-east to north-east winds offer good protection along this section of coast.

MAP 56 WRIGHT BAY

Situated just a short drive from Cape Jaffa, this delightful piece of coastline offers quality surf fishing and beach launching for small boats. It can be accessed from the main road between Kingston and Robe or those with a four wheel drive vehicle can take the road south of Kingston through to Cape Jaffa.

The middle and northern ends of Wright Bay are recognised as the best areas to surf fish. The beach is famous locally for its ability to produce trophy-sized fish and each year mulloway over 20 kilos are caught by anglers particular with tackle and bait. School, gummy and bronze whaler sharks are also a common catch at night. Snapper are mainly targeted from the northern end of the bay, where sandy channels run between the reef areas.

Drifting for flathead is popular within the bay and natural baits of pilchard and fish fillets work well, as do soft plastics at times. Whiting, snapper and snook are best targeted on the anchor over broken reef bottom.

MAP 57 BOATSWAINS POINT

This popular weekend fishing venue is situated at the northern end of Guichen Bay, just south of Cape Thomas. Vehicles can travel north from Robe along the Kingston road for 16 kilometres before turning left and heading to the beach and shack sites.

Boating in this area often produces impressive catches of King George whiting, trevally and snapper, but local knowledge is essential to pick your way through the inshore reefs to safer water. Other popular species targeted in the area include flathead, snook and sweep.

Fishing outside the shelter of Baudin Rocks is considered dangerous, but when weather conditions allow, exceptional catches of snapper, groper, sweep and large trevally can be expected.

snapper directly out from Evans Cave Beach, south of Cape Lannes. Using your depth sounder, look for the drops-offs near good reef formations anywhere from 800 metres to 2.5 kilometres offshore, which will put you in prime snapper water. The offshore reef areas off West Beach also account for good catches of snapper. These snapper generally aren't the large models as found up Gulf waters, but are good eating size fish averaging two to four kilograms.

MAP 57 Robe Lakes

Situated just off the Millicent Road on the outskirts of Robe is a series of small lakes linked together as a result of the South East drainage scheme that was cut through to the sea in 1915. Each of the lakes produces bream, but the most popular is Lake Battye. The small jetty and a number of access points give land-based anglers the chance to tangle with bream to two kilos. Best baits include cockles, prawns, clickers, shrimps and whitebait.

Anglers keen to experiment will find that bream will eagerly take small diving lures trolled slowly behind a kayak or an electric-powered boat. Small hard body lures such as Jackalls, Rebel, Rapalas and Attack lures will all work nicely, but treble hooks need to be needle sharp to penetrate the hard, bony mouth of the bream. Mullet of all sizes and even a few mulloway frequent the lakes throughout the year. Small boats can easily be launched from the bank immediately to the left of the jetty on Lake Battye.

MAP 57 Robe

The historic township of Robe is not only one of the prettiest coastal towns in the South-East, it provides access to some truly wonderful fishing. A popular holiday resort during the summer months, Robe offers the full range of accommodation options, from motels, caravan parks and cabins to comfortable camping grounds.

A good place to start fishing for the visiting angler is the boat haven (Lake Butler) at the western end of the town. During summer, schools of small mulloway swarm in from the sea through the channel to feed on the mullet and salmon schools that shelter in the harbour. Most of these fish will be under the 75 centimetre minimum size limit and should be immediately released. Good baits for the mulloway include live mullet, pilchards and squid. Casting weighted soft plastic lures into the deeper water and

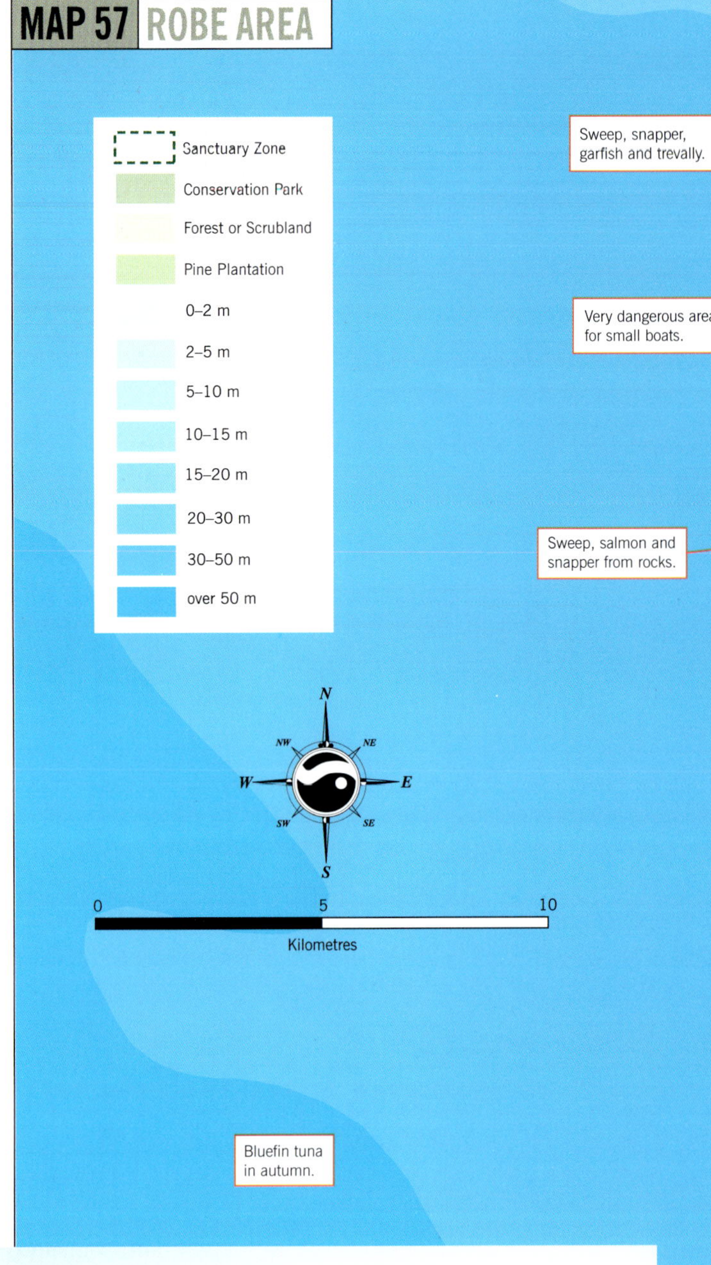

BELOW: Robe, a picturesque location on the Limestone Coast.

retrieving slowly also works very well and it's often possible to hook a legal fish from among the undersized ones. Bream are also a common catch around the pylons and the occasional flathead also joins in the action.

The breakwater outside the boat haven and the jetty further along the beach both fish well for salmon, mullet, garfish, flathead and whiting. Mulloway of all sizes are also a chance. Fishing from the rocks and ledges around Cape Dombey produces sweep and snapper. Try pilchards for the snapper and cockles or craytail for sweep. Float fishing is an ideal way to target the sweep and be prepared to lose a few rigs on the rough bottom if snapper fishing.

There is an all-weather, dual lane boat ramp located inside the marina at Robe which can be used for a small fee. The offshore fishing from Robe can be exceptional, when the weather conditions allow. Some barrel-sized Bluefin tuna in excess of 100 kg have been caught in recent years, along with albacore and big mako sharks. Bottom bouncing the deeper reefs and shoaly bottom produces Jackass Morwong (Terakihi), flathead and gummy sharks. The continental shelf is relatively close to the mainland at Robe, offering access to deep water fishing for larger vessels. Deep dropping baits over the edge of the continental shelf produces some blue-eye trevalla, gemfish, knifejaw and a few prized hapuka.

Robe Jetty where salmon, mullet, flathead and a few whiting can be caught.

ROBE TO BEACHPORT

This is a beach fisherman's delight, but like a lot of this coastline, it is very exposed which makes it mostly weather dependent.

MAP 57 Robe's southern beaches

There is four wheel drive access right through the Little Dip Conservation Park. Intelligent positioning of tracks for four wheel drive anglers gives the option of beach driving or the safer and easier alternative of using the tracks that run just behind the beach. Four wheel drive tracks running from behind the town rubbish tip down through the Little Dip Conservation Park towards Nora Creina provide access to some fantastic surf fishing beaches and rocky headlands.

Anglers without the luxury of a four wheel drive vehicle can still reach a number of spots off Robe. The Nora Creina to Robe road running behind the Little Dip Conservation Park has tracks that go all the way to the beach. West Beach is the first of these and produces trevally during the spring months. Trevally will take pilchard, fish flesh and squid baits. Schools of yellow eye mullet also frequent the sand patches around the rocks, while mulloway and snapper can be caught anywhere along the beach during summer.

Evans Cave Beach is a short, deep beach that is often very soft and can create dramas, even for the experienced off-road drivers. The track running just behind the beach gives adequate access without the risk. The beach regularly fishes well for mulloway, snapper, sharks and trevally. Trying from the rocks further south around Stony Rise on a good sea and low tide can result in catches of sweep and snapper.

Gummy sharks are regular captures from the beaches of the south east.

Back Beach is the best salmon proposition in the area, particularly during winter. Casting lures or bait fishing with pilchards are the best methods for this location.

MAP 57 Domashenz Beach

This is another good one for the surf fisherman, often producing good catches of mulloway and small sharks. Berleying here can add snapper and trevally to your catch. The beach is normally very soft to drive on, so make sure you have recovery equipment in your 4WD and it's wise to fish in tandem with a second vehicle if practical.

Fighting salmon in the surf on light tackle.

MAP 57 The Boundary

This very popular fishing location is accessible by two wheel drive vehicles. Travel 14 kilometres south of Robe along the Nora Creina Road and take the track to the beach. The Boundary is a top salmon producer during the winter months and at times, when the bigger schools are around, it is common to hook a fish every cast. Bait fishing at night when the salmon are in the area could also result in school sharks and mulloway are always a chance.

Further east along the beach are several other top locations for salmon. These can only be accessed on foot due to the rocky headlands and private property blocking vehicular access.

SBTs are a caught in the Robe area.

MAP 57 Nora Creina

The pretty bay at Nora Creina is a terrific spot for the whole family to enjoy a spot of fishing, swimming or boating. The waters inside this small bay are very well protected and provide shelter for both the fish and the anglers. The land surrounding the bay is private property, however access is no problem as long as a few simple rules are followed. Make sure to observe the speed limit signs and take all rubbish home.

Boats can easily be launched from the beach into sheltered waters that are home to whiting, flathead, trevally and sweep around the inshore reefs. At times, large schools of salmon hole up in the bay, providing plenty of action for anglers. Fishing outside the protection of the bay gives experienced boaties the chance to tangle with snapper, sharks, trevally and sweep. However, boat owners should be aware that this area of coastline is considered quite dangerous due to the many reefs east and west of the bay and it is for this reason that the area is only lightly fished.

Flathead underwater

Some nice mulloway are caught from the surf around Beachport.

MAP 58 Beachport

The population of Beachport swells dramatically during holiday breaks as vacationers flock to take advantage of the fabulous fishing and superb surf beaches in the area. The town jetty is one of the longest in South Australia at 772 m and is a great place to start for any visitor. Mullet can be readily caught from the shallows, while further out mulloway, whiting and flathead are a chance.

Each year a few mulloway in excess of 15 kilograms are landed from the jetty, but several more are lost to inexperience, inadequate gear or just plain bad luck. At times, schools of smaller mulloway in the two to four kilogram bracket mill around the jetty, providing plenty of action. The smaller fish will take baits of pilchard or squid, while the larger specimens seem to prefer live baits like mullet, salmon and mackerel.

BEACHPORT TO PORT MACDONNELL

This lengthy stretch of coastline offers a heap of attractive fishing options, from beach and rock to small boat and blue water. It is arguably the most productive section of the South-East coast, but much depends on the wind, swell and general weather patterns.

MAP 58 Rivoli Bay

The waters inside Rivoli Bay are good for all-round boat fishing. Boats can be easily launched from concrete ramps at either Southend or Beachport into relatively safe waters. The cray boat

Five Mile Rocks
Beachport Conservation Park
Rooney Poi
Three Mile Rocks
Point William
Post Office Rock
Snapper Poin
Snapper
N
NW
NE
W
E
SW
SE
S
0
2.5
5
Kilometres

MAP 58 BEACHPORT TO SOUTHEND

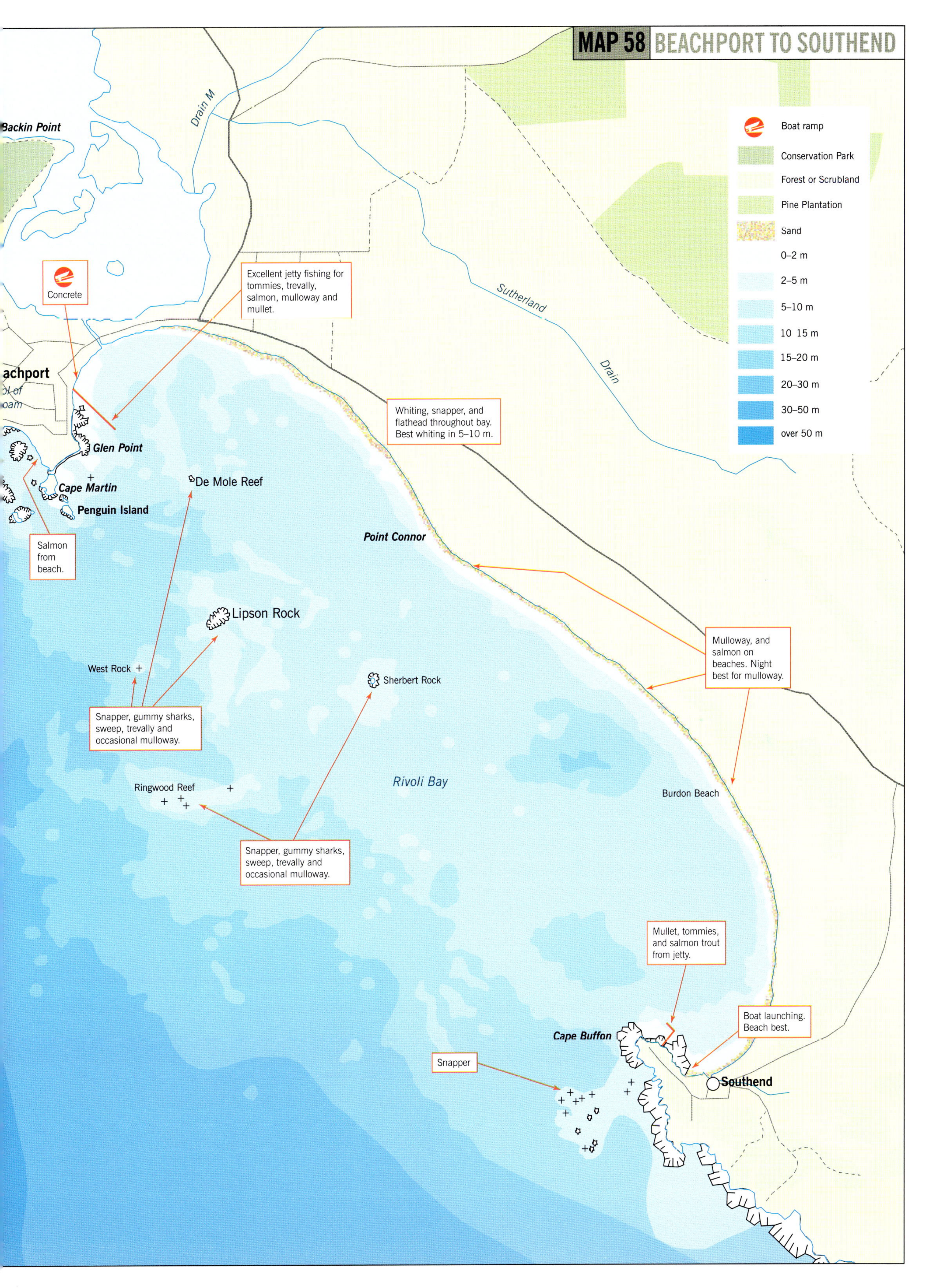

Mulloway of various sizes can be sometimes caught in Rivoli Bay.

anchorages are good areas to start if unfamiliar with the area.

Whiting, flathead, snapper, mullet and salmon can all be caught, along with the odd mulloway.

On reasonable seas and a low to moderate swell, conditions are ideal for exploring outside the anchorages for snapper, flathead and whiting. Look for patches of reef amongst the sand or around the outside of the kelp beds. The better whiting grounds are in the sand areas amongst patches of ribbon weed in water depths ranging from 6–10 metres. When berleying in these deeper waters, it is very important that you make sure the berley goes straight to the bottom and doesn't drift away with the current, taking the fish away from you.

Snapper can turn up anywhere, but tend to frequent the kelp beds and reef areas. Only use sinkers for snapper if your unweighted baits are not reaching the bottom. An unweighted bait is also less likely to snag up on rough bottom. The offshore reefs, namely the Sherbert, Lipson and Ringwood, break in all seas and provide good holding areas to try for snapper, sweep, trevally and whiting. School and gummy sharks can also be caught anywhere in the bay, particularly if using fish flesh baits.

MAP 58 Southend

The small fishing and holiday village of Southend experiences little fishing pressure and provides excellent surf and rock fishing. The town jetty regularly yields good catches of mullet, salmon trout and tommy ruffs, while the beaches and rocks along the Canunda National Park to the east of the township can really fire for mulloway and sharks. The action usually hots up around November and continues right through to the winter months.

To access the top rock and surf fishing locations east of Southend, turn left just over the drain in the township, then follow the four wheel drive tracks down through the Canunda National Park. The beaches along this stretch of coast are treacherous and should not be driven on.

The Southend boat ramp is not a good one, as it runs at right angles to the swell and can create problems for the larger aluminium and fibreglass boats. Most recreationals choose to launch their boats from the beach, leaving the limited parking space at the boat ramp for professional crayfishermen.

MAP 59 Livingstons Bay

Livingstons is one of the best spots for garfish in the South-East. Fish up to 40 centimetres in length are quite common and catches can easily mount into the dozens. Using a feeder float together with

Livingstons Bay is a good location for garfish.

size 12 hooks and gents (blowfly maggots) generally brings good results.

Snapper are sometimes caught around the outer reefs in the deeper areas, however the waters outside the shelter of these reefs are only fished during ideal conditions.

Whiting are seldom targeted in the bay, but sometimes schools turn up in the berley trails meant for garfish and readily take float rigs in the shallow water. Large snook frequent the shallow waters of the bay during the summer months and a favoured method here is to slowly troll dead garfish around the kelp and ribbon weed beds.

Often large schools of salmon visit the bay, providing fabulous sportfishing. Most are caught from boats trolling lures. Shallow diving minnows, metal lures or trolled pieces of plastic tubing all work well. The pieces of tubing create a bubble trail on the surface that salmon can't resist.

Boat launching is difficult anywhere along the beach due to the shallow water. The easiest spots for launching lie at either end of the bay or alternatively launch at Blackfellows Caves on calm seas only. Wading out through the shallow water and berleying can result in catches of garfish, mullet and, to a lesser extent, whiting.

Salmon shelter from the weather inside the reef at Cape Banks Lighthouse area.

MAP 59 Nene Valley

This is one of those places that has something to offer everyone and this includes good beach and boat fishing and safe swimming areas for the family. The town was named after a ship travelling from London and bound for Portland that was wrecked on reef nearby in 1854. The township has no public facilities or accommodation and consists mainly of holiday shacks. The beach in front of the shacks holds good numbers of King George whiting, garfish, salmon and mullet.

MAP 59 Cape Banks

The Cape Banks Lighthouse area, just north of Carpenter Rocks, is one of the most popular beaches in the area. It is a favourite with anglers targeting salmon during the winter months. When rough seas prevail and most other beaches are unfishable, this spot really fires. The salmon shelter from the weather inside the reef and provide fantastic action for lure casters. The best spot to try is just to the right of the rocks below the lighthouse. The reef here runs at right angles to the beach and this is usually where the salmon shelter.

King George whiting is a popular target throughout the area.

To the left of the rocks in the corner of Red Rock Bay is another good spot to try. It is an ideal location for lure casting, as the wind is usually behind you during winter. If bait fishing, try further along the beach, as the bottom is quite snaggy near the point. A favourite technique with locals is to wade through the channel between the two large rocks and climb onto the smaller rocks on the left, giving access to deeper water.

The beach is suitable for four wheel drive vehicles only and provides opportunity to launch aluminium and smaller fibreglass boats. This is best done in the small, sandy channel up towards the large rocks where the sand is firmer. The whiting fishing is at its best during summer and autumn when the water is stirred up following rough seas. Good whiting can also be caught off the beach, with small pieces of squid being the ideal bait.

Red Rock Bay to the east of the lighthouse provides good boat fishing for whiting and garfish. Fish the edges of the weed beds and reef areas for best results. Boat launching off the beach can be done at either end of the bay, with the eastern end the easiest.

MAP 59 Port MacDonnell

The Port MacDonnell area offers the full range of fishing options, including jetty, surf, rock, boat and offshore fishing. The jetty is a popular place for the family to fish in relative comfort and safety. It fishes well all year round, with the summer months the most productive. Mulloway are occasionally caught and are usually taken on live baits such as salmon, mackerel or squid.

Tommy ruffs are often prolific around the lights during the night, although they can be difficult to get into a feeding mood.

Cape Buffon
Southend
Canunda Conservation Reserve
Millicent
Cullen Bay
McIntyre Beach
Canunda National Park
Canunda Sanctuary Zone
Nangula
Snugge
Canunda National Park
Lake Bonney
Boat ramp
Sanctuary Zone
National Parks
Conservation Park
Forest or Scrubland
Pine Plantation
0–5 m
5–10 m
10–15 m
15–20 m
20–30 m
30–50 m
50–100 m
over 100 m
Benara Creek
Salmon during winter from beach. Good location for lure casting inside reef when it's too rough outside.
Cape Banks
Carpenter Rocks
Carpenter Rocks
Bucks Bay
Pelican Point
Bungaloo Bay
N
NW
NE
W
E
SW
SE
S
Nene Valley – good beach fishing for King George whiting, garfish, salmon and mullet.
0
5
10
Kilometres
Bluefin tuna, albacore and sharks.

Wepar
Lake Leake
Allendale
Lake Edward
Tarpeena
Glencoe
PRINCES
HIGHWAY
Dartboogie
Burrungule
HIGHWAY
GLENELG
VICTORIA
Mitchell
Sutton Town
Compton
Attamurra
Mount Gambier
Burnda
Valley Lake
Blue Lake
Willowvale
Glenburnie
Kongorong
Road
Neechy Flat
Murrawa
Moorak
O B Flat
Days Hill
Yahl
Coratum
Road
Sisters
Road
Kongorong
Gums
SOUTH AUSTRALIA
Caveton
ellows Caves
Mount Gambier Forest Reserve
Livingstons – big garfish inshore and snapper offshore.
Nene Valley
Glenelg
River
Rock
Punt
Snapper
good concrete
Allendale East
Lower Glenelg National Park
Road
Jetty fishing for whiting, tommies and the odd mulloway.
Eight Mile Creek
Douglas Point
Port MacDonnell
Eight Mile Creek Road
Brown Beach
Nelson
Middle Point
Riddoch Bay
Brown Bay
Danger Point
Green Point
Sweep and salmon from rocks.
Cape Northumberland
Stoney Point
Piccaninnie Ponds Sanctuary Zone
Salmon and whiting from breakwater.
Ruby Rock
Bluefin tuna, albacore and mako sharks offshore. Autumn best.

ABOVE: A tuna nearing the boat

BELOW: Bluefin Tuna are caught offshore from Port MacDonnell

Salmon to around a kilo also visit the jetty during the day and berley will help hold them in the area. King George whiting can be caught off either side of the jetty and particularly at the end. Best baits for the whiting are cockle or small squid pieces, but you need to cast well out for the bigger fish.

The Port Mac breakwater is another option for land-based anglers, but be prepared to climb over the rocks towards the end for best results. Fishing on the inside produces all the species previously mentioned and also offers protection from the cold southerly winds. Fishing on the outside of the breakwater can produce the odd snapper, gummy shark and sweep, but the bottom terrain is rough so be prepared to lose a few rigs.

The concrete boat ramp and dredged channel make boat launching easy and the large open car park provides safe storage for vehicles. Small boat fishing inside the breakwater almost guarantees you a feed on most days. Whiting, salmon, mullet, flathead and garfish can all be caught in good numbers, however be prepared to move a number of times until the fish are located.

On the calmer days good boating can be found outside the shelter of the breakwater. A kilometre or so to the east in front of Orwell Rocks is a good area to try for snapper, whiting and garfish. Anywhere from 200 metres off the rocks out to about 500 m is a good area to start. Surf fishing around Orwell Rocks can also result in catches of snapper during the summer months.

Port MacDonnell's close proximity to the continental shelf makes it an ideal location to target the deep water pelagic species like southern bluefin tuna, albacore, blue sharks and mako sharks. The tuna usually make their way along the coast between the months of February and July, and vary in size from 15 – 20 kg school fish, all the way up to trophy-sized Bluefin over 100 kg. Skirted lures and heavier 37 kg tackle is recommended when the bigger fish are in the area. This is big boat territory and a degree of local knowledge is mandatory to fish outside of Port MacDonnell safely.